Praise for *Sustainability Generation*

"The business case for sustainability has been made. Behaving in ways that enhance the earth and people is simply better business. Mark Coleman goes beyond this increasingly conventional wisdom, however, to argue that it is also the basis for greater happiness, and the best route to find yourself. This is exciting stuff."

—L. Hunter Lovins
President & Founder, Natural Capitalism Solutions,
www.natcapsolutions.org

"Mark Coleman says we are all part of the *Sustainability Generation.* Indeed we are, regardless of age. He lays out a compelling story for how you can make a difference. Humanity needs to transform our 'container ship brimming full of stuff,' much of it toxic and dangerous, into a new model of living, connection, and consumption. Mark writes with passion, humor, and solid substantiation; you will be energized to reassess your life and come away with renewed vigor, tools, and hope for our planet."

—Marilyn Tam
author of Living the Life of Your Dreams *and* How to Use What You've Got to Get What You Want, *co-founder of the Us Foundation, and former CEO Aveda Corp., President Reebok Apparel & Retail Group*

"Mark Coleman's book can be considered a major milestone towards directing sustainable development to a new dimension that exceeds the typical business context that we were used to. He sets the right perspective, which can't be other than the personal one. It takes a change of mindset rather than a mere change of business strategy. It is a challenge of character and ethics that undoubtedly will shape and carve the generations to come.

"Sustainability is a battle that we mainly have to win within ourselves.

"A much more demanding task, a much more rewarding win . . ."

—Stelios Voyiatzis
CEO Enolia Ventus SA

"If we're going to move our world toward sustainability in all its many forms, we'll also have to move ourselves, our families, our communities, and our institutions. Mark Coleman describes how a new generation, born of the notion that 'more' is not always better, is rethinking what it means to 'have it all.' He provides guidance and hope for an increasingly fragile world that seems to be spinning ever faster."

—Joel Makower
Executive Editor G
Author of Strategies

"How many new century authors can write intelligently about entitlement, indulgence, and taking personal action in the same book? Mark Coleman has done this with grace, force, and insight for executives, consumers, and social leaders alike. This is a book for the now generation in a new way. Use this book often."

—Bruce Piasecki

Founder & President, www.ahcgroup.com
Author of Doing More with Less: A New Way to Wealth

"Sustainability is often put forward as the responsibility of governments, companies, and activists. Mark Coleman brings this complex field to a personal level: how can each of us bring our values and our dreams to the decisions we make every day? Just as Mark's life felt transformed as he gazed at his newborn child, each of us is challenged to open our eyes to the interconnected web that binds us to the generations before and after our brief lives."

—Barton Alexander

Chief Corporate Responsibility Officer
Molson Coors Brewing Company

"The maturation of the concepts surrounding sustainability has been like watching the growth of the Internet ... only faster. The most fascinating aspect of this transformation has been that business has led the charge. Business is adopting concepts and principles faster than individuals and pushing the boundaries in all directions at once. Mark Coleman not only consolidates and categorizes these learnings, but captures the soul of sustainability—finding personal responsibility in a global context. He contributes a HUGE needed piece of the puzzle that ties the concepts together to suggest that a 'never satisfied' humankind and sustainability can happily coexist."

—Richard Walker

Program Leader—High Performance Buildings,
Trane Commercial Services Global Services and Contracting

"In a time when so many are describing lofty thoughts and very green what-ifs, Mark Coleman has produced an informative tool with depth and supporting backup, that could benefit anyone who is really serious about making a difference."

—Bob Bechtold

Founder and President, Harbec, Inc.

"I have an old friend that tells me he doesn't mind change as long as it doesn't happen to him. He would hate Mark Coleman. Not only does *The Sustain-ability Generation* accurately depict the underpinnings of the global tsunami which is sustainability, the book challenges to reader to grab a surf board and ride the wave—another thing that would terrify my friend."

—Derrick Mains

Recycling, software, and sustainability entrepreneur

"Mark Coleman has a unique way of explaining and showing us that we must accept personal responsibility for creating the sustainable future we all desire. It does not need authoritative top-down government or corporate leadership. It is organic and very personal—starting with little actions taken by millions of people and beginning with each of us accepting our part. Mark's work is clear, concise, and irrefutable. The responsibility rests with us. Mark's passion, wit, and charm show through in his work and make the argument even more compelling. Generations to come will look upon Mark's work as provocative and liberating, showing us the way."

—Paul A. DeCotis
Vice President of Power Markets
Long Island PowerAuthority

"Coleman's book underscores the truth that we can't mandate, regulate, and legislate our way to a sustainable world. He eloquently describes the moral imperative that we must nourish multigenerational solidarity around preserving the precious natural resources that make up the finite foundation of humankind's ability to thrive. Through an enthralling series of personal revelations and case studies, Coleman leads us to the understanding that environmental protection isn't simply something we do . . . it's who we are, and each individual must decide if they are the kind of person who wastes or replenishes, even when no one is looking. No doubt, Coleman's children will one day thank him for writing this book, as will the children of all parents who read it and put it into practice."

—Jill Buck
Founder and CEO, Go Green Initiative
www.GoGreenInitiative.org

"A transformational read for those concerned about the fate of this and future generations. Mark Coleman provides a unique perspective on the trade-offs this generation has to wrestle with if we are to balance the needs and opportunities in our economy, environment, and energy futures. The time is now for 'clean' energy and this book is a primer to understanding the issues we face with dwindling natural resources and how this issue of personal responsibility will shape the future of clean energy development."

—Dr. Carole Inge
President and Chief Executive Officer
National Institute for the Commercialization of Clean Energy

"After reading this book, Mark Coleman will have you motivated to change some habits and look at life on this planet from a very different perspective."

—Robert Franzblau
Master Scheduler, Supply Logistics, Roche Molecular Systems

"Ultimately, sustainability is about balance and the interconnections of our actions. Mark Coleman's book provides the framework for an inside-out, bottom-up approach to creating positive change. Starting from the assumption that we are all designers of our future, this book provides the roadmap to a journey that starts within. Get ready for the ride of your life!"

—Chandler Van Voorhis
Managing Partner of C2I, LLC
Managing Partner of GreenTrees
2002 Recipient of the ChevronTexaco Conservation Award

The Sustainability Generation

Best Wishes!

Mark Coleman

gift

The Sustainability Generation

The Politics of Change & Why Personal Accountability Is Essential NOW!

Mark C. Coleman

SelectBooks, Inc.
New York

This edition published by SelectBooks, Inc.

For information address SelectBooks, Inc., New York, New York.

First Edition

ISBN 978-1-59079-233-9

Cataloging-in-Publication Data

Library of Congress Cataloging-in-Publication Data

Coleman, Mark C.
   The sustainability generation : the politics of change & why personal accountability is essential now! / Mark C. Coleman.
      p. cm.
   Includes bibliographical references and index.
   Summary: "Examines how indulgences from individual and generational entitlement impact the environment and society, resulting in depletion of natural resources to the detriment of future generations' ability to meet their needs. Presents options for change to rally the emerging Sustainability Generation to take action toward a more balanced, sustainable future"—Provided by publisher.
   ISBN 978-1-59079-233-9 (pbk. : alk. paper)
   1. Environmental responsibility. 2. Environmental ethics.
   3. Sustainability. I. Title.
   GE195.7.C64 2012
   338.9'27--dc23

2012005321

Text design by Kathleen Isaksen

Manufactured in the United States of America

10 9 8 7 6 5 4 3 2 1

Dedicated to my loving family:
My wife Aileen McNabb-Coleman and two sons,
Owen Patrick and Neal Garrett

You are my inspiration, joy, and love!

Contents

Foreword

L. Hunter Lovins

President and Founder, Natural Capitalism Solutions,
www.natcapsolutions.org

This is a book about taking responsibility and thereby creating a wonderful life for yourself and for the entire world. It is a book about opportunity and innovation. Most of all, it is a book about change.

Margaret Mead said that the only person who likes change is a wet baby. And I'd argue that a baby squalls all the way through the process.

Yet change is upon us. Consider that from summer of 2010 on:

Four Middle Eastern governments fell in the Arab Spring. More may fall in the months ahead;

Two European governments fell in the PIGS (Portugal, Ireland and Italy, Greece and Spain) economic crisis, more may, as well, perhaps bringing down the entire Euro-zone;

Over a several week period in August and September, 1,253 people protesting the proposed Keystone pipeline were arrested in Washington, D.C. But it was worth it: the pipeline decision was delayed, perhaps killing the project;

On Sept 17 a few hundred protesters "occupied Wall Street," launching what has become a global Occupy Movement involving hundreds of thousands of people and events in over 2,000 cities around the world. Official over-reaction resulted in the arrests of thousands of young organizers, grandmothers, business people, and every imaginable slice of the 99% of society who have been dispossessed by the banks, lobbyists, and venal politicians—the 1 percent that has most of the wealth. Viral videos of police brutality against Iraqi veterans, beer-bellied cops pepper spraying peaceful students, and leaderless general assemblies convened by young activists have caused an irreversible shift in the attitudes of young people the world around about the need for them to take charge of their future;

The Sendai earthquake destroyed a major portion of the world's third largest economy, triggering the Fukushima nuclear disaster in which, but for the incredible bravery of the workers at the plant, we could have lost Tokyo. Nuclear programs around the world are now being questioned, particularly given that solar is now cheaper than building any new nukes and wind is cheaper than just running the existing ones;

Pakistan test-fired nuclear tipped missiles, then went underwater, as climate change induced floods that displaced twenty million people. Its instability and the vast mineral wealth in Afghanistan mean that the United States will have a military presence in the region for the foreseeable future;

Floods swept Queensland, Thailand, New England, Guatemala, and many other locations, as global weirding drove intense rain events, cyclones, hurricanes, and melting glaciers. 2010 was tied with 2005 for the hottest year ever in recorded history;

If it wasn't too wet, it was too dry: droughts swept Somalia, killing thousands, displacing hundreds of thousands, threatening millions. The two-year and counting drought in Texas, while not as devastating, caused record wildfires and may have permanently altered agriculture from Arizona to Louisiana. In 2011 the United States suffered ten separate weather disasters, each costing over a billion dollars;

China surpassed Japan as the world's largest economy and for being the country building the most wind turbines. Westerners scoff that the Chinese cannot innovate past us, but there are more honors students in China (and in India) than in the United States;

Unemployment soared, especially for young people, to levels equivalent to youth unemployment rates in the countries that launched the Arab Spring. Student loan debt in the United States is now larger than consumer debt—and 60% of the jobs that will exist in ten years haven't yet been invented.

These changes and hundreds more are emerging in a time of unprecedented peril and narrowing possibilities. The 2010 report Global Biodiversity Outlook 3[1] makes clear that all ecosystems on Earth are threatened. Three are tipping into collapse and—sorry scuba divers—if business as usual prevails, there are unlikely to be living coral reefs on planet Earth, perhaps by as early as 2050. The Amazon, cut by illegal loggers and burned to convert the rainforest to cropland, could lose 85% of its trees from rising temperatures from climate change.

Perhaps most scary, the oceans are acidifying. The increasing carbon dioxide in the atmosphere—levels increased by 6% in 2010 alone, the largest annual increase ever recorded—is creating carbonic acid in the oceans. Shelled creatures from oysters to phytoplankton, the source of almost half the oxygen on the planet, cannot survive in even mildly acidic waters. Left unchecked, this trend could lead to the sixth great extinction event in the earth's history, threatening life as we know it.

Clearly today's Sustainability Generation has its work cut out for it.

Yet good news abounds. Young entrepreneurs around the world are creating jobs, profiting, and building lives based on solving the gnarliest problems to face humanity. The Unreasonable Institute[2] mentored twenty-five young entrepreneurs from seventeen countries on five continents, and then unleashed them and their fledgling companies to save the world. One is bringing solar cookers that also produce electricity and heat to villages in Tibet, another is bringing renewable energy to Native American Villages in Canada, and others are bringing clean water to villages in India, recycling to China, sustainable food production to Africa—and all are making a living following their passion.

Prices for solar panels (and other renewables) fell dramatically. It's become apparent that Moore's law (the computer maxim that prices halve and output doubles every eighteen months) also applies to renewable energy.[3] Countries from Scotland (by 2020) to Germany (by 2050) are on track to become 100% renewably powered. Cities from Dardesheim, Germany (already 100% renewable)[4] to San Francisco (by 2015)[5] are rejecting fossil energy and implementing the clean energy options that drive job creation (10 times as many jobs are created by investing in renewables as in fossil energy), clean the air, and lay the basis for a prosperous future.

Schools like Bainbridge Graduate Institute, where I teach, have transformed MBA curricula to integrate sustainability into every class, graduating young people to run sustainability programs at major corporations, in municipalities, and in new entrepreneurial ventures that feature local food, fair trade, and a wide array of exciting new technologies. When I helped found this transformation to education there were only a few schools interested. There are over two hundred MBA programs that feature sustainability in the United States alone, and more are emerging each year. The challenge now is to take this transformation digital, bringing the expertise of the world's sustainability thought leaders to your tablet and smart-phone, like TED talks, but organized so that you can get a sustainability degree from leading universities, affordably from anywhere in the world. A team of us is now working on this (check out www.madroneproject.com, and http://www.youtube.com/watch?v=nhk1y4Qz-n0)

There is now a very solid business case for behaving more responsibly toward people and the planet. When those wild-eyed environmentalists at Goldman Sachs tell us that the companies that are the leaders in environmental, social and good governance policies have 25% higher stock value than their less sustainable competitors,[6] I'd argue that any business school that is NOT teaching sustainability is being irresponsible. There are twenty-five separate studies from the likes of IBM, Deloitte, McKinsey, and virtually all the big management consulting houses. Even *Harvard Business Review* has picked up my phrase "the sustainability imperative," stating that sustainability isn't the burden on the bottom line that many executives believe it to be. In fact, becoming environment-friendly can lower your costs and increase your revenues. That's why sustainability should be a touchstone for all innovation. In the future, only companies that make sustainability a goal will achieve competitive advantage. That means rethinking business models as well as products, technologies, and processes."[7]

Smart corporate managers agree. A 2010 study by Accenture found that 93% of CEOs surveyed believe that "sustainability will be critical to the future success of their companies and could be fully embedded into core business within ten years."[8] Market for sustainability continues to grow.

A study conducted by MIT Sloan Management Review and Boston Consulting Group found that 69% of companies plan to increase their investment in and management of sustainability in 2011.[9]

Dr. Eban Goodstein, Director of the Bard College Center for Environment, and founder of the new Bard MBA in sustainable management,[10] in a letter to students, stated,

> We are living at an extraordinary moment in human history. The work that today's young people will do over their lives will have a profound effect on every creature that will ever inhabit the planet, from now until the end of time. This is truly the most exciting, most decisive, most human time to ever be alive.
>
> Today, there are so many ways to have an impact, to be an agent of history. And there are multiple entry points into this good work. The jobs are there.
>
> Students who get sustainability, and who get how important their lives' work might be, do not have the luxury of delay. To stabilize the global climate, they have to start changing the future before they turn thirty.

Eban's right. The challenge now is not to get a job and fit in, but to transform an entire economy, a whole society.

Change is hard. But consider the caterpillar. When it enters the chrysalis it has no earthly idea what's fixing to happen to it. Have you ever broken one of these things apart? There's no worm in there, no butterfly ... it's just goo. To become a butterfly, the creature undergoes a complete transformation.

Perhaps our society is like that. If things feel a bit gooey just now, perhaps it is because we are in the midst of the most profound transformation human kind has ever undergone. (Looking at the forces arrayed against us, we'd better be ...) We have all of the technology we need to solve all of the world's challenges to, in the words of Buckminster Fuller, "make the world work for 100% of humanity, in the shortest possible time, through spontaneous cooperation, without ecological offense or disadvantage of anyone." Doing this will build resilient communities, improve our quality of life, and unleash the greatest prosperity humankind has ever known.

In the chrysalis the goo begins to coalesce and a butterfly begins to emerge, fragile at first, uncertain, but as the transformation completes, the new creature takes wing, bringing delight to all who marvel at its beauty.

This book will help you through this time of transformation to find your own wings.

Enjoy!

L. Hunter Lovins
June, 2012

Preface

A Personal Note about Change, Adaptability, and Sustainability

I have centered this book on sustainability around personal accountability because I truly believe success, spirituality, and sustainability derive from within ourselves. While material goods, recognition from peers, and other external factors validate our sense of self, it is who we are inside that makes the difference. When I began "thinking" about this book project, it was around the time my first son, Owen Patrick, was born. Two years later, Owen's younger brother Neal Garrett was born. It is incredible, humbling, energizing, and life-fulfilling to bring children into our world. Before parenthood you are essentially accountable to yourself. Once you have children you have to answer to yourself, but are also responsible for the caring, nurturing, loving, and 24/7 support for new lives that fully need your attention While personal accountability changes throughout life, at the core is our self-identity, values, morals, beliefs, and behaviors. While our influence and responsibility to our families, work, children, and communities may change over time, who we are inside can make a profound impact on those we choose to spend our time with and how we engage with them in our family, work, and community.

Change happens that can often impact your life in profound ways. My story about my son, Owen, illustrates personal resiliency, adaptability, and perseverance, each of which I believe are traits that the Sustainability Generation will require if it is to address and succeed in finding balance among the social, economic, and environmental challenges of today.

Owen was born March 12, 2008, by emergency Cesarean section. My wife Aileen was in labor for nearly thirteen hours. After a long day in labor, baby and mom were beginning to show signs of stress. Around 8:15 p.m. doctors made the decision to perform the surgery. The next fifteen minutes seemed like an eternity. Aileen and I were very nervous and anxious. Owen was our first baby. As Aileen was prepped for surgery and I put on a white gown, face mask and hat, a number of questions ran through my head. "Why had Owen not been born yet? How much stress were he and Aileen under? What is involved in a C-section?"

Childbirth is all about the clock: timing contractions and figuring out how long it will take to get to the hospital. Yet there is a moment when watching the clock simply doesn't matter anymore. It as if you enter a new phase of time, like just before takeoff. Sometimes when I fly, just before takeoff and right before the plane hits maximum altitude, I experience a moment of letting go. A self-awareness and realization that the moment, as much as I'd love to control it, has very little to do with me other than my being a participant as a passenger and observer of it. So all we can do, really, is to relax and try to enjoy these life moments.

I sat outside the surgery room where a nurse had left me, all prepared. The doctors had finished washing their hands. As I had watched them it struck me how deliberate and careful they were, much more than I was when washing my hands at home. But they were performing surgery on a person! My wife! Random thoughts entered my brain, some very scary, others quite lovely as my anxiety mounted. This is real, right? I'm really going to have a baby in a few minutes. Aileen will soon be a mother and I, a father. Wow! I hoped she was doing alright and feeling comfortable. Then I wished the same for the baby. Was the baby scared? Aileen and I chose not to find out the sex of the baby until it was born, so, my attention shifted briefly whether it be a boy, or girl? Either way, I though, our lives would be forever changed in a few minutes.

I had stopped watching the clock. The area where I sat, dressed in my whites, likely pale in the face, knees bouncing in a nervous rhythm, became eerily quiet. Suddenly the experience became surreal. Colors became clearer, my mind stopped having random thoughts, and a focus came over me. I felt an inner peace. Then the nurse called me into the surgery room, saying "We are all set." I could not see her mouth but I could tell from her eyes that she was smiling. It brought warmth to the moment. As I entered the room, my senses were swirling. I had never been in a surgery room before. There seemed to be one hundred people, but more likely around six. There were a lot of machines, equipment, lights, and at center stage were Aileen and our baby to be born. As I took a first row seat, right near Aileen's head, I realized this was an incredible moment, one which she and I had tried our best to prepare for over nine months.

Trust was put into the hands, wisdom, strength, and experience of those doctors and nurses whom I did not know or could not see behind their surgical masks. Watching and listening, I could tell they were in their element, doing what they were born to do in this world.

My attention focused on Aileen. She was radiant. She had tears, perhaps of fear, joy, and love. You could see all the emotion of the day and moment on her face. I did my best to look into her eyes, held her hand and head, and tried to be as supportive as I could. At 8:45 p.m. our first baby boy we named Owen Patrick, was born. He came into the world screaming, demanding to be heard, and with a fury on his face that seemed to be the look of impatience, as if he would have liked to breathe life a couple of hours earlier.

I felt a great sense of relief as the next few minutes passed. The baby had arrived. Aileen was doing just fine, and I thought this birth experience was not so bad. But when you have not gone through something like this before, you focus on the newness of the situation, the excitement of the big picture, and not the dangerous undertones that in retrospect were right in front of us through the entire experience. Owen and Aileen did not get one-on-one bonding time right away. It turned out that his breathing was labored. X-rays of Owen's chest revealed he had either fluid or a trapped air pocket within his lungs. His oxygen levels were low so they needed to administer oxygen.

Owen stayed in the ICU for the first three days of his life. It was a very tough time for Aileen and me. Although we knew the infant would eventually be fine, not having him with us and in our arms through those first days felt horrible. When he finally slept with us in Aileen's room at the hospital, we each had the best night sleep in days; everyone seemed to feel each other's presence. Calmness ensued, enriching this life-moment for this new family. Owen's lungs cleared up and he was finally released, but we were told that he had asthma.

The first twelve weeks were typical of two first-time parents who bring their child home and readjust their lifestyle and reprogram their brains about what they thought they knew of themselves and taking care of a baby. In short, everything is out the window! Read the books, listen to war stories from parents and friends, and seek out counsel from priests and bartenders. In the end, it is you alone at 3 a.m. with a screaming child, and fatigued and drunk from lack of sleep and a steady diet of Red-40 saturated Swedish Fish candy. Who you are in those moments says a lot about people's ability to deal with change. While the first few weeks seemed typical, we did compare notes with friends and family. We learned that Owen seemed to be crying, frustrated, and cranky more than most other babies. It finally sank in: we had a very colicky baby. We took Owen to the pediatrician to be assessed several times. We tried switching brands and types of baby formula, but the changes seemed to have little effect. The three days he spent in the hospital in ICU had made breast feeding challenging. Aileen tried diligently several times over those three days to breast-feed Owen. But in the end, the bottle won out. Aileen, to this day, feels a heavy regret about that even though the situation did not allow for any other course of action.

One day, after eating a bowl of cereal with milk, Aileen had given Owen a kiss on his cheek. His cheek broke out in hives. Within a day we gave him a bath using a milk-based soap. His skin all over his body became red and irritated. He was equally uncomfortable and screamed after the bath, while wheezy and short of breath. Soon we brought together our collective memories of similar moments of Owen's early life. Connecting the dots, we developed our hypothesis that he had an allergy to milk. We had Owen's skin and blood tested for food and other allergens. The outcomes were shocking to us. Owen had, and continues to have, severe allergies to all dairy products, eggs, peanuts and tree-nuts, soy, bananas, and other foods and substances, including an allergy to dogs and reactions to seasonal allergens. We felt overwhelmed and almost negligent. How could we have missed this for weeks? We should have realized sooner when we knew Owen was colicky that he must have food-related allergies. And what were we going to do going forward? How would we feed this baby? What foods were OK? How would we know? Would he be getting proper nutrition?

The next few months were full of discovery. We began to reach out to others with children with food allergies. We talked with doctors, nutritionists, and allergists. We attended food allergy and anaphylaxis support meetings locally. We tried to absorb as much data and information as we could. It helped us understand the disease, but it also opened up a new world of change, uncertainty, and concern for us as a family.

For example, we learned more than 12 million Americans have food allergies, or one in every twenty-five people. And, children have the highest incidence of food allergies: one in every seventeen children under the age of three has food allergies. There are eight foods which account for ninety percent of all food-allergic reactions: milk, eggs, peanuts, tree nuts, fish, shellfish, soy, and wheat. Owen had an allergy to five of the eight! We also learned that some of the allergens may be outgrown, but others often remain lifelong allergies. We also discovered that people can develop allergies to foods at any time during their life. Perhaps the scariest fact we learned was that there is no cure for food allergies, and even trace amounts of a food allergen can trigger a reaction. This left us feeling very uneasy about Owen's future, particularly as he enters his school age. By the way, an excellent resource for data and information about food allergies is the Food Allergy & Anaphylaxis Network (FAAN), www.foodallergy.org.

Following this discovery phase of Owen's food allergies we were overwhelmed. But we knew it was time to take action. Feeling sorry for ourselves was inappropriate and inexcusable. We needed to be accountable to him. We introduced certain foods to Owen's diet that we hoped he would not be allergic to. He was able to have chicken, turkey burger, sweet potatoes, peas, and other foods regularly. To this day he has a steady diet of these foods plus other fruits, vegetables, and snack foods made by companies that dedicate their facilities to make products that are allergen-free.

As we learned about Owen's food allergies, we also began to transform our lives. We all went on a diet! Out of the need for safety and concern for our child we began choosing to not eat certain foods like milk, cheese, and eggs in the same room or the same time as Owen. We also made some lifestyle changes in our dietary habits in our interactions with family and friends. For example, Owen's allergy to dogs was and remains an emotional issue. My family and parents have had dogs for years. I grew up with family pets, dogs, and fish. My parents still have a dog, a welcoming black lab, Hannah. But we've seen first-hand, following family visits to a variety of relatives' houses, how quickly the onset of allergy symptoms can occur. We've seen wheezing trigger Owen's asthma and skin reactions like hives, itching, and swelling affect him within seconds of an exposure to an allergen. We feel a sense of obligation to not have Owen in environments where dogs or any other source of allergens are prevalent, if at all possible.

We carry an EpiPen with epinephrine[11] everywhere we travel with Owen. We have never administered the EpiPen. But there were times in which we should have. On two occasions in his first eighteen months of life Owen had to go to the emergency room. The first time he spent two nights, literally inside a metal cage, receiving oxygen for his breathing. We believe an allergic reaction brought on low blood pressure and shortness of breath, to the point where he was in need of oxygen. After two nights in the hospital, Owen recovered. It is then we were prescribed his "breathing treatments." When seasonal allergens are high, or if we experience his wheezing, we typically give Owen routine nebulizer breathing treatments. Others with asthma are very familiar with this. As new parents, neither of whom is or was asthmatic, this was another change to be accepted into our daily life.

Owen is now a happy and healthy three-and-a-half-year-old. Recent blood tests suggest that his peanut and tree nut allergy could potentially be decreasing. Since this data point is a positive signal, and we remain hopeful that this becomes a sustained trend, we are encouraged by this information. We must, however, always be vigilant. There have been too many instances when letting down our guard has resulted in a reaction in Owen, hindering his health and quality of life. But what I like to tell people is that Owen is one of the healthiest three-year-olds I know. He eats fruits and vegetables, lean meats, and has never even had fast foods. His only knowledge of French fries is baked sweet potatoes with nothing on them, maybe a sprinkle of salt time-to-time. He eats high-quality nutritious foods. And we hope the silver lining in this early life experience for Owen, and us, is that we set him up for a life of healthy eating, personal awareness, and advocacy and support.

Although it is difficult, change is necessary. As Owen is getting older, we are becoming even more deliberate in our food choices. Yes, we occasionally eat chicken wings with bleu cheese or have an occasional ice cream cone or breakfast sandwich with egg (nowhere near Owen). But we are consistently removing foods from our diet which Owen is at risk of reacting to. And the result is that we don't miss them. We actually find that we eat in a healthier way and feel better. More importantly, we feel great that as Owen's curiosity in foods expands, we are doing the right thing by not having him exposed to food allergens in the house. It is our personal responsibility and accountability to him.

My personal story envelops personal change, accountability, resiliency, adaptability, and perseverance and shows why it is critical for me (and I hope you) to figure out how we can leave the world in better place for our children. I was inspired to write this book because in my heart and mind I want a better world for my children to live in. And I want them to grow to be responsible individuals in their own lives and in greater society. It is my hope that my children ask of themselves and others the right questions, never settle for the status quo, and continually work to find their sense of balance as they grow with the world.

My experience is not necessarily atypical of the experiences others are going through right now in life: caring for loved ones, living with cancer, MS, or other diseases, and managing the emotional and physical aspects of new challenges. Individuals have the power within themselves to adapt to the influences upon their world and have the responsibility to do so. Those who care for our children and our natural resources are stewards for today and tomorrow. When we have knowledge in hand that we know will lead to a better quality of life, shouldn't we make the necessary changes? I am a believer that we should.

In the context of sustainability this means we need to ask ourselves very tough questions. And while we may not always like the answers or the results that may come from change, one thing is certain: we can adapt, we are resilient, and we will persevere.

Our perspective on education and parenting is directly related to our ability to "grow and nurture" a generation of informed, caring, compassionate, and concerned citizens. Since having children, my life is much different. I have a special and unique responsibility to myself, my wife, and my family to use every skill I have to raise children who can think for themselves, have strong, positive values and beliefs, and become responsible and accountable individuals. Simply put, my job is to be a parent! As parents we need to show our children what we've done wrong, what works, and what doesn't. We should not limit their imagination or potential. And while we need to protect our children, we also need to keep them aware of the world around them, including the realities that we face as a society in an interconnected globalized world.

While we won't be able to solve all of the social and environmental challenges before us, we should, at a minimum, provide the solid grounding in education that prepares our children to live as a "Sustainability Generation. "They will be successful only if the transfer of knowledge can take place between older and younger generations to correct the wrongs of the past by making better, more sustainable choices toward the future. It is up to the existing generation to define the skills, morals, traits and tools required to teach our children how to be critical thinkers, innovators, and educators for positive change.

Institutions of American education are in need of a makeover. Our educational system is suffering from too much focus on pre-defined tests and test scores and by a lack of integration between traditional academic disciplines. Math, science, language, and history are critical disciplines in education; however we also need philosophers, artists, musicians, trades people, farmers, communicators, writers, and diplomats. Support for humanities, social sciences, music and arts, and other ways in which humans engage and learn, is required if we are to develop a generational capacity for holistic, critical, and systems thinking. In considering what sustainability is and is not, should be the understanding that sustainability is inherently multi-disciplinary and collaborative. There is no one technology, no silver bullet, or one answer to addressing the complex and interrelated challenges of this and future generations. We need to do prepare this and future generations to be critical thinkers, endless tinkerers and willing participants to do more than just sustain our earth in the present. We can also thrive on this planet of fixed resources, but limitless potential, in the years to come.

This book was written in an effort to try to create awareness about society's entitlement to have natural resources, clean air and water, and enjoyment of the bounty of our earth. I hope that our current generation can be not only reflective and responsive to this, but also builders of a new Sustainable Generation where entitlement to have sustainability is an ethic to live by, not just a goal to be pursued. Our generation will be the architects, designers, builders, policy-makers, investors and philosophers of this movement. For our generation to achieve this, personal accountability is essential now!

I hope this book aids your personal discovery of leading a more sustainable, fulfilling, and enlightened life.

Introduction

"People do not change when we tell them they should; they change when their context tells them they must."[12]

—Thomas Friedman

∞

"I can't understand why people are frightened of new ideas. I'm frightened of the old ones."[13]

—John Cage, U.S. Composer
(1912–1992)

∞

"To waste, to destroy our natural resources, to skin and exhaust the land instead of using it so as to increase its usefulness, will result in undermining in the days of our children the very prosperity which we ought by right to hand down to them amplified and developed."[14]

—Theodore Roosevelt, 26th President of United States
(1858–1919)

The quotes above portray the human emotion associated with fear of change. It is surprising that we have such a hang-up about change. The world is in a constant state of flux, sometimes for better, sometimes for worse. The natural environment, human built environment, political systems, economic models, and religious sects are essentially ever-changing. People inherently don't want to be told what to do. Thus the human aversion to change stems in part from unwillingness to change exclusively at the hand of others. People like to reach their own conclusions about the right time, place, and impetus for change. Because the decision for change can be personal, often it comes later than desired with impacts and externalities that could have been avoided. This book is a reflection on a significant change happening throughout the world today—and a call to try to accelerate individuals to decide to make this change in their own lives. The context of how humans work, live, play, pray, and love is changing throughout the world. An ethic of personal accountability toward a more sustainable way of life now and for the future is a change happening in our society today and is both inspiring and challenging. For those who have accepted this change, a more balanced, fulfilled life has begun. For those who continue to push this change away, continued fear and uncertainty persists.

When I began writing this book, I wanted to focus the content and message of greater accountability and personal responsibility exclusively for the Baby Boomer generation. As a Generation Xer I have felt a sense of pent-up anxiety about the future and a disdain for the condition of the world that Boomers are handing down to their children and grandchildren. I have been guided by many advisors to focus the message of this book on the Millennial Generation, those that will next inherit the earth and the human built environment from the Boomers and Generation Xers. A leading social-change agent put it to me this way:

> "The Boomers are the generation that built and set-sail an enormous ocean liner filled with oils, chemicals, toxins, management and consumer behaviors and other stuff. But the ocean liner was not designed to hold all of this stuff, and what's worse is that the ship is now off-course and set to hit an iceberg. It will be the Millennial Generation that grabs the wheel of the ocean liner, steers away from the iceberg, while simultaneously cleaning up what's left on the boat."

This analogy is interesting because within it are several metaphors and subtleties: first, the ocean liner is going in the wrong direction; second, the boat is filled with "stuff," including obsolete business models, policies, and behaviors that need to be curtailed, and cleaned-up; and third, an iceberg will cut it down the middle if some directional and operational changes are not made soon. The size, scale, and impact of the proverbial iceberg are the big unknown factors. The iceberg envelops climate change and ecosystem and natural resource damages, including the future ability of ecosystems to give us the life-essential services of providing clean water, delivery of food, and sustaining the embodiment of diverse life. In a sense, the BP Gulf of Mexico disaster is only a tip of an iceberg that runs deep, long, and wide.

The author of the quotation, David Gershon, is the author of *Social Change 2.0: A Blueprint for Reinventing our World,* and founder and CEO of the Empowerment Institute.[15] David himself is a self-effacing Boomer who himself admitted that his and prior generations have played a significant role in the current state of the environment and the issues of energy security and natural resources. But as he rightly points out, it is his generation that has been also diligently launching life rafts from the ocean liner for years as the Boomer Generation has tried to decrease the size of the ocean liner. As the ocean liner grows more encumbered, so too does the probability of hitting the iceberg because making mid-course corrections for the direction of the ocean liner is more challenging. Thus, it is his belief that the ocean liner needs to trim down, find new direction, and set new sails toward a more sustainable future. And he is of the belief that Millennials, with the help of Boomers and others, will be the essential part of this necessary change.

Like no other time in history, there is a coalescing of social and environmental challenges that pose risk and detriment to the ongoing sustainment of human and ecologic life on Earth. While there are many social, economic, and environmental challenges for the existing generation, there are an equal number of opportunities for us to take action individually to effect positive behavioral change.

Individual and generational entitlement has led *to erroneous indulgence* of our natural resources, particularly in industrialized counties. In addition, our thirst for the here and now has led to the detriment of future generations' ability to meet their own needs. We need to bring to light a different perspective on the philosophic, individual, and societal notions of sustainability and how we as both individuals and generations can make positive changes during our lifetime. Themes of individual constraint, personal responsibility, increased critical thinking, and leadership are addressed in the book.

At a time of so much concern about our social and environmental challenges and needs, including climate change, water and air pollution, consumerism, and increased incidences of natural and human disasters, this timely book should enable readers to think in a new way about their behavior and how they those actions impact the state of human health and environment, for both today and tomorrow.

Unrestrained individual and generational entitlement is in many ways the root cause of our current social and environmental challenges. However, there is hope. By gaining a greater awareness of our daily behaviors, and by a reexamination of both individual and generational responsibility toward protection, conservation, and enhancement of our natural resources, we can engage with those older and younger than us to create solutions.

A new **"Sustainability Generation"** is evolving throughout all facets of society and throughout the world. The empowerment and enlightenment of this generation can change the course of ecologic damage and social ills that now hinder the ability of the existing generation and future generations to meet their needs and to sustain a civilized quality of life.

In my research about social change through interviews with industrial, government, and academic leaders, I realized from the wisdom of those older and younger than I am that every new generation has a certain amount of apathy for the preceding generation. And older generations will always have a bit of fear and doubt about the promise they see in younger generations. This book is not written to chastise Boomers or put the burden of making the world a better place exclusively on the Millennial Generation. Instead, my intention is to highlight that the current generation—all of the people alive today and throughout the world, Boomers, Xers, and Millennials alike, are the Sustainability Generation. But I do believe that the younger Millennial Generation will be the first generation to truly "own" sustainability as a concept and endeavor and bring it to life as a daily practice, and not just a theological pursuit. Generation Y will have more impact on global society and economy than the industrial revolution of the 20th Century. Thus I do hope and intend that the core messages of this book will reside first and foremost with the Millennial Generation. Much the way it takes a village to raise a family, it will take a collaborative global approach to achieve sustainability. Buy-in and collaboration across all age, sex, ethnicity, creed, and socio-economic groups are necessary for sustainability to move into its next phase of enlightenment and action to create a better world.

Taking action on sustainability will require an "all hands on deck" approach to personal accountability, which is then magnified to generational accountability if we are to change the course of the ocean liner from its current trajectory to hit the proverbial iceberg. However, getting "all hands" to want to come on board, and to acknowledge necessity for change and acceptance of personal accountability, remains a challenge.

My intent is to help people to visualize how a "Sustainability Generation" of all age groups is emerging throughout the world. I want to encourage more open and honest conversation among all generations of people who are alive here and now about our needs and aspirations. This includes a desire for greater balance in our lifestyles, our government and politics, and in our industry and economy.

Catastrophic events of the past few years have caused a great deal of uncertainty in the lives of Americans and many throughout the world. The convergence of significant economic, social, political, and environmental issues brings complex global challenges to the present generation that can no longer be dismissed as another person's, another country's, or another generation's problem. Extreme anxiety about the future contributed to the feelings of loss and despair with the people who lived in the Lower Ninth Ward and throughout New Orleans in the aftermath of Hurricane Katrina, and added to the overwhelming feelings of helplessness after the disastrous earthquake in Haiti and the tsunamis in Asia and nuclear plant disaster in Japan. Anxiety about our economic future fueled the fury and disgust over the financial markets' collapse in 2008 and the fear and chaos at the time of the London riots of 2011. As a result of the financial crisis and a myriad of other geopolitical, environmental, social, and energy issues, society has become more impatient, and less forgiving of, large institutions and organizations that have struggled in recent years to meet the evolving needs of their customers.

The convoluted protests on Wall Street and in other large U.S. cities in 2011 expressed the fears and anxieties of the current generation, as well as a demand for attention and a call to action. On the 23rd day of "Occupy Wall Street" a CNN article,[16] *"As 'Occupy' protests spread, some politicians rebuke"* began to unveil the real and raw motivation behind the protests. The article noted:

> The remarks [from New York City Mayor Michael Bloomberg] drew criticism from Tyler Combelic, a spokesman for Occupy Wall Street, who claimed Bloomberg "hasn't really represented all of New Yorkers. The fact is there are thousands and thousands of us out on the streets, and he's not really recognizing that we're a movement," Combelic said Saturday. "We should be heard by New York politicians."

> Lately, the movement has been spurred by support from unions and other groups.

> "Social and economic inequalities are the tipping point, and people are hungry for getting involved and trying to do something to change it," Jim Nichols, who has been involved in Occupy Atlanta protests, said Saturday. "It's almost like, 'I want the American dream back.'"

> President Barack Obama acknowledged that protesters "are giving voice to a more broad-based frustration about how our financial system works," even as he defended the need for a vibrant financial sector.

> The No. 2 Republican in the U.S. House of Representatives, Eric Cantor, slammed what he called the "growing mobs" who he claimed were "pitting ... Americans against Americans."

Combelic, the New York spokesman, said the movement chiefly is trying to showcase "active democracy and (show that) everyone has a voice in government." He said the protests—which have been associated with progressive causes—are "a rebuke of government, that includes the left and the right."

On Saturday, U.S. Rep. Charles Rangel backed the demonstrators—whom he has been visiting regularly over the past three weeks—for venting their frustrations and exercising their constitutional rights.

"Their dreams are being shattered," Rangel, D–New York, told CNN's Don Lemon. "They may be an inconvenience to a whole lot of people in that area, but people are going to sleep at night with an economic nightmare."

He also dismissed criticism that the demonstrators don't have a coherent purpose, saying despite their varied issues and lack of organization, their sentiments are raw and real.

Hero Vincent, one of several unofficial spokesmen for Occupy Wall Street, acknowledged last week that "we're here for different reasons."

"But at the end of the day, it all boils down to one thing," he said, "and that's accountability."

The imperative for the current generation is to find a common voice and leadership amid the turmoil of continued social and geopolitical unrest. This generation wants the economic war games and partisan politics of today to end. The current generation has had enough of short-term politics that negatively impact long-term outcomes for individuals, families, and communities.

The Sustainability Generation is rising in the wake of huge manmade environmental disasters, such as the 2010 BP oil disaster in the Gulf of Mexico, and is growing quickly in scale as it evolves in our global "flat world" coined by Thomas Friedman to describe the connectivity the Internet has brought the world. As it grows in the face of unsustainable production and consumption behaviors, including the uncontrolled greed that led to financial, energy, and market volatility throughout the past two decades, individuals are now asking more from governments, industry, and their peers. The "more" that the Sustainability Generation seeks is not based on individual entitlements or social programs, but "more" by way of accountability, responsibility, and greater transparency in government and industry.

This generation wants more critical thinking (better use of data, information, and personal and professional judgment), and greater consciousness about the world. While sustainability is often valued and viewed as a "green" or environmental initiative, it is much more than that one dimension. The advent of a "Sustainability Generation" is about finding greater balance to empower people to be good critical thinkers and tinkerers capable of building a new economy. This cannot be accomplished through petty political positioning, but instead requires grounded, innovative, and pragmatic approaches to meet the needs of the present by defining and pursuing common priorities and goals. This means short-term action and long-term thinking from all facets of society—young and old, Republican and Democrat, rich and poor.

Personal, generational and societal accountability is essential as the ideas of the Sustainability Generation become established in our local communities, governments, and economy. There are four dimensions where concepts of sustainability are forming in the "here and now" that will influence future generations:

- Work
- Family
- Spirituality
- Entertainment & Living

Within these "sustainability dimensions" there is a set of questions that will help to clarify how we are accountable to a more sustainable future personally as individuals and as entire generations and an entire society. At the heart of a more sustainable future is a consciousness about ourselves and the world around us at any given moment. Being present is essential to understanding one's own selfish needs and the needs of others.

The key is in asking the right questions and pushing for the most balanced decisions—because not all decisions are going to appeal to everyone or work for all of our needs. Think about minerals extraction and the chase for more "green" technology. This approach is one-dimensional. By this I mean that we are simply trying to patch up a wound by stitching it, while a new wound is being cut. While some minerals offer great efficiency and promise (lithium for batteries to enable lower emission "cleaner" transport), when they are in a system-wide global supply chain they will bring with them huge sustainability issues (economic security, waste, and materials handling). So while we solve some issues, such as mobile emissions, others are created, such as hazardous waste and environmental liabilities at mining sites. A question we need to ask as we pursue cleaner technologies is,

"Are we playing a zero sums game of using innovation and technology to buy time?"

Thus, this generation "here and now" needs to address underlying issues of consumption and reasonableness about our choices and decisions. This takes strong leadership and tact, as well as an ability to be self-aware and conscious of our decisions and their impact on the world. Think about the powerful impact of President Kennedy's statement "Ask not what your country can do for you, but what you can do for your country" and how it remains the ultimate call to personal action and accountability in context of an engaged citizenry. During the past ten years Americans seem to ask continually less about what they can do toward the common good of all and increasingly more about "What can you do for me?" Unfortunately, this kind of narrow self-centered thinking is not going to get our generation anywhere except more in debt, less secure and more vulnerable on a global stage. This flawed thinking will not allow this or future generations to advance in science, explore deep oceans or deep space, or reach our fullest potential as a society.

To have a sense of clarity about the four sustainability dimensions as you go on your journey to have personal accountability in your life and take action for a more sustainable future, I hope you will ask these questions:

- **Work** Does your work provide a value to the economy, the community, and the environment? Are you passionate about what you do? Does your work have meaning to you, or are you simply collecting a paycheck? What values, capabilities, and strengths do you bring to your work?

- **Family** Do you have enough "family time" in your life? Is your family "engaged" and "active"? Does your family live with purpose and meaning?

- **Spirituality** Do you feel "spiritually engaged"? Do you allow spirituality to be a part of your life to influence your thinking and behavior? Do you dedicate enough time to spirituality?

- **Entertainment and Living** In what ways do you spend your spare time? Are sources of entertainment intensive? Is your form of entertainment relaxing or a "crutch" for your lifestyle? Where and how do you live? Are your home, belongings, and behaviors at home built on consumptive behaviors and patterns? How can your living environment be improved to bring a better standard of living?

All stakeholders who want sustainability need a push-and-pull to make changes. At the heart of this are our behaviors and perceptions about consumption and our stubbornness toward making change. And we need to break free from conventional thinking about the past and how it affects the future. If we run out of natural resources, if the country is less secure, if we owe too much money to China, there will be no one to bail us out. As a global society, there are big issues before us. To remain economically innovative, competitive, and conscious and active about sustainability, we need to reinvigorate an ethic to have personal accountability and a desire to "get it done" in our work, family, spiritual life, choices of entertainment, and everyday living. Thanks for being a part of the Sustainability Generation! I look forward to sharing the discovery, excitement and hard work, in the pursuit of sustainable living with you.

Summary

- Global changes that affect our life and the life of our children are happening now! We need to respect and embrace that fact.

- Through individual decisions and behaviors you have control over your life and can influence the life of others and the world around you. By choosing to take action on individual accountability, you choose to engage in a life of purpose and consequence for today and the future.

- Deferring decisions to take action can increase probabilities for negative consequences in our future.

- Living a lifestyle just to keep the status quo negates the possibility of sustainability. To work for sustainability means continually looking at your life and asking "What can I do to improve this condition? And the condition of those around me?"

1

The Societal Shifts before Our Eyes

A societal enlightenment for a new generation focused on sustainability has been underway for forty years. However, only in the past few years, while we were in the middle of a self-induced economic recession brought on in part by our self-indulgence, have dramatic shifts occurred in our industry, governments, and colleges and universities. This new enlightenment has launched the "Sustainability Generation." This generation will be measured not on its ability to wage and win a war, land on the moon, or be a global economic powerhouse. It will need to become empowered and enlightened to work to solve pressing social, economic, and environmental challenges of this and future generations. It will need to solve the dilemma of how we can live in harmony on a planet of fixed assets, yet limitless potential. The magic, art, and science of humanity give us an understanding that we have everything we need—yet we have also an internal desire to struggle to get more. A renewal of our thinking and behaviors about the balancing of our desires with what we truly need is now more crucial than ever.

We need to advance discussion about the "social side" of sustainability—namely the people, faces, emotion, and intellect behind change. Too often, an attempt to define sustainability is anchored in technologies, processes, policies, and financial terms. Those are all essential elements of enabling sustainability practices and ensuring checks and balances and return-on-investment. But for sustainability to be fully immersed in society *people* need to find value and meaning in their decisions and actions. Many in society at-large, whether confused and disgruntled youth in London, or thousands of protesters ranging in age and ethnicity who are "Occupying" cities in

2 The Sustainability Generation

the United States, are standing up and proclaiming to Wall Street and Main Street that they have had enough of greed, corruption, partisan politics, inattention to social and environmental challenges, and the perceived lack of concern over their future.

On October 1, 2011, more than 700 protesters were arrested in New York for occupying and blocking the Brooklyn Bridge. Articles in mainstream news networks like CNN[17] noted that the mass protesters appear to "have a lack of a coherent message." However they were being effective in uniting masses of people to come out in droves in other cities across the United States. The tag-line, "Occupy Wall Street" inspired "Occupy Chicago," "Occupy Boston, "and "Occupy Los Angeles" and "Occupy Oakland" and "Occupy D.C." campaigns and similar protests in other U.S. cities and towns. The protesters in New York centered their demonstration on Wall Street and did so for many weeks. Messages from the protesters touched on corporate greed, high gas prices, insufficient health insurance, foreclosure prevention, climate change, and social justice-related issues. In essence, the raw emotion of the protesters came down to issues related to generational entitlement, accountability, sustainability, and social equity. An October 3, 2011 CNN article[18] noted:

... The motto atop a website for "Occupy Los Angeles," which kicked off Saturday with a march from Pershing Square to City Hall, reads: "The revolution is happening ... It's just not in the news."

There are 34 organizations—from unions to ethnic organizations to activist groups focused on everything from foreclosure prevention to climate change to justice-related issues—listed as being involved in a like-minded activist coalition in Boston. This group, which held a festival and march Friday and Saturday and has explicitly targeted Bank of America in recent weeks, states on its website that its aim is to "stop their greed," "fight for an economy that works for all of us" and "build cities that are democratic, just and sustainable."

The website of Seattle demonstrators describes the nationwide effort as "a leaderless resistance movement with people of many colors, genders and political persuasions."

The one thing we all have in common is that We Are The 99% that will no longer tolerate the greed and corruption of the 1%," the statement continues, referring to what it sees as a sharp divide between the wealthiest Americans and the rest of society.

And other news organizations captured some of the personal perspectives and intentions of the protesters:

"Our beautiful system of American checks and balances has been thoroughly trashed by the influence of banks and big finance that have made it impossible for the people to speak," said protester Marisa Engerstrom of Somerville, Mass., a Harvard doctoral student.[19]

The Boston demonstrators decorated their tents with hand-written signs reading, "Fight the rich, not their wars" and "Human need, not corporate greed."

Patrick Putnam, 27, a chef from Framingham, said he's standing up for the 99 percent of Americans who have no voice in government.

"We don't have voices, we don't have lobbyists, so we've been pretty much neglected by Washington, D.C.," said Putnam, wearing a red bandanna across his face. The bandanna isn't just to hide his face from the multiple surveillance cameras on the Federal Reserve building, he said, but to show solidarity with several other demonstrators wearing similar masks. Putnam slept in a sleeping bag on a tarp in the open air Sunday night and said he plans to keep coming back as long as his work schedule allows it . . . "People are finally coming together in this country," he said.

Given the actions and diversity of messages from protesters on Wall Street and outside Bank of America in Bean Town, the "Sustainability Generation" has taken root and wants its voice to be heard. There is gaining momentum toward a universal call for greater accountability in the very foundations that have created independence, individuality, and freedom in the United States for the past two and a quarter centuries, namely government, capitalism, and an engaged citizenry. An October 5, 2011, blog post "Think Occupy Wall St. is a phase? You don't get it"[20] written by Douglas Rushkoff, a media theorist and the author of *Program or Be Programmed: Ten Commands for a Digital Age* and *Life Inc: How Corporatism Conquered the World and How We Can Take it Back*, summarizes how the tactics of current generation differentiate from other movements in the past:

> . . . To be fair, the reason why some mainstream news journalists and many of the audiences they serve see the Occupy Wall Street protests as incoherent is because the press and the public are themselves. It is difficult to comprehend a 21st century movement from the perspective of the 20th century politics, media, and economics in which we are still steeped.
>
> In fact, we are witnessing America's first true Internet-era movement, which—unlike civil rights protests, labor marches, or even

the Obama campaign—does not take its cue from a charismatic leader, express itself in bumper-sticker-length goals and understand itself as having a particular endpoint.

Yes, there are a wide array of complaints, demands, and goals from the Wall Street protesters: the collapsing environment, labor standards, housing policy, government corruption, World Bank lending practices, unemployment, increasing wealth disparity and so on. Different people have been affected by different aspects of the same system—and they believe they are symptoms of the same core problem.

Are they ready to articulate exactly what that problem is and how to address it? No, not yet. But neither are Congress or the president who, in thrall to corporate America and Wall Street, respectively, have consistently failed to engage in anything resembling a conversation as cogent as the many I witnessed as I strolled by Occupy Wall Street's many teach-ins this morning. There were young people teaching one another about, among other things, how the economy works, about the disconnection of investment banking from the economy of goods and services, the history of centralized interest-bearing currency, the creation and growth of the derivatives industry, and about the Obama administration deciding to settle with, rather than investigate and prosecute the investment banking industry for housing fraud.

Anyone who says he has no idea what these folks are protesting is not being truthful. Whether we agree with them or not, we all know what they are upset about, and we all know that there are investment bankers working on Wall Street getting richer while things for most of the rest of us are getting tougher. What upsets banking's defenders and politicians alike is the refusal of this movement to state its terms or set its goals in the traditional language of campaigns.

That's because, unlike a political campaign designed to get some person in office and then close up shop (as in the election of Obama), this is not a movement with a traditional narrative arc. As the product of the decentralized networked-era culture, it is less about victory than sustainability. It is not about one-pointedness, but inclusion and groping toward consensus. It is not like a book; it is like the Internet . . .

. . . The members of Occupy Wall Street may be as unwieldy, paradoxical, and inconsistent as those of us living in the real world. But that is precisely why their new approach to protest is more applicable, sustainable and actionable than what passes for politics today. They are suggesting that the fiscal operating system on which we are attempting to run our economy is no longer appropriate to the task. They mean to show that there is an inappropriate and correctable disconnect between the abundance America produces and the scarcity its markets manufacture.

Given the greed, corruption, and sense of entitlement exhibited from politicians, captains of capitalism, and some of the protestors themselves in late 2011, it seems that U.S. society has become imbalanced, and the citizenry of the current generation is not taking responsibility to bring a sense of balance back to this great country. The protesters on Wall Street initiated a new generation of activism and leadership that will look, feel, and behave much differently than our traditional notion of "here are our demands, or else!" Even activism in the past had a sense of entitlement about how it was carried out. The current generation is looking for much more from its government and industry than corrective actions and "meeting their perceived demands." The Sustainability Generation is looking for fundamental change in how society currently functions, and wants a focus on greater balance. This generation is seeking to change the politics of change to be less entitled and more accountable. Only time will tell if, and how much, this societal shift will impact our future. But, it is a shift that has forty years of momentum behind it.

A Societal Shift—40 Years in the Making

Since the late 1960s and early 1970s there has been a fundamental transformational shift among U.S. consumers. While the oil crisis of the 1970s spurred some early energy and fuel conservation efforts as well as fuel efficient vehicles introduced by Toyota and Honda, it's really been the past five-to-ten years where we have witnessed a coalescing of business performance with consumer preferences and values.

Today's American consumers are different from the past. As Patricia Aburdene, best-selling author of *Megatrends 2010: The Rise of Conscious Capitalism* notes: "... there is a rise in the conscious consumer and conscious capitalism." Consumers are now purchasing products that align with their values, often very individual and complex, that include elements of spirituality, environmental responsibility, and ethical conduct.[20]

The modern day state of "environmentalism" in business has undergone three transformations and is on the cusp of a fourth transformation, marked by the emergence of the Sustainability Generation:

- ***Transformation 1 (late 1960s to late 1970s)*** This era was marked by social transformation and the emergence of environmental law. The first Earth Day was held in 1970. The 1970s witnessed a surge in environmental legislation and regulation focusing on protecting human health and the environment. The national environmental policy act (NEPA) of 1969, the Clean Air Act (1970), Environmental Pesticide Control Act (1972), Safe Drinking Water Act (1974), and Toxic Substances Control Act (1976) are some notable examples of the era (NRDC: Environmental Law).

- ***Transformation 2 (late 1970s to early 1990s)*** This era was marked by a decade of hazardous waste response and clean-up. In the late 1970s and in 1980 public awareness of hazardous waste impacts on humans became a national issue when Love Canal emerged from a local homeowner association issue to a classified national disaster (EPA and Love Canal). The 1984 industrial accident and disaster at Bhopal triggered societal concern on the safety of industrial facilities. There are many great resources covering this social history of the environmental movement.

- ***Transformation 3 (early 1990s to today)*** This era was marked by more market-based mechanisms to improve the operations of corporations. Corporations increased the roles and responsibilities of environmental managers from compliance activities to operational excellence and efficiency experts. Corporations learned that they could not only reduce compliance costs by being environmentally responsible—they could also reduce operating costs and improve their margins. This era brought rise to ISO 14001 environmental management systems, certification and auditing of environmental programs, and a focus on a slew of metrics that measured energy efficiency, waste reduction, water conservation, hazardous waste handling and reduction, recycling, and air emission reductions for most major firms. The era sprouted the modern day focus on corporate social responsibility, product stewardship, pollution prevention and corporate environmental strategy.

The world is on the verge of a new economy driven by a more socially and environmentally aware generation of global citizens. We can call it Transformation 4 of the modern environmental movement focused on the evolution of the Sustainability Generation. It is one that is being shaped by a myriad of past mistakes, promise for the future, and real-time transaction. This is occurring at a furious rate of speed. And businesses have taken on a new role in transforming this new economy by advancing "socially responsive" innovation to provide value not only directly to customer demand, but to all stakeholders. Consider some of the following trends:

- **Social Investing** In 2010, and in the United States alone, greater than $3 trillion of the investment dollars under professional management are invested in socially responsible companies that have been screened for their governance, environmental, social and corporate responsibilities efforts globally. The $3 trillion under management in the U.S. represents a 380% increase in socially responsible investments (SRI) since 1995. According to the Social Investment Forum Foundation, SRI assets in the U.S. experienced "healthy growth" during the most recent financial crisis (2007–2010) while the balance of professionally managed assets remained relatively flat.[21]

- **Eco-Innovation** Making better products: products that have social, environmental, and sustainability virtues and values embedded in them is the current state of the competitive business world. Look at companies like Toyota, Boeing, Sun Microsystems, HP, GE, Green Mountain Coffee, Suncor Energy, Interface and Siemens. What you see is a strategic choice to offer products that compete not only on price and quality, but also on a new dimension of product value: social response. Toyota's hybrid vehicles, Boeing's fuel efficient 787 Dreamliner, Sun's UltraSPARC T1 eco-responsible microprocessors, and Suncor's commitments to integrating renewable energy technologies into their portfolio are all examples of this strategy unfolding in the marketplace. This is not a "green" trend; it is a strategic decision to differentiate better products for a better world on behalf of these corporate giants.

- **Growth in Renewable Energy** The renewable energy market is exploding with force and fascination for the near future. Global wind and solar markets reached $11.8 billion and $11.2 billion in 2005—up 47% and 55% respectively from the previous year. The market for biofuels exploded to $15.7 billion globally in 2005 up more than 15% from the previous year. Multinationals like Archer Daniels Midland, BP, GE, Sharp and Toyota are all partly responsible for this strong growth in the renewable energy sector. These companies are stoking these technologies' aggressive growth, leading the way with billion dollar divisions dedicated to solar, wind power, ethanol, and hybrid electric vehicles, among other technologies," According to Clean Edge, growth in renewable energy and clean technologies is anticipated to continue through 2015.[22]

- **Responsible Lending** More than forty-five banks and financial institutions representing more than $4 trillion in assets under management have subscribed to the Equator Principles,[23] a set of voluntary guidelines for environmental and social investment for international project finance. Financial institutions including Citigroup, HSBC, Bank of America, ING, JPMorgan Chase, Wells Fargo, Wachovia, and Royal Bank of Scotland are just a sample of the global finance leaders that have adopted the principles into their lending practices for project finance. Large financial institutions have acted on concerns over climate change to improve procedures of hazardous waste handling. Brownfield redevelopment will incorporate social responsibility into their lending practices with institutions and corporations. This change is driving a transformation in capital markets as they are more cognizant of the risk of financial investments in new development and the need to maximize capital return by minimizing environmental and governance related risks. Banks are essentially requiring that businesses have a sound governance, energy, environmental, and social responsibility policy and program to implement before they move forward on large scale global development initiatives.

- **The Power of Philanthropy** The year 2006 was an incredible year for billionaires. Not only did they have a successful year of returns, they also returned billions to society. In June 2006 Warren Buffet announced that he would give away 85% of his fortune he built in Berkshire Hathaway, and the largest share, some $30 billion, would go to the Bill & Melinda Gates Foundation.[24] The Bill & Melinda Gates Foundation have committed billions of dollars toward fighting disease globally as well as reducing poverty and hunger.[25] And with a focus on energy and climate change, global health, poverty alleviation, and mitigating religious and ethnic conflict, the Clinton Global Initiative emerged in 2006 with a $7.3 billion pledge from 215 sponsors to continue these efforts globally.[26]

- **Fundamental Shifts in the Philosophy of Environmental Protection** The environmental movement in the United States and in other developed nations was born in part out of a need to curtail the creation of hazardous wastes and minimize human and environmental exposures to such risks. The risk-based approach toward environmental protection has undoubtedly protected human health and the environment for the past forty years. There has been an advancement of a "sustainability ethic and philosophy," particularly since 2000, as a voluntary and strategic opportunity for business and as a new philosophical paradigm for government. It is notable (see text box on *Key Players Question EPA's Ability to Lead New Sustainability Approach*) that in 2011 U.S. Environmental Protection Agency Administrator Lisa Jackson introduced a "new approach" required for government and industry leaders to collaborate and address contemporary environmental issues using a holistic sustainability approach. USEPA Administrator Lisa Jackson's vision for a "new approach" is the kind of leadership, forward thinking, and innovation that will be required for the Sustainability Generation to balance economic and environmental goals into the 21st Century. The science, policies, and politics that set the environmental movement in motion forty years ago are not the same requirements, necessarily, that address the complexity of sustainability related issues today. The current generation now needs to revisit, redefine, and reframe its policies, politics, and practices so that there is greater balance and equity between government, industry, and the needs of greater society.

Key Players Question EPA's Ability to Lead New Sustainability Approach

Source: Inside EPA, 1/6/2011, by Bridget DiCosmo

As EPA takes steps toward building an operational framework for incorporating sustainability measures across the agency, a landmark effort that Administrator Lisa Jackson calls **the "new approach" to environmental issues,** key former agency officials and other observers are questioning the agency's ability to lead sustainability efforts.

While Jackson recently announced the creation of a National Academy of Sciences (NAS) panel to advise the agency on **how it can replace its current risk-based approach with a more holistic sustainability approach,** some former EPA officials and current state officials say that EPA as a regulatory agency is not the right orchestrator for the responsibility.

Ann Klee, a former EPA general counsel during the Bush administration now serving as lead lawyer for the General Electric Company, suggested at a Dec. 14 meeting of the NAS panel that for EPA to adopt a truly sustainable approach across the agency, it must be willing to consider a move beyond a "binary compliance-noncompliance" regulatory framework, which Klee argued will serve to stifle current sustainability activities industry is doing on its own, to a more flexible paradigm.

Klee argued that innovations in sustainability are "driven from the bottom up, not in response to a regulatory mandate, but letting all the creative, smart thinking bubble up. It's clear that success depends on more than the traditional environmental crowd."

EPA research chief Paul Anastas announced last September the move to re-structure the agency's Office of Research & Development (ORD) to ramp its sustainability focus and more "closely align" its research with Jackson's priorities, plans that included consolidating the agency's dozen research programs into four larger programs.

The four proposed consolidated programs are safer products for a sustainable world (SPSW); air, climate and energy; sustainable water resources; and safe and healthy communities. They are aimed at replacing fragmented research with integrated transdisciplinary methods to work toward developing more sustainable, "system-based" solutions approaches to environmental issues, rather than the agency's current risk-based approach.

Anastas has described the push toward sustainability as a "seismic shift" in how the agency views challenges, with the goals being to move away from "chemical-by-chemical" risk assessment approaches in favor of systemic solutions that avoid the trap of addressing one environmental problem to have another crop up in its place.

And last month, Jackson announced EPA's plans to ask the NAS to craft novel "Green Book" recommendations advising the agency on how to integrate ORD's existing sustainability efforts into all EPA decision-making, and move the current risk assessment and risk management paradigm into a more holistic, sustainable framework. Jackson touted the drive for sustainability as "not an initiative, not a program," but a "new approach" to environmental protection.

The NAS panel faced with the task of drafting the Green Book recommendations must determine the parameters of EPA's role in advancing sustainable solutions, but many former officials and others say EPA is not the right orchestrator for the responsibility.

At the Dec. 14 meeting, Klee also urged EPA to provide more flexibility for state and local governments, saying that "states are great incubators for sustainability. We ought to let them incubate freely." Klee suggested the "blue sky proposal" of creating a new interagency team to address sustainability, saying that EPA should have a more limited role, with involvement from the Department of Energy, Department of Education and Interior

Department. This new team, which Klee said should be housed within the White House Council on Environmental Quality, should serve as a "clearinghouse for evaluating best practices."

One state official appeared to agree that EPA may not be able to provide the kinds of flexibilities needed to advance sustainable approaches to managing of water resources. Ellen Gilinsky, of the Virginia Department of Environmental Quality, said at the Dec. 14 meeting that EPA should accept and help to promote some of the department's "creative solutions" to developing more sustainability-minded water programs, such as watershed-based permitting and water quality trading. "We need to think outside the box . . .," Gilinsky said, highlighting a need for a "more flexible regulatory framework" that could offer permit incentives for water reuse and reclamation activities.

Linda Fisher, a former EPA deputy administrator during the Bush administration now serving as DuPont's vice president for sustainability, largely agreed with Klee that sustainability is a concept better driven by entrepreneurial catalysts than regulatory ones, but said **that the question "is bigger than just 'what is EPA's role?' It's 'what is government's role?' It's 'how do you define problem-solving tools to address bigger problems than are mandated in statutes?'"**

Fisher pointed to EPA's voluntary Design for the Environment and Energy Star programs, saying that non-regulatory programs tend to be more successful in encouraging innovation. And Fisher and Klee both agreed that there are opportunities for EPA to offer some consistency across the various sustainability initiatives—such as developing consistent life-cycle analysis guidelines and establishing other metrics for better characterizing sustainability.

Klee cautioned that development of such metrics could easily become a "new set of stovepipes" that would further hamper innovation. "If we tell EPA to consider what approaches drive water use down the most, that's going to have unintended consequences."

Paul Gilman, a former EPA research chief in the Bush administration now serving with Covanta Energy Corporation, asked whether the possibility of EPA developing standards within a sustainability framework that took into account a wide variety of long-term consequences, not just human and environmental health effects but water use, economic performance, and environmental justice issues—"a mishmash of sustainability issues"—make innovation easier or harder for industry.

Fisher responded that the scenario Gilman described would stifle innovation and make sustainable solutions "way harder" to implement by adding to existing regulatory burdens and making the approval process more costly and unwieldy. "It's not something you want government to have to sign off on."—Bridget DiCosmo

Reprinted with permission from Inside EPA available at http://insideepa.com/ and http://environmentalnewsstand.com/.

Lessons in Leadership: Working toward a Better Future Requires Patience and Humility

I once heard a senior executive at the New York State Energy Research and Development Authority (NYSERDA) tell an audience of college students in upstate New York that when he got into the energy business in the early 1970s he was full of optimism and focus. His intent, he said, was to dedicate a career in transforming how industry, businesses, government, and consumers perceive and use energy in the United States. Thirty years later, with a tone of regret and humbled defeat, this senior leader issued a word of caution to his audience, "don't listen to conventional wisdom ... seek out answers to the complex energy and environmental challenges of the day ... and find ways to work together."

The NYSERDA leader noted that his career began with a desire to develop new energy technologies, reduce energy demand, promote energy efficiency, and deploy renewable energy technologies on a broad scale. Reflecting that the amount of renewable generation in the United States continues to be marginal, that the fuel economy of vehicles has stayed roughly the same along with increases in energy demand and prices, the senior leader admitted that he wished his career had created more of an impact.

The story about this energy industry leader is a case study of the past thirty years. I hear similar sentiments from senior managers at large electric utilities and at big chemical, oil, and automotive companies. Their reflections of the past are rich with reasons why not more change has occurred. But one hears from them a new urgency to want to make good on the last few years of their professional careers and often their desire to launch new careers in "retirement" to take advantage of the new opportunities for advancing alternative and renewable energy.

Across the globe the race has started. Instead of one whose outcome will be judged by who lands on the moon or proliferates nuclear weaponry first, this race is more peaceful. But it is just as significant as our past technological missions. With a burgeoning population of seven billion people and a growing global economy, the demand for energy, material, and natural resources are at an all-time high. We are now seeing price signals in the marketplace that tell us that constraints to our growth include the availability, reliability, and dependability of energy and natural resources like water. In 2007 the price per barrel of oil exceeded $100 for the first time in history. Reports of global energy demand brought on by growth in China and Asia

Pacific indicated energy demand was higher than supply. In addition the political environment of 2001–2010 marked a shift in debate about global climate change and how humans should think about their carbon footprint.

Globally and regionally new economies are also being formed and reshaped by corporations designing better products influenced by a new era of philanthropists and by a transformational shift in how we think about, invest, spend, use, and make, our money. These evolving trends on money and markets are built in part on the shoulders "of Business Past." Social response to capitalism is being shaped by all of these forces and shows no signs of receding.

While no particular tipping point can be referenced, a fundamental shift of government, industry, non-government organizations (NGOs), trade associations, intergovernmental coalitions, and consumers is underway. This shift spans multiple generations and is the spawn of the Sustainability Generation.

Rebalancing Your Future

Several times a year I receive alerts from my financial investment brokerage reminding me to make the effort to annually rebalance my retirement portfolio. As the theory goes, rebalancing the initial allocations of one's retirement portfolio helps to maintain the right percentage of dollars in investment (i.e., stocks, bonds, international, and so on) that fit your stage of investing, stage of life, and future financial goals. This makes sense to me as a basic investment strategy. Hopefully it pays to rebalance and realign your portfolio so that your allocation of dollars meets your ideal positioning for growth, stability, or sustainment over the long-term. I like the alerts I receive from my brokerage.

Many of us spend time, energy, and focus on rebalancing our financial portfolios. This is a necessary and obvious need to keep our financial futures on track with our goals, expectations, and hopefully in alignment with market forces. What is interesting is that we do not necessarily spend the same time, energy, and focus on rebalancing our lifestyles in the context of societal, individual, or generational goals and aspirations, or as a reflection of signals from natural or spiritual forces. When we do make the decision to focus on this or respond to these signals, it is often reactionary, like the clean-up of the BP oil spill in the Gulf. With our rebalancing and reallocation of our retirement accounts, we are as strategic, thoughtful, guided, deliberate and anticipatory as we can be with information at hand. Yet when it comes to things that enrich, nourish, and sustain life, we do not exercise the same care and commitment to protect our future.

Rebalancing for our future, in the context of sustainability, is much like the maintenance of a retirement portfolio. This requires a deliberate and consistent assessment of the health, vitality, and abundance of the earth's natural resources in the context of sustaining human life, but also maintaining a balanced ecosystem. Humans are impacting the earth's ecology, atmosphere, water, natural resources, and energy systems in many ways. The earth's ledgers are recording human-induced positive and negative impacts. What we do not necessarily know, however, is just how much rebalancing is needed to keep the existing and future generations on track for ecologic security.

Financial security, I would argue, is directly tied to ecologic security. The conservation, protection, and enhancement of the earth's natural resources and ecologic services for providing clean water, clean air, and abundant food sources, is not just in our long-term best interest for survival; it is also our long-term best interest for financial growth and security.

To rebalance for our future we need to begin to ask the right questions, as individuals, citizens, and as generations, to keep our ecologic portfolio in check with our goals for growth, spirituality, and stewardship of our collective home, planet Earth. As you go about your daily life, consider these questions:

- Are you a "successfully" engaged citizen? What does that mean to be a "successfully engaged citizen"?

- What belongs to you as an individual? What do you own? What are your rights, privileges, responsibilities? Do you exhibit "entitlement" for goods, services, and resources?

- What belongs to "us" as society? What do "we" own? And, what are our collective rights, privileges and responsibilities? Does society exhibit "entitlement" over Earth's natural resources?

- What belongs to your "generation"? What impacts on the positive and negative side of the ecologic ledger has your generation made?

- Does "conformance" in society, either individual or generational, lead to an unbalanced ecologic (or economic) portfolio?

- How can modern innovations, technologies, institutions, and networks be deployed to help individuals and generations rebalance the ecologic portfolio for long-term sustainment?

As you can tell, there are no simple answers to these questions. In each one there are moral, ethical, and perhaps legal justifications and perceptions that can shape perspective. And in many ways, this is the point. Sustainability is not an end-state to be achieved. Sustainability is not just reacting to what has been right or wrong in our past. Rather, sustainability is a process of rebalancing the portfolio to meet the needs of the short- and long-term investors, the generation here and now, and the future generation.

The origins of a cultural shift is happening right now, in real-time throughout society. This shift is being led by individuals in a variety of demographic, geographic, and socio-economic standings. Leaders in the world's largest corporations, smallest family owned businesses, and throughout government, academia, not-for-profit organizations, and inner-city business incubators and suburban strip malls have begun to take action toward a sustainable future. The diversity and breadth of knowledge of individuals concerned about their economic, environmental, and social futures are creating a "culture of sustainability" within their organizations, networks, and generation. These leaders are challenging the assumptions of how society operates and are innovating solutions that attempt to balance and economic, environmental, and social needs. The question now becomes how these early influencers can further advocate, align, and empower a higher order of individual and generational intelligence that can support sustainability in this, and in future, generations.

Generational Accountability

The earth is a natural, dynamic, and living system. The landscape of the earth has never been static; it has changed over the millennia through the forces of nature, geology, and humans. Each of these forces have eroded and built new landscapes. Each of these forces has positive and negative impacts on the earth. While humans cannot directly influence natural and geologic earth systems, we can be accountable to our own behaviors and influences upon the earth.

Much as the way greater governance and accountability have infiltrated financial markets, the current generation needs to have greater accountability toward the sustainment of our natural resources. From a consumption point of view, humans began their relationship with the earth by taking only what they needed to survive. The arduous tasks and human systems built around hunting and gathering, and then small scale agriculture communities, was constructed to achieve survival needs of food, clothing, shelter, and procreation.

However, somehow in human existence, and particularly in the past century of our evolution, we have shifted our notion of survival to an extreme. We now burn a proverbial candle at both ends of the stick. On one end, developed countries represent highly consumptive behaviors. On another end, growing populations, particularly in the poorest regions of the world, suffer from a lack of sufficient food, clothing, shelter, and medical attention. Since humans have invented tools and gadgets, anything that allows us to shape the earth more quickly, easily and effectively—we do.

A high rate of consumption of goods and services coupled with unfettered population growth is placing incredible and damaging demands on the earth's natural resources and the ability for ecosystems to provide the services that historically enabled humans to simply survive (clean water, abundant food reserves, abundant fuel sources, and so forth). In short, humans have evolved from a relationship of "small payments from the bank" to "drawing huge loans that are now defunct." We are not paying our interest on our loans from the earth, let alone addressing the principle that we use annually by way of natural resources and the impacts associated with a consumption society.

Like no other time in history, humans face "survival" challenges. A burgeoning global population places greater demand on natural resources, and also heightens the potential catastrophic impacts that can cascade from disease, hunger, or collapse of ecosystems. The current generation has a variety of tools and solutions to adapt and manage the imminent change that will occur in our lifetime and that of our children. We already have the tools to make the world a better place in our common intellect, humanity, and sense of humility. In my personal view, a social enlightenment about individual and generational restraint along with intelligent innovation is necessary if we are to continue living in any harmony on the earth.

We are now improving, in general, the culture of behaviors that have created excess, waste, and many of the inefficient systems in finance, industry, and government. I recently heard at a regional "Green Jobs Summit" a "business generalist" say the past decade has been like a slap in the face or a splash of cold water in the face of business. The generalist represented a small architect and engineering company in Rochester, New York—not a big three-auto or nation-state. The point here is that the "small guys" have caught on, and it is from there where I feel innovation will be born, momentum gained, and a quickening of social transformation begun.

But the small business transformation will take time, and it will take us only so far. I do believe a necessary correction in the form of individual and generation behaviors remains. That is, more foundational and philosophical questions need to be asked of consumers, industry, government, and society at large: What is too much? Who decides what is too much? And where are we collectively going? As the world gets smaller—do we become more ambitious as a society and risky and daring? The BP spill would have one believe so, as we search greater depths of our oceans for oil, or consider the search for water on Mars. Or do we cap our human ego of conquering our natural world and relearn what it means to be a care-taker of this fine planet, much like the way we began? These are questions that we should be discussing daily—not putting this off for technology to decide.

The existing mix of generations (young, middle-aged, and old) can work toward a more sustainable existence with the earth. The solution is simple, yet difficult to implement. Society needs innovation, creativity, and entrepreneurship. This will provide us with the products and services that reduce demand for natural resources or help us clean-up past environmental damages. Society also needs proper governance, policies, and controls to help us protect ecosystems, financial markets, and people. And, society needs to reestablish its role as a steward of the earth, not just a taker. The Sustainability Generation shares a common humanity. We have the ability to unlock the ways in which we can work as individuals and as generations to sustain a focused and shared effort to adapt to environmental change, and to adopt new consumptive behaviors to seed the development of innovation and technology that can enable us to meet our needs, not just for today, but also for tomorrow.

Going Beyond Generational "He Said, She Said"

Generation X and Y (those typically in mid 20s to early 40s) have an enormous weight on their shoulders. As a Gen Xer I will try not to sound too whiny here, but being born after the Baby Boom generation is no picnic. No, Gen X and Yers not have not had World Wars, a Great Depression, or a major pandemic flu epidemic to completely change or define our generation. But what we do have is a lot of asymmetrical and distributed "issues" and lot of baggage from the past.

While the threat and acts of terrorism, health epidemics, environmental pollution, and economic woes are not new with our generation, these issues are becoming more prevalent and cascading. With more than seven billion people now on the planet there is much greater potential for economic and environmental chaos that can directly affect us as humans. We don't have just one or two major issues to address as a society. We have hundreds of small issues that if not monitored, analyzed, remediated, or acted upon can become big issues very quickly. For example, since 1970 the following significant events impacting human health, our natural environment, and global economy have happened:

- Love Canal disaster, August 7, 1978
- Bhopal disaster, December 2, 1984
- Chernobyl disaster, April 26, 1986
- Exxon Valdez oil spill, March 24, 1989
- Gulf War
- World Trade Center Bombing, February 26, 1993
- Oklahoma City Bombing, April 19, 1995
- Terrorist Attack on World Trade Center, September 11, 2001
- War in Iraq
- War in Afghanistan
- Decade of Greed (2000–2010)—Enron, Worldcom, Tyco, Bernie Maddoff and other financial debacles
- Hurricane Katrina, 2005
- Global Financial Meltdown, 2007–2010
- BP Gulf of Mexico Oil Catastrophe, May 2010
- 9.0 magnitude earthquake triggering the devastating tsunami off the Pacific coast of Thoku, Japan, March 2011

Figure 1.1 further illustrates how environmental sustainability has been evolving over the past thirty years. The ability to monitor, adapt to, and effect change is the heart of sustainability. The post-Baby Boom generations that will comprise the beating heart and new age vision of the "Sustainability Generation," are the generations that accept the changes before us and works together to move society past one of entitlement toward empowerment and enlightenment.

Figure 1.1

Ongoing Evolution of Environmental Sustainability

Created by Mark C. Coleman

1950s–1970s

Era of Disdain & Discovery

Illustrative Events:
Silent Spring by Rachel Carson is published (1962)
Clean Air Act (1963)
National Environmental Policy Act (1969)
Clean Water Act (1972)
Small Is Beautiful by E. F. Schumacher is published (1973)
RCRA (1976)
Love Canal (1978)
The Nature Conservancy, Environmental Defense and Natural Resources Defense Council were all formed.

1980s–1990s

Era of Awareness, Regulation/Enforcement & Clean-up

Illustrative Events:
CERCLA (1980)
Bhopal Disaster (1984)
Chernobyl nuclear disaster (1986)
Water Quality Act (1987)
Brundtland Report introduces "sustainability" (1987)
Intergovernmental Panel on Climate Change (IPCC) is established by UNEP and WMO (1988)
Clean Air Act Amendments (1990)
GEMI is formed (1990)
ISO 14000 environmental management standards (1996)
Kyoto Protocol is agreed upon (1997)
Dow Jones Sustainability Indexes launch (1999)

Figure 1.1 (continued)

Ongoing Evolution of Environmental Sustainability

2000s–2010s

Era of Disclosure, Financial & Global Assessment "Stock Valuation & Taking Stock" on Impacts

Illustrative Events:
- Millennium Ecosystem Assessment (2001)
- EU WEEE Directive (2002)
- United States Sarbanes Oxley Act (2002)
- Chicago Climate Exchange (CCX) launches (2003)
- The Equator Principles are developed (2003)
- EU RoHS (2006)
- EU REACH (2007)
- SEC Guidance on Carbon Disclosure (2010)

Beyond 2010

Era of the Sustainability Generation: Accountability & Action

Illustrative Events:
- BP Gulf of Mexico Oil Spill (2010)
- Japan's Nuclear Crisis post 2011 Tsunami and Earthquake
- London Riots of 2011
- Continued Uncertainty on Carbon Regulations and the long term impacts of Climate Change
- Social Response Capitalism Corporations taking leadership role in social response capitalism—delivering superior products that address social needs and improve the environment. See the books "World Inc." and "The Surprising Solution" by Bruce Piasecki
- A need to address natural resource constraints in the context of a burgeoning world population
- Access to "commons" including clean air, water, fisheries, and minerals more and more a competitive factor globally.

However, those born after the Baby Boomer generation cannot achieve this alone. The United States has an aging population. The sector of those aged 55+ will grow nearly three times faster than the U.S. population as a whole between 2000 and 2020. Thus younger generations must understand, appreciate, and tap into the intellect and knowledge that comprises what Tom Brokaw calls the "Greatest Generation." If Generation X and Y are the beating heart of the Sustainability Generation, then Baby Boomers are its spirit and mind, offering wisdom and guidance from their experience.

The "Sustainability Generation" will require all generations to work together in concert with one another. The challenge in the next decade will find ways for those that are growing up to work with those that are grown up in ways that are constructive, collaborative and consequential. The Sustainability Generation will help to save not just the planet, but also the people that make up this vast land we call Earth.

The challenge before us has become dramatically more transparent in the past generation. As the world population has grown from an estimated one billion in 1810 to seven billion 200 years later, there has been an incredible amount of damage from human error in the earth's ecosystem. That error is in the form of overconsumption, environmental degradation, air and water pollution, and irreversible damage to sensitive natural resources and ecosystems. Several global studies monitored by organizations have reported on our human errors in the past decade in particular. Global organizations have in many ways fallen short in their goals to set policies and practices to create swift change to impact the correction of our human error. *Why is that?*

Part of the answer is generational "**entitlement.**" Entitlement, a belief that one is "entitled" to certain privileges is the common denominator in why the current generation has more "baggage," all of those little but highly explosive issues, than past generations. This is not stated as reason for whining about our lot in life. It is given as a matter of fact and a prelude to why and how our generation (Baby Boomers, Gen Xers and the Millennial, Gen Yers) and future generations must move beyond issues of entitlement toward empowerment and enlightenment. We see this transformation happening in society right now. Cars, homes, computers, and clothes are getting greener. Corporations have begun to transform the entire product life-cycle, from cradle-to-grave-to-cradle as new-age model of responsible product development and consumer consumption.

Small-and-large corporations, including some of the world's best know bands like Coca-Cola, Green Mountain Coffee Roasters, Patagonia, Johnson & Johnson, Nike, Sharp, and Wal-Mart have instituted sustainability policies and supply chain practices. These and many in industry are accepting the drivers of change before them: changing customer preferences for more sustainable products, stricter rules governing greenhouse gas (GHG) emissions and climate change impacts, higher uncertainty in the volatility of energy and commodity prices, and investor requests for greater transparency and reportable progress on sustainability goals.

There is a fundamental shift happening in people and subsequently the systems and institutions that people have created: government, industry, capitalism, and even religion. Too often we, as a society, decouple the individual (the person) from the systems and institutions we've created. It is as if those systems and institutions have a mind of their own. It is easier to point the finger and place blame on capitalism, industry, or big government when things are not going our way. In many ways, there is legitimacy to this. However, at the heart of every institution is its decision-makers, policies, and practices—all of which are defined by its people. As people, generically, begin to shift their beliefs and values toward greater accountability and responsibility regarding sustainability, our systems and institutions will catch up. The following sums up an approach for facilitating a value-shift in people and institutions so that the Sustainability Generation not only emerges, but also thrives in managing imminent change:

- *First* The key to unlocking a change in people, and having an impact on institutional policies and practices, is first an individual and then societal recognition that living with entitlement is unsustainable. This is happening today as "eco-innovators" come to life inside college and university business and technology incubators or from within corner coffee shops or behind their corporate cubes.

- *Second* This belief has to be reinforced by empowering people to accept and act upon change. People are now influencing many new social-networks, start-ups and corporate product development efforts that pull away from "entitlement" and toward empowerment.

- *Third* Public-and-private institutions and human-built systems need to be enlightened. We see top-down shifts in government, industry, and religion. It was telling when Pope Benedict XVI made direct ties to climate change and the sustainment of religion and society. Embedded in the Pope's message is one of hope, but also caution and warning that if society cannot come to grips with our view of entitlement toward Earth's abundance (natural resources), we may fall victim to an uncertainty that cannot be predicted nor ignored.

- *Fourth* Society needs to co-exist with the earth in balance, a share eco-equity that can benefit people and planet in harmony. With a focus on equity, people, and our institutions we can define the balance that is needed to sustain, improve, and enhance life for humans and for the Earth's ecosystems. By instilling a culture an ethic of eco-equity, we can remove entitlement from the masses and eventually shift generations away from having negative baggage to having equitable holdings.

Figure 1.2 summarizes some of the forces and influences upon how the Sustainability Generation is being shaped. While GenXers and GenYers are wrestling with entitlement from a negative sense, entitlement can be positive.

Figure 1.2

Elements Impacting the Evolution of a
Sustainability Generation

Created by Mark C. Coleman

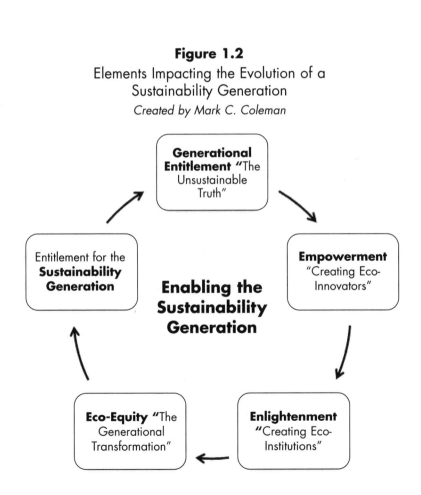

Sustainability is a Human Endeavor

The Sustainability Generation is about embracing the intellect, passion, power, and resilience of humans. The underlying bedrock of sustainability lies in our ability to invent, innovate, maintain, what is necessary to our survival and well-being and to destroy what is harmful. Each of these actions are led by humans within the context of the perceived needs of any given generation and the natural forces of nature, the physical and chemical processes of Earth and Earth's relationship with the cosmos. Humans can currently only influence certain aspects of sustainability: our relationship as givers and takers and stewards of the earth. Conceptually and practically, sustainability of humans resides, in what we can control, within ourselves in both our individual (self) and collective (generational) relations with the world around us. At the heart of this is our ability to be accountable to ourselves in our daily life, as we age and as we nurture new generations into this world. The decisions and actions we made 100 years ago and the decisions we make and actions we take today and tomorrow about our relationship with the earth ultimately determine our sustainability. Thus we have collectively an enormous power and great responsibility as the highest form of life on Earth. As the Sustainability Generation evolves globally, we need to ask ourselves individually, and as entire generations comprising a global society, are we:

- *Informed* to have the right balance of data, information and knowledge?

- *Governed* to be representative of all nations and people on earth make responsible societal decisions in the context of a diverse value and belief system that accepting of all humans?

- *Empowered* to take action in our individual daily lives toward bettering the world. and toward the organizations, enterprises, and human-environmental-societal systems we live and work within?

- *Enlightened* to have an awareness and openness to the external world in the context of one's self, and to remain open to phenomena, events, situations, and occurrences that fall outside of our control, understanding, knowledge, and intellect?

- *Accountable* to ourselves, our families, communities, and current and future generations? Accountability is the underlying key to sustainability success.

Humans continue to assess, understand, and make sense of the world and universe around them. We do not have all the answers, but are a curious species that seeks facts and accepts shared beliefs. By being informed, empowered, and enlightened there is greater probability that we as individuals and generations will be in tune with ourselves, and the world around us. In doing so we can be more conscious of our choices and decisions related to living a more sustainable and healthy lifestyle. By having the right information, perspective, and knowledge individuals can determine their role within the Sustainability Generation.

As individuals that make up broader society, finding balance is essential to our collective and future sustainability. As a society, whether we are deep-ocean drilling for oil, mass-producing solar cells, converting vehicle fleets to run on cleaner fuels, or re-evaluating how we source and consume food, we have choices and we will make mistakes. The point of the Sustainability Generation is to not necessarily be afraid of change, and not to be afraid of trying new things. The Sustainability Generation is now operating in a very ambiguous time in history. Great uncertainty surrounds the future of natural resources, ecologic biodiversity, and ecosystem services that provide society with critical life-support "commons" such as clean air, water, and food resources. It is as important to how the Sustainability Generation deals with natural or man-made changes and disasters as it is to creating a culture that can define what sustainability means within the context of the current generation so that there are balanced approaches toward determining that future generations have the resources they need to exist. Our ability to sustain the earth's natural resources and ensure that our needs and those of future generations are met, resides only with us—the current generation.

Chapter Summary

- Global economic, environmental, and social challenges continue to unfold with seemingly greater pace and impact, particularly in a world nearing 7 billion people.
- We live on a planet with fixed resources; thus there are limits to traditional methods of production and consumption.
- Sustainability is a human endeavor. It is about people and our interaction with one another and the natural world around us.

- There is little to be accomplished if we put ourselves at odds with one another in a "he said—she said" or "older versus younger generation" debate. The challenges and needs of society far outweigh the pettiness of politics and ego for us to delay a more collaborative spirit of innovation and change toward sustainability.

- The Sustainability Generation is forty-plus years in the making. There have been significant societal shifts and transformations that have contributed to the current state of play and affairs in sustainability. Further, a convergence of new data, information, leadership, and public participation is helping to substantiate and drive the evolution of the Sustainability Generation.

2

Entitlement and Indulgence

In Your Backyard:
A World of Erroneous Consumption

Imagine a world where vehicles that get 9 MPGs rule the road and are the lawn ornaments of 3,500 sq. ft. homes chockfull of consumer products, electronic gadgets, and "stuff," most of which will be obsolete within two to three years or worth very little on the dollar. In this world many conveniences are available twenty-four hours a day: breakfast-lunch-or-dinner, carwashes, pharmacies, movie theatres, grocery and retail stores, and gas stations, among many other establishments. In this world the dollar is king and consumption is a close second. In this world it is acceptable for families to eat out at fast-food establishments seven days a week. It is acceptable to have a vehicle that gets a whopping 9 MPG (as long as it looks cool and has a nice sound system to boot). In this world it is acceptable and understood that consumer products and "daily life" create waste and that this waste, whether it goes into the trash, down the drain, or up the stake, is something that everyone deals with. And therefore is OK that we have to deal with it as well. In this world we've come to accept our unconscious use of resources and our thoughtless consumption of goods, whether it is accepting cars that get 9 MPG, or fast food meals that are high in fat, or accepting that the life-cycle for many consumer electronics is two years or less. And in this world it is acceptable to "buy-buy-buy" your way to a life of perceived happiness and wealth.

When described in this way, the ways of this world sound wasteful, unrealistic, and perhaps downright stupid. People are unaccountable for their impacts today and tomorrow. Yet this world is our reality, the one we have as individuals and generations created as our "modern and civilized" society. In relatively few years the problems of energy price volatility, the scarcity of water and swift changes in the global economy have greatly affected developed nations. But our transformation from this unsustainable world has just begun with our awareness of this crisis. For the sake of simplicity let's say we hit bottom, were scared sober, and are now beginning our ten-step plan to recovery. But recovery is not just a plan to be put into place. Recovery is about a behavior change that requires leadership, focus, and vigilance over a sustained period of time.

Since World War II we have been on an erroneous consumption addiction, particularly in the United States. We buy products and services sometimes for no good reason other than "I want that," or "My neighbor has that, so should I." or "That is the latest, newest, and best, so I need to have it." These justifications for erroneous consumption are false and do not lead to wealth creation or personal happiness. Instead, these traits of consumption in U.S. society are leading the United States and many developed nations down a slippery and unsustainable path of economic and ecologic damage. The middle classes of many developed countries have more wealth than any time in history. However, how this wealth is measured and how money is invested will be the true determination on whether the "wealth" of the middle classes is a legacy or simply a one-time flashy show, like a Dennis Kozlowski birthday party for his wife. I argue that as a broad generalization, the Baby Boomer, Generation X, and Millennial generations are failing superbly at creating lasting wealth and are very much caught up in the here-and-now "it's all about me and my wants" perception of wealth.. The post WWII generations generally have fleeting notions of money and wealth. Somehow in the past fifty years or so, three generations of people have earned more, spent more, and destroyed more than any other time in history. Let's say the current post World War II generations are partying and spending their money and behaving like Dennis Kozlowski.

Welcome to the world of Erroneous Consumption. It is difficult to pinpoint when erroneous consumption began. It likely can be traced back to the first introduction of wealth in society, where the financial and class divide between the haves and have-nots became demarcated by power, prestige, and the accumulation of "finer things," basically just stuff. Many have argued that a well- functioning capitalistic system needs to have wealthy and less wealthy individuals and that there is nothing wrong with a division between the wealthy and not so wealthy. In the roaring 20s and in many industrial eras prior to this one, wealthy industrialist's often put their wealth into sprawling estates, philanthropic endeavors, or toward self-indulgence in the "finer things" in life. Since World War II the middle classes in the United States and other countries and regions of the world (Europe, Asia, China, and India) have begun to have a higher standard of living and to have many choices to make as they create wealth.

As more masses of individuals and entire generations of people have begun to have more money, they also have begun to accumulate more material things. Well functioning capitalism, right? I'm defining erroneous consumption here as a "mindless, heartless, and unconscious desire to accumulate stuff to fulfill one's perceived notion of wealth and class, worth and identity." What that means is that the more stuff I have, the better I feel, and the more others will admire me and see that I am financially successful. Call it the middle class keeping up with the Joneses phenomenon or one similar to what Alan Greenspan termed "Irrational Exuberance," an unrealistic and fevered optimism to over-speculate in the stock market. The point is that erroneous consumption began as a trickle post-World War II and has become a full flood in the middle classes in many developed nations. The effect and impact of this on individuals and generations, if left unfettered, will yield unsustainable economic and ecologic systems throughout the world. There have been signs of this happening and growing in force and severity in the past decade. Now, it is true that my purchase of a new coffee maker at Wal-Mart is not likely to result in the next global financial meltdown or new political unrest in North and South Korea. However, when hundreds of millions of people with more purchasing power than ever before choose to invest their money in more objects to give them a perceived sense of wealth, these unconscious, unsustainable behaviors and impacts on economic and ecologic systems can cascade very rapidly.

But now imagine a world where people live free of disease, hunger or political unrest. Imagine a world where wars are not waged over natural resources and celebrations are held when saving fragile ecosystems. Imagine a world where the new capital is ecologic and where wealth is measured not just by what vehicle sits in the driveway, but in how many tons of CO_2 were diverted or never created. This is the world that the current generation is beginning to define. This new world is being charted by green entrepreneurs, educators, industrialists, housewives, and dads, and major corporations.

This Sustainability Generation has sprouted out of the failures of erroneous consumption that has been occurring over the past fifty years (and more rapidly in the past twenty). The real implications of unsustainable erroneous consumption have been seen and felt by many in the past two years. The global financial meltdown left many investors with a mere pittance of their original retirement portfolios. The sights of the BP oil catastrophe in Gulf of Mexico slowly becoming the worst man-made environmental disaster in history have been alarming and sobering. The current generation has some tough questions to address in the next few years and throughout its life-time. Questions of constraint, how much is too much, and what constitute wealth and happiness, are all on the table for conversation and reflection. Modern society is grateful for having a standard of living that allows us to get medications at 3 a.m. or eat breakfast at 3 p.m. or have millions of choices before us across many products and services. In this way capitalism is not flawed; it is reacting well to consumer demand. What we as individuals and generations of consumers need to do, however, is to become more conscious of the choices before us, and more educated about our perceptions about the reality of wealth creation for ourselves and for future generations. The following examples illustrate how erroneous consumption has infiltrated and impacted our lives.

Our Love of Free Products: The Baby Formula Example

Getting free stuff in the mail is not something new. When our second son Neal Garrett was born in May 2010, we received many free packages of baby formula. My wife was breastfeeding our son when he was born, so the formula was not of use to us at that time. Had my wife decided not to breastfeed Neal perhaps the free baby formula in the mail might have been welcomed. Since that time I began to think more about the idea of free products in our society and how much waste they create. I'd personally much prefer that a company send me a coupon offering to ship us at no cost a free product if we choose to try it, versus a company that makes the assumption that we will try the free baby formula they ship to us, with their additional assumption that my family is accepting of wasteful consumption. My wife and I didn't have any options except to throw the formula away. Our friends and family with new babies were either breastfeeding or using a different brand of baby formula.

There are many instances of this kind of presumption throughout our society from governments and corporations that impact our daily consumptive decisions and our sense of entitlement. Many people might love receiving free baby formula in the mail. I love free things when they are of use to me or my family, but in the case I see it as nonsensical waste. In the end, energy, materials, water, and financial and human capital were expended just to try to entice my family to try that brand of baby formula. Perhaps this is accepted and justified as the price of earning new market share and new loyal customers. But from my perspective, consumers and corporations need to become smarter at earning and maintaining each other's trust if we are to rid ourselves of entitlement and work toward a more sustainable world. Both companies and consumers perpetuate a sense of entitlement throughout our society. However, consumers have a great deal of power. We can shift corporate behavior and this change starts with our being more aware, more responsible, and more critical of those that sell or provide free products to us.

Our Disengagement within Families

There seems to me to be an unfortunate disengagement of members within the family structure in the United States and in many other developed nations. Perhaps this is a natural evolution of family and society; or perhaps it is a reflection that the more wealth that is created and the more stuff we bring into our world, the less engaged we are with one another. A great deal has been written on the disaggregation of families and the fact that greater than 50% of U.S. marriages end in divorce. But what is not written about frequently is the impact of divorce and the breakdown of family structure on human health and the environment. There are the emotional impacts on children, husband and wife and extended family, and friends that are unfortunate and damaging effects. But there are also impacts like increased consumption of goods and services, greater reliance on fast foods, less social interaction, and often the gifts resulting from parental guilt that are building a sense of entitlement in our youth as opposed to a sense of character and strength.

Families of divorce often divide assets and go separate ways. They go from living in one house with one kitchen, one bathroom, and one entertainment center, to dividing children between two households with double the things that they used to have. Now, I'm not going to suggest that those who divorce should reconsider their situation to help save the environment. But it is interesting to consider that families with divorced parents usually consume more. I often see divorced fathers and mothers at shopping malls with their children. The children ask their parents for the latest pair of $100 jeans as they are texting their best friend. I imagine that in many cases the reluctant "OK" from the parents is due to a sense of guilt about the emotional damage of their dissolved relationship. I'm not going to pass judgment on other parents, but as individuals and society we should be aware that buying the $100 jeans out of guilt does not teach our children anything except entitlement and the idea that if they feel wronged they should automatically get something. I do believe that the dissolution of family structure in the United States is a critical societal challenge that directly impacts the wellbeing of our youth and also our natural environment. If we are to heal our ecosystems we must first heal our egos and our families to be stronger.

Our Disengagement with the Natural Resources, Agriculture and Energy

Another critical societal challenge before us is a general disengagement we have with the natural environment. Many environmentalists have over the decades, especially when celebrating Earth Day, proclaimed a need for us to get back to basics and become closer to the natural world. Yet year by year we seem to actually become more distanced; that is, unless we make a conscious effort to engage with the natural world around us. I love the outdoors and the entire splendor it has to offer. However, if I don't make the time to take a hike, ride a bike, go fishing, or simply sit and have a picnic under a tree, I will not experience the natural world. I observe from my house and car the changes I see in my neighborhood. But much of the landscape has been engineered, maintained, and re-structured by humans.

Many children in larger cities have little knowledge about where beef, milk, or cheese comes from, let alone how electricity is generated and distributed. As we distance our stomachs and our thermostats from the sources of the products we consume, we become less aware of our impact on natural resources and the natural-and-human built systems that enable our quality of life. There is so much assumption and entitlement built into our daily lives in developed countries. We have, in a very short period of human existence, engineered incredible systems for delivering power, water, food, clothing, and shelter. We have also engineered amazing infrastructure to handle our waste streams and in many cases to clean them up or reutilize them. But with these systems in place the average consumer acts like a "black box." Stuff comes in and stuff goes out with little awareness, recognition, or conscious thought about what is too much, what the impact is on the resources consumed, or what the impact might be on future generations. The human-built environment and systems protect us and alleviate our concerns for clean water, reliable energy, and dependable food supplies. But what if these systems fail to perform? What if these systems become too constrained? I would argue that much of our built environment is becoming constrained and is now in need of modernization, adaptation, and a realignment with what our true natural resource needs are beyond what we feel we are entitled to.

Our Desire to Stroke the Ego: Viagra, A Gateway Drug into Self-Indulgence

You've likely seen the commercials on television. A man and woman sit in bathtubs overlooking some scenic vista. Or a man and woman suddenly get a romantic urge while doing laundry and then find themselves in an oasis of a rainforest engulfed in pleasure. Usually in these commercials it is an older man and woman and much of the male enhancement drugs on the market are targeted to older men. Now, as a man, I confess that should I find myself at an age and physical condition where my unit doesn't work as well anymore, I am all for some form of performance enhancement. This is a personal, individual choice. But it is also ego-driven and entirely focused on self-indulgence. There is nothing wrong with this. It is interesting to note however that sexually transmitted diseases are rising fast in young adults under the age of twenty-five and in older adults over the age of fifty-five. Drugs like Viagra help revitalize a sense of youth, agelessness, and freedom in males. I bring this example up to make the point that ego, entitlement, self-indulgence, and erroneous consumption are intricately linked. We are driven by our ego, that thick headed voice that is tough to reason with and which likes to justify our behaviors.

Our ego makes us believe that we are entitled to things, even if they are at odds with the health of ourselves or our ecosystems. As we self-indulge in medications, are we demonstrating a new kind of erroneous consumption? There are seemingly drugs for every ailment: for enhanced sexual activity, for restless legs, for sleepless nights, for hypertension, for over-anxiousness, for dieting, for chronic dry eyes, etc. Some ailments are truly negative and dangerous and I don't mean to sound insensitive, but some of the drugs advertised seem ridiculous. The drugs are a patch to our erroneous consumptive lifestyles. They mask the real cause of our ailments and mask the truth of our behaviors. Instead of treating the problems we encounter in our daily lives, we treat the symptoms with prescription drugs thinking that we will be better. For a time, perhaps the symptoms go away (we are less anxious, we lose some weight, we sleep better), but eventually other problems occur, such as the disclaimers on many drugs that state how this drug may cause nausea, vomiting, dizziness, dry mouth, loss of eye-sight, etc., and we are told not to operate heavy machinery or try to carry on an intelligent conversation. Why can't we skip the drug fixes and instead focus on proper health, good nutrition, and sound physiological and emotional well-being? The challenge for the Sustainability Generation will be to move society beyond unsustainable characteristics of entitlement, instant gratification, continuous self-indulgence, and unconscious and erroneous consumption. Our generation needs to question its consumption of goods and services in the context of what is right and wrong, sustainable and unsustainable, and whether consumption is masking hidden truths or truly addressing our needs.

Examining Entitlement in Society

In August 2011 London experienced some of the heaviest and worst rioting it had seen in decades. Triggered by the tragic event of the April 4, 2011, a fatal shooting by police of Mark Duggan, a 29-year-old father of four during their attempt to arrest him, thousands of England's youth took to the streets in a revolt that went on for many months. Rioters went on a looting rampage throughout London and surrounding districts causing destruction and chaos as they showed their disregard for authority and social structure. In total, more than 2,800 people were arrested. During this time British Prime Minster David Cameron issued remarks, blaming "a culture of entitlement and irresponsibility among British youth" as the culprit of the events. He went on to state how greed and irresponsibility had infiltrated big government and the banking industry, and that the need to restore a sense of civility and accountability needed to happen for a better functioning society. In August 2011 Prime Minister Cameron stated,[27]

> ... *"We have been too unwilling for too long to talk about what is right and wrong ... [Moral Collapse happens in a society when there are] children without fathers, schools without discipline, reward without effort, crime without punishment, rights without responsibilities and communities without control. ... In the banking crisis, with MPs' [Military Policy] expenses, in the phone hacking scandal, we have seen some of the worst cases of greed, irresponsibility and entitlement. The restoration of responsibility has to cut right across our society."*
>
> —British Prime Minister David Cameron, August 2011

The August 2011 riots in London were dramatic. I remember seeing an interview of a woman, perhaps in her mid-thirties, crying and pleading for answers to why London's youth seemed to have lost all control. The woman in the interview was a mother of young children. They were not involved in the riots. She was clearly terrified and perplexed about what was happening all around her. The remarks by British Prime Minster Cameron were a reaction to the chaos that engulfed greater London in the weeks and months following April 4, including the feelings of helplessness that filled the faces and minds of many like the woman in the interview. Reviewing many articles, blogs, and seeing the reaction of many people interviewed during the event, it was clear that Prime Minister Cameron's comments struck a chord with many. Some people agreed with his critical review of "moral collapse, "yet others were critical of his depiction of what was occurring. What was clear to me was that "entitlement" can be a sensitive word. As a result, I will attempt to offer perspective on what I mean by "entitlement" and how in many ways, I agree with the sentiment of Prime Minister Cameron. There does appear to be an underbelly of indifference and a mounting frustration within society.

Entitlement is a belief that one is "entitled" to certain privileges. Those privileges may include access to clean potable water, or the availability of electricity, or affordable healthcare. Privileges, in the context of entitlement, are defined by both individual and societal beliefs and values. An individual who works long hours as a server at a busy Italian restaurant in Boston may feel after a 10-hour shift, "entitled" to a free glass of wine and perhaps taking home a spaghetti dinner. What if the server after a busy shift invited three friends to the restaurant, enjoyed a full bottle of wine with them and then took home a prime-rib dinner and dessert for free? Is the individual abusing his or her entitlement and the employer's views of entitlement? There are beliefs, values, and boundaries we as individuals and as society place on entitlement. These beliefs and values are assembled through personal and shared experience. The monetary value of a spaghetti dinner and one glass of wine seems somehow reasonable as an "entitled" privilege after a long days work. A bottle of wine, a prime-rib, and dessert seems excessive and perhaps a bit presumptuous and greedy as a privilege.

If, however, the Italian restaurant server did an incredible job when the restaurant was busier than usual, or the server waited on a table with an enormous bill with a high degree of service, perhaps the range of entitlement privileges changes and a prime-rib dinner with dessert and wine are reasonable privileges. The restaurant owner of course would be the bearer of how the privilege is determined and whether the server is entitled to it.

In every facet of modern society, the simple scenario of the Italian restaurant server and questions of entitlement are played out. There are questions of morality, ethics, and professional conduct in many scenarios, but at the heart of each case is a pure and basic question: Why is an individual or an institution (or society for that matter) entitled to something?

Generational entitlement is the set of privileges a particular generation feels that it has, and is owed, and what the generation seeks based upon that generation's beliefs, values, and accumulated knowledge and experiences. Generational entitlement is justified on the basis that "If everyone else is doing it, why not me?" This is a huge deficiency in modern society, one that contributes in our view to critical flaws in our healthcare and educational systems to shortcomings in natural resource, energy, and environmental policies. Some of the recent economic crisis may also be attributed to generational entitlement issues, including perceived notions of how pension plans should be funded and invested and the amount of healthcare coverage retirees should have access to.

Examples of entitlement are ever-present and recurring in our society. Probably you or someone you know has been in situations where you took or consumed more than necessary. Perhaps you or someone you know has rationalized a decision on the basis that "Others are doing it, so why not me?" or "There is so much of something that no one will miss a little being taken." The control of personal impulse and temptation is difficult. It takes maturity, experience, sound judgment, a moral compass, and knowledge of what the recourse may be if impulse and temptation lead to undesired consequences. Entitlement is experienced individually and justified by large groups (including entire generations). The following examples help to further examine what is meant by "entitlement in the context of sustainability."

Having Your Cake and Eating It, Too!

Entitlement starts at a young age. Unfortunately, most don't have the capacity to rid ourselves of this human condition that is directly tied to our inability to fully realize the potential of sustainability. When the impulse of a child at a birthday party leads her or him to break off a little piece of cake it seems benign, perhaps cute. Children's temptation increases when they realize they did not get in trouble the first time, so the child may go back for more and in a swift motion take a larger piece. This can recur until the child gets caught and is embarrassed at being yelled at, or the child realizes he or she has taken too much cake and others will notice, or the cake is taken away. The impact of one child swiping some cake may be small. Sure some frosting is gone; there may be finger prints, maybe even a non-graceful chunk of cake is entirely missing. But, all in all the cake is intact and still in a quantity and condition to be enjoyed. However, what if ten of the child's friends caught on to what was happening and decided if their friend is grabbing some cake, "Why can't and why shouldn't I?" Without any rules, guidance, recourse, or oversight the temptation and impulse of the children might lead to a cake that is devoured, or when served doesn't even look like a cake!

Grass Is Always Greener: Keeping Up with the Kardashians

Don't you just hate it when your neighbor's lawn looks so perfect? It is nicely landscaped, nicely trimmed and GREEN! Your neighbor provides that extra attention in the form of fertilizer and extra water to keep that baby plush, green, and as if every blade of grass were specifically engineered for perfection. Well, you should have that too! Right? The psychology of "everyone is doing it so why not me" is complex. In the back of one's mind the knowledge that fertilizers contribute to water pollution and other ecologic degradation exists, but it cannot compete with the human ego and desire to have, or be entitled to, as green a lawn as one's neighbor. This is fundamentally the crux of many sustainability challenges. We know our moral boundaries and obligations, yet we often dismiss them or make justifications for why our actions go outside those boundaries. Like a child taking cake, adults in many instances don't have positive or negative reinforcement for decisions that impact human health and environment. If the grass is dying, add more water. If the weeds are sprouting, add more fertilizer. The direct and indirect impacts of keeping up with the neighbors are not immediately felt. When you drive mile after mile through the suburban jungle, you think "everyone is doing it so why not me?" We see this sense of entitlement play out in society, in our backyard, and in "reality" television shows like "Keeping up with the Kardashians." Until the individual and society wrestles with our flawed notion of entitlement, we will not be in a position to be true stewards of our lawns, our communities, our educational systems, or our natural resources.

Living the "American Dream"

The analogy between individual and societal entitlement with "Keeping up with the Kardashians" (aka, the Joneses) transcends almost all mass consumptive behaviors in industrialized countries. In the United States the automobile, the home, and the consumer products of everyday life are all examples of feelings of entitlement gown awry. Why do disconnects exist between the utility of many products for consumer needs and what is available for purchase and consumption? From the point of view of entitlement, there are huge disconnects in many product segments. For example, automobiles exist to get us from point A to point B and back again in a safe and reliable way. Yet in most car commercials human desires for luxury, comfort, power, speed and high performance are pushed and sold to the consumer. Consumers are fed a steady diet of "this is possible" and "you need this" and "you work hard, you deserve this" as opposed to "this is what you need and this is what we have." What if the options for a vehicle were not grounded in this notion of "high performance and high technology" but rather in low cost, high reliability, and safety? What would that car look like? In modern society there is the ongoing challenge of who drives the messaging and who is influencing decision-making. Consumers have incredible power, as does government and industry. Yet as consumers we often consume what is fed to us because (1) it exists; (2) we may not have all the facts behind what is right, wrong, or possible and (3) we don't know any better until we try. Greater constraint and greater accountability is needed in consumer behaviors across all product categories.

This is not a blanket de-facto position to try to change product innovation or the fundamentals of capitalism. The magic of capitalism should always be organic and allowed to be dictated by the forces at work. However, more critical thinking about the true needs of society is required if we are to truly make significant shifts toward more responsible use of natural resources and sustainable development. Not to pick on the Baby Boom generation again, but that generation in many ways drove the modern ideals of consumption and over-consumption. As they came out of the Great Depression and the World War era the U.S. Baby Boom generation believed that the more they had, the better-off in every way they would be. If they had two cars, a big house, and a nicely manicured lawn they were "living the American dream." That "dream" is a nirvana vision of life that the Baby Boomers (and other) generations bought into, sold to themselves, and built an economy of consumer products around. Initially, it did not appear that Baby Boomers questioned or made decisions based on generational restraint, personal consumer responsibility, or global resource conservation. Baby Boomers looked like they had it made as post-War era opportunists ready to take a drive into the sunset. Well, the sun has set and we've learned that over-consumption is irresponsible. The Baby Boom generation learned this, and in the late 1960s and early 1970s began the environmental movement that spawned a generation of environmental activists and leaders.

Just because the next-door neighbor has a shiny H3 Hummer in the driveway does not mean that we need one. Owning, driving, and maintaining a car is a privilege and bears with it an individual responsibility. In the past thirty years that privilege has been abused. The right to own a car and the right to pollute the environment through combustion of fossil fuels are thought of as two different things by most consumers. Ask someone if she or he has the right to own and drive a car and the person will say a resounding YES! Ask that same individual if people have a right to burn twenty gallons of gas in an open pit, just because they can and the answers might be different. The individual might see the burning of the gas as wasteful, pointless, or harmful to them or the environment. Yet we burn millions of gallons of gas daily while thinking about what we're going to order at the drive-thru on our way home from work. The issue of entitlement is not just about what products we have as consumers to choose from, but also our personal choices and responsibility in how we use those products. In the case of cars, we can buy more fuel-efficient models, and we can also consciously drive less and curb our fuel-consumptive behavior. Again, just because we can do something doesn't mean we should.

Our ego will tell us that we need to compete with the neighbors and have that H3 Hummer or maybe something bigger, faster, sportier, or more luxurious. But for us to become a sustainability generation we need to get past our ego and sense of entitlement and recognize, through an individual and generational enlightenment, that less can be more and that we need a redefinition of who we are, what we need, and how we will survive beyond the prior generation's notion of "living the American dream."

Shop 'til Ya Drop

"Buy! Buy! Buy!" CNBC's Jim Cramer's push button voice-over shouts. Companies are not recession-proof, but in a down economy consumers want good quality at low or competitive prices. The global economic meltdown has taught many lessons to business and individual consumers. One important lesson is that "thoughtless consumption" is irresponsible to our wallet, our bodies, our minds and our environment. Industrialized society loves to shop. Investors and consumers typically cheer Buy! Buy! Buy! when the economy is good. But when things turn south, we hear Save! Save! Save! and

Conserve! Conserve! Conserve! The ebb and flow of economic growth is inevitable and in a well-functioning economic system there will be growth and recession. The idea of unfettered growth is at face value unsustainable. At some point a retraction is needed so that new growth can occur. The "shop 'til ya drop" mindset was in need of an overhaul. But changing consumer, individual, and generational behavior is not so easy. Behavior change happens through positive and negative outcomes and through tactics for reinforcing the change. We are bombarded with a slew of messaging from social media, television advertisements, news stories, and direct marketing promotions focused on getting us to "Buy! Buy! Buy!" In contrast there is very little positive reinforcement by way of direct marketing, advertising, or social media targeted to consumers to push them to reduce, shift, or even think about their consumption. But one way behavior is changed, particularly consumptive behavior, is by having a direct and immediate crisis. While unfortunate and sometimes deadly, crisis moments can curb behaviors dramatically.

Fast Society, Fast Food, But Where's the Fasting?

In the case of child obesity in the United States many say we've at a crisis. According to the Centers for Disease Control and Prevention (CDC), "the prevalence of obesity among children aged 6 to 11 years increased from 6.5% in 1980 to 19.6% in 2008. The prevalence of obesity among adolescents aged 12 to 19 years increased from 5.0% to 18.1%." The CDC also points out that "Obese youth are more likely to have risk factors for cardiovascular disease, such as high cholesterol or high blood pressure and diabetes. In a population-based sample of 5- to 17-year-olds, 70% of obese youth had at least one risk factor for cardiovascular disease. Children and adolescents who are obese are at greater risk for bone and joint problems, sleep apnea, and social and psychological problems such as stigmatization and poor self-esteem." Close to two in ten children are obese. And the trend in childhood obesity is increasing. Without direct and immediate attention childhood obesity impacts not just the unfortunate children dealing with the issue. It impacts their families, their schools, their communities, and our educational and healthcare systems. Childhood obesity is akin to many societal and environmental issues of our time. If left alone, the problem will fester, spread, and eventually adversely affect other human and environmental systems. In the case of childhood obesity there are direct and indirect impacts on the cost of healthcare, the cost of education and undue burdens on society.

The basic causes and opportunities to "fix" childhood obesity are well known, but it is not until the "crisis moment" has arisen, particularly in the United States, that anything is being done to address the issue. Associating childhood obesity with entitlement is not as farfetched as some might think. The example of children eating too much cake is typical of many childhood obesity issues. The overconsumption of sweet and fatty foods coupled with a lack of physical activity is a simple recipe for obesity. Core to the definition of entitlement is the word "privilege." What started as an option or a "treat" after a well rounded diet has become the baseline diet in itself. Rather than having a diverse mix of fruits, vegetables, whole grains, and protein, many children now feast on high-fat processed foods as their core daily diet. Somehow in one generation the "privilege" of fast food has resulted in a steady diet of fast food. And ironically the market for organic fruits and vegetables now charges consumers a premium price as if food grown directly from the earth is now a "privilege." Again, this notion of entitlement is core to our long-term sustainability, health, happiness and environmental quality.

As demonstrated in the issues of childhood obesity, we should not be waiting for a crisis to make changes that can positively affect human health and environment and reduce our future financial burden. We need to ask, as individuals, as a society, and as a generation of like-minded people: Are we consuming too much food? Are we consuming too much oil? Are we consuming too much water? What do we really need to survive and live a life of purpose? What can we do to not only recognize our behaviors of consumption but to shift those behaviors before they become, like childhood obesity, a crisis situation for society to deal with?

Addressing the Challenges through a New Age of Global Cooperation

In 2000 Kofi Annan, Secretary General of the United Nations, called for an assessment of global ecosystems and determination of what future actions need to happen to enhance, conserve and sustain those life systems into the future. In response to the Secretary General's request, in 2001 the Millennium Ecosystem Assessment was launched. Involving more than 1,300 science, technology and social experts worldwide the Millennium Ecosystem Assessment (MA) was one of the largest multi-disciplinary and multi-stakeholder initiatives established to collaborate on assessing the status of our land, water and air. The collective work of the MA resulted in five technical volumes and six synthesis reports that provide *"a state-of-the-art scientific appraisal of the condition and trends in the world's ecosystems and the services they provide (such as clean water, food, forest products, flood control, and natural resources) and the options to restore, conserve, or enhance the sustainable use of ecosystems."*

The MA was developed, in part, to improve decision-making regarding the use of natural resources and the services global ecosystems provide. Major findings of the MA are available at (http://www.millenniumassessment.org/en/Index.aspx). The MA's governing board, which oversaw the MA process and which is comprised of representatives from the U.N., nongovernmental organizations, academics, business, indigenous peoples, and governments issued some key concluding statements:[28]

Millennium Assessment Findings

- Everyone in the world depends on nature and ecosystem services to provide the conditions for a decent, healthy, and secure life.
- Humans have made unprecedented changes to ecosystems in recent decades to meet growing demands for food, fresh water, fiber, and energy.
- These changes have helped to improve the lives of billions, but at the same time they weakened nature's ability to deliver other key services, such as purification of air and water, protection from disasters, and the provision of medicines.
- Among the outstanding problems identified by this assessment are the dire state of many of the world's fish stocks; the intense vulnerability of the 2 billion people living in dry regions to the loss of ecosystem services, including water supply; and the growing threat to ecosystems from climate change and nutrient pollution.
- Human activities have taken the planet to the edge of a massive wave of species extinctions, further threatening our own well-being.
- The loss of services derived from ecosystems is a significant barrier to the achievement of the Millennium Development Goals to reduce poverty, hunger, and disease.
- The pressures on ecosystems will increase globally in coming decades unless human attitudes and actions change.
- Measures to conserve natural resources are more likely to succeed if local communities are given ownership of them, share the benefits, and are involved in decisions.
- Even today's technology and knowledge can reduce considerably the

human impact on ecosystems. They are unlikely to be deployed fully, however, until ecosystem services cease to be perceived as free and limitless, and their full value is taken into account.
- Better protection of natural assets will require coordinated efforts across all sections of governments, businesses, and international institutions. The productivity of ecosystems depends on policy choices on investment, trade, subsidy, taxation, and regulation, among others.

Environmental leadership in this new century is about collaboration to work together to understand these challenges, and make a worldwide commitment to implementing solutions. With a population exceeding 6.5 billion, people's demand for natural resources and ecosystem services are at an all-time high. The future of our lands, water, and air is now just as much influenced by humans as it is by unpredictable events of nature from volcanic eruptions, earthquakes, and other earth events to cosmic influences like radiation and asteroids. We need to continue to understand the status of our ecosystems and how they impact our living Earth. We need to use the findings of the MA and future assessments to develop universal policies that ensure that the present ecosystem services needs are being met equitably and fairly and to ensure that resources are available for future generations.

A Tragedy of the Commons: A Need to Exercise Common Sense

First published in the journal Science in 1968, the "Tragedy of the Commons" written by Garret Hardin examined how individuals, when acting independently and in their own self-interest, can ultimately lead to the depletion of a limited and shared resource, even if it is in their long-term interest not to deplete the resource. The concept of the "commons," resources that are shared by humans, is not new. Many contemporary public policies and regulations like the Clean Air Act (CAA), the Clean Water Act (CWA) and the Sustainable Fisheries Act (SFA) were designed, in part, to protect our "commons" including clean air, clean water, and vibrant fishery habitats and populations. The "commons" can be viewed as "life critical," those things that humans cannot live without, or which are critical elements of a well-functioning eco-system that supports human life. Clean air, water, and habitat for plants and animals fall into natural commons that need protection and stewardship. As modern society advanced, almost ubiquitously, to access to radio frequencies and, in some cases, electrical power, some might view these man-made technologies as public resources, perhaps also justified as critical to human well-being and life on the merits of human health, protection and security.

As the global population has grown, especially in the past two centuries, we as humans have struggled with how to best utilize, manage, conserve, protect, and account for our collective "commons." Water is one of the most critical "commons." Access to clean water was not an issue when the earth's population was in the hundreds of millions. Two hundred years ago there was more water to go around; water contamination and pollution were not a concern on the scale they are today; and there was a perception that water was everywhere and limitless. We know today, just how precious water is to our survival. The entire basis of life is built from water resources. Without clean, potable water we simply cannot survive. Yet we have for the past century, treated how water is used almost equally for all of its uses. Is a gallon of water for medical breakthroughs more valuable than a gallon for agriculture or industry? Is a cup of water for enabling the life of a child in Africa more or less valuable than a cup of water for a child in the United States? The modern day "Tragedy of the Commons" continues to exist in the form of generational entitlement. Years and years of continued "thoughtless consumption" of our commons, has led us to a point where we need to be much more vigilant and aware of how we consume, protect, conserve, and sustain water resources. A great deal of emphasis, rightfully so, is placed on global climate change and the impact of greenhouse gases (GHG) like carbon dioxide.

Climate change will have a dramatic impact on the availability of water into the future. We need to empower a new generation of people to break away from a philosophical generational entitlement to "commons" and work toward a sustainability generation that is dedicated to the long-term stewardship, conservation, protection and even enhancement of the "commons" that provide not just basic life, but our everyday quality of life. Science, technology, and innovation will be enablers for the sustainability generation to take action and create change. However, and just as important, a new generational ethic toward conservation, frugality, and responsibility will be required. The world's consumption of oil as a primary source of energy is just one example where new thinking and paradigms are needed so that our "commons" can be protected and enhanced. The following text box examines the oil resources in the context of our commons and entitlement. As shown in Figure 2.1 the future our commons (natural resources including: clean air, water, and land) are impacted by several intersecting satellites of influence and confluence. There are many unknown factors about the future of our natural resources, including the convergence of technology, growth in global population, the migration of people to cities, and continued "geo-political-social" challenges that will inform the daily context of the Sustainability Generation.

Figure 2.1

The Future of Our Natural Resources:
Satellites of Influence and Confidence

Created by Mark C. Coleman

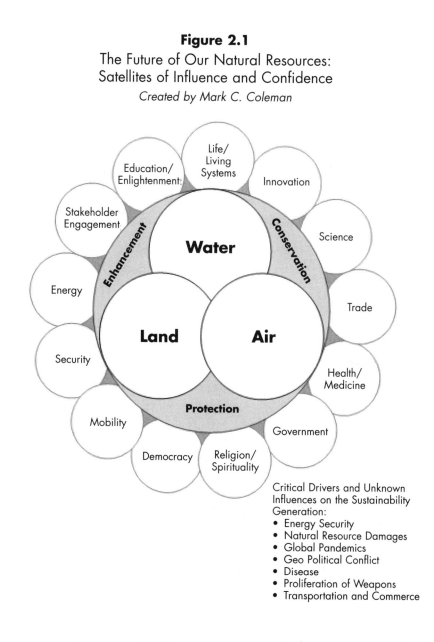

Critical Drivers and Unknown Influences on the Sustainability Generation:
- Energy Security
- Natural Resource Damages
- Global Pandemics
- Geo Political Conflict
- Disease
- Proliferation of Weapons
- Transportation and Commerce

fOILed by our spOILs: Ending Our Indulgence in Oil

Is continued economic growth in the U.S. and the world obstructed by the price and availability of oil? Is the lifeline of modern society clotting, or is it simply thinning out and offering no substantial pressure to continue its legacy of economic growth? Are the days of plundering ending or just beginning?

Oil has given society many rewards: the ability to transport people, goods and services; the ability to heat and electrify; the ability to produce quality products and services; the ability to shelter, feed and clothe billions of people; the ability to advance civilization through education, health-care, telecommunications, and scientific advancement.

The World Factbook published by the CIA lists the top economies of the world. In the list of 193 nations, firms like Wal-Mart and Exxon Mobil would rank in the top 30 largest economies of the world. If you totaled the sales of the following eight oil giants (Exxon, Shell, BP, Total, Chevron, ConocoPhillips, Pemex and Petrobras), they would equate to one of the top ten economies of the world. In 2011 the total sales of the eight oil giants exceed $2.3 trillion and their combined net incomes exceeded $166 billion. Together these firms employ more than 660,000 people worldwide.

Oil is one of the most widely used commodities on Earth. Some 85 million barrels of oil are produced and used per day globally according to the Energy Information Administration, the data and analysis arm of the U.S. Department of Energy (DOE). In 2008 oil prices hit record highs, topping more than $120/barrel. Over the past decade the price of oil has increased more than 1000%. On December 28, 1998 the price of oil was approximately $10 barrel. And during the week of April 22nd 2008 the price of oil flirted with $118, $119, and $120 per barrel. In March of 2012 crude oil futures continued to be above $106 per barrel, and energy analyst forecasts suggested higher prices to continue amid global energy related geo-political and oil supply challenges.[29]

The world has a love hate relationship with oil. When the economy is strong and the pocketbooks fat, we forget about the price of oil. When the economy struggles and our pocketbooks empty, we focus intently on the price of oil and point to it as the root of all economic evil. Every Greek tragedy needs a lead antagonist, and in the story of the rise and fall of global industrialization the antagonist is oil.

TOILING TOWARD A BALANCED ENERGY DIET

Oil has been the consummate enabler for industrialized nations to feed the veins of commerce with a "performance enhancement" and "mood adjusting" supplement. It's almost too bad that there were not product disclosures and warnings 100 years ago before we became fully addicted. You know those commercials where they say "side effects may include nausea, vomiting, fatigue, etc." Perhaps the disclosure for oil would have read, "side effects may include sluggish economy, natural resource damages, global warming, geo political and economic warfare, social inequity, and detachment from living due to chronic idle time spent driving."

But the truth of the matter is that 100 years ago we had no idea about the scale and magnitude oil would play in everyday life, our economy, our standard of living, and our ability to sustain critical infrastructure and networks. As oil has pumped through the veins of commerce, we've grown. But like the overuse of performance enhancement drugs in top athletes, too much can result in serious injury, suspension of play, or even death. In the case of oil, perhaps we've grown so quickly and have become so strong that we simply cannot score enough performance enhancement oil to help us keep pace. Or perhaps we're now overweight, bloated and ready to suffer a massive heart attack due to one or more blockages in our system (e.g., global demand, climate change, availability of refineries, aging infrastructure, and cost pressures).

Oil is not bad. It's just a performance enhancer that has been oversold and over used. Sure it has its side effects, but no technology or energy source is without their fair share. And, with 6.5 billion addicts around the world a premium can be placed on the availability, price and quality of oil. Oil is an earth-based commodity with a man-made purpose. Sometimes that point is lost. We've created a flat world whose pace of growth has quickened, all in part to our friendly performance enhancer, oil. We have the ability to transform our flat world into a new dimension, neither round nor flat, but shapeless bound by only our imagination and innovation to bring to it new life not bound by technology, resource or ideological constraints. Oil will have a place in this new shapeless world, but so too will other forms or energy that will displace and yet balance our traditional thirst for petro-based nourishment.

bOILING THIS DOWN

When it comes to high energy prices and environmental challenges related to oil, we need to move beyond blame and get serious about creating real change. It's so easy to blame the Bush Administration or point the finger toward OPEC or hedge fund managers that are perceived to be in cahoots with big oil executives padding their wallets and patting each other on the back for influencing oil markets and reaping huge profits. Are their inefficiencies, potential back door deals, unneeded confusion in how the price of oil is set? Sure, but blaming one administration or one company will solve nothing and will only fuel more wasted time, money, and oil.

The 21st Century challenge before each of us as consumers, industrialists, policy makers, shareholders, innovators, scientists, students and conservationists is to collaborate on a way to reduce our appetite for oil while simultaneously working toward performance enhancement supplements that we can develop and use to round out our energy diet.

So often I hear references to the "silver bullet" technology that will transform our energy diet. According to the Schlumberger Excellence in Educational Development project, oil was first drilled in 347 AD. Since that time oil has been somewhat of a "silver bullet" for the energy needs of human kind. Oil has provided us with heat, electricity, transport, cooling, and that performance enhancing high that has fostered economic growth. But we now know that oil cannot be the "silver bullet" for our future prosperity or sustainability.

A well balanced diet has a mix of energy sources rich in nutrients. A well-balanced energy diet may include exercise (energy demand reduction), it may include a balanced approach (combined heat and power, distributed generation), it may include options low in proverbial cholesterol—that is, carbon (wind power, solar, geothermal, etc.) it may include fortified vitamins and minerals (engineered petrochemicals and biofuels) and it may include new age supplements yet to be fully qualified (fuel cells, hydrogen, carbon sequestration techniques). The point here is that we need an energy diet that is balanced, nutritious, and that positions us for longevity, not just performance enhancement. The performance enhancement will come from a renewed focus on energy research and development and new innovations. Besides are we foolish enough to believe the best we can do as a society is to rely primarily on an oil-based economy? Is that the extent of our ingenuity and imagination? Oil has given us so much, but it's time to transition to more secure, reliable, and economic sources of energy that promote independence and sustainability.

AVOIDING eENERGY MARKET turmOIL: MORE ENLIGHTENED AND RESPONSIBLE ENERGY DEVELOPMENT

It's time for the oil economy to be shaken up, agitated, and churned. It's certainly causing enough turmoil at its current state of being today. High energy prices, environmental degradation, water and soil contamination, air pollution, climate change, inequitable distribution of wealth, socio-political conflict. These are the spoils of oil? I don't believe that's what we had intended.

If the state of civilization were equated to the life-cycle of a human, we're still in our infancy. We've been formula fed with oil for a few weeks or months and now it's time to introduce new nutrients into our everyday diet so that we can grow, mature, and lead a balanced life. The largest economies of the world, from industrialized nations to the wealthiest of corporations, are taking strategic, proactive, and leadership actions to prepare them for an exciting childhood, adolescence, adulthood, and old age.

Companies that are rounding out their energy diet are becoming better investments. As they transition from the one-dimensional oil based economy to a multi-dimensional energy services economy they ultimately hedge on the price of energy in the future. In addition they are more apt to compete over a longer term and offer better products at a better price as they are less reliant on price fluctuations associated with oil. We call companies with well-balanced energy diets social responsive leaders because they are positioning themselves for future growth in alignment with societal needs and values. Examples of companies innovating new products and adopting better energy management strategies include:

- **Boeing**—is developing lighter and more fuel efficient airliners. This is a social response product innovation that is adaptive—meaning it seeks to optimize efficiency and reduce demand for aviation fuel. In the absence of other forms of energy, Boeings fuel efficient 787 Dreamliner is a dream. Boeing is contributing to a new era of efficiency in air travel that will reduce side effects of a petroleum-rich diet like carbon emissions. With greater fuel efficient aircraft, Boeing stands to fly 30,000 feet above its competition toward a balanced energy diet.

- **Canadian National (CN)**—is a Canadian rail company that operates the largest rail network in Canada and the only transcontinental network in North America. The company operates in eight Canadian provinces and 16 U.S. states. As part of its equipment upgrade policy the company is upgrading its fleet of locomotives with models that are at least 17% more fuel efficient than their predecessors which reduces air emissions and enables more efficient delivery of goods. The company also remanufactures its older locomotive engines which reduces waste, recaptures energy used in manufacturing processes and minimizes the need to produce new materials for locomotive engines. CN optimizes the flow of goods through the use of rail, a demand side response to energy use in our transportation sector.

Corporate leaders are now more proactively balancing their energy diet within their operations, their product portfolio, among their employees and within the communities in which they operate. Ultimately their more balanced energy diet is translating into a stronger business and a stronger bottom line due to operational efficiencies, cost recovery, product innovation, margin improvements, and enhanced reputation.

Every day we see more and more companies making conscious decisions to evaluate their firms' energy diet and ways to enrich their diet. Share with us some of the corporate leaders you are aware of that are creating a more balanced energy diet for their operations, employees, customers, shareholders, and communities in which they operate.

Tragedy in the Water Commons

Our water resources are precious, perhaps more so than any other resource. Once an undervalued resource, water has become sold on a per-unit (gallon) basis, a valuable resource and commodity. At the end of 2011 a gallon of water in the United States cost approximately 132% more than a gallon of gasoline, even at $93 barrel for oil.[30] To do this back of the envelop calculation I assumed that the water was purchased at a convenience store for approximately $1.25 for a

20 ounce bottle and that gasoline cost $3.45 a gallon. Both numbers are conservative. But the point is that water is much more monetized than ever before in our history, and will likely continue to be so into the future. What is an amusing aside is the fact that the convenience store where I purchased gas and water had a deal. If I were a "card member" of the retail outlet I could get a discount on in-store purchases (like water) for the more gas I purchased.

It seems our consumption of oil is now actively subsidizing our water costs directly. We can sustain life without using another drop of oil. We have thousands of years of human existence that validate this. Serious concessions on our standard of living would need to take place, but it is possible since it was humans that discovered oil, and likely we who will find an energy replacement for it. We cannot however survive without an adequate supply of fresh water. Global resource wars of the future may continue to spawn from our petrochemical addictions of the 20th century, but without water to nourish our thirst, no war for oil is worth fighting for. Availability of clean and potent water may just be the determinant of winning societies into the future. Consider these water facts:

- The blue planet Earth is covered 75% by water. All life requires water for survival.

- Only 3% of Earth's water resources is fresh water. Of that 68.7% is in the form of glacial ice, 30.1% is captured as groundwater and 0.9% as surface water.

- Globally, and in the United States, water resources are constrained by demand from power generation, agriculture, industrial use, and human consumption.

- According to the United Nations Environment Programme Global Environment Monitoring System/Water Programme: unsafe water and poor sanitation cause an estimated 80 percent of all diseases in the developing world.

- In the United States, consumers drink more bottled water annually than any other beverage, other than carbonated soft drinks.

It is estimated that U.S. consumers spent a whopping $12 billion in 2007 on bottled water, representing close to 9 billion gallons of water. Worldwide demand for bottled water is very high and has risen a great deal in the past decade. The top ten global markets for bottled water consumed more than 35 billion gallons in 2006, up 9.1% from 2001. On a per capita basis, nine countries consume more bottled water than the United States: Italy, United Arab Emirates, Mexico, France, Belgium-Luxembourg, Germany, Spain, Lebanon, and Switzerland.

Global debate is underway on consumer fascination with bottled water. On the one hand, bottled water provides a certain utility for millions of thirsty consumers. On the other, bottled water has unintended consequences for the environment. The waste associated with plastic bottles, emissions from transporting water in bottles to consumers, emissions from storing water at retail outlets, and increased energy use used to produce bottled water, all adds up. Once left in the hands of municipal water authorities, water has become a privatized big business with Nestlé, Poland Spring, Coca-Cola, Pepsi and others discovering new revenue from a once "perceived free" commodity.

The future of water is uncertain. One thing that is certain is that we need to protect this valuable resource to ensure that future generations have access to clean water, and ensure that we don't leave them more environmental damages from our desire to make water overly accessible through bottling. The following box about water resource issues highlights how some companies and global organizations are working together to offer a social response solution to the world's thirst for clean water.

The Global Thirst of Entitlement: Addressing Water Resource Issues in the 21st Century

By Mark C. Coleman
Originally published July 10, 2007
http://worldincbook.blogspot.com/

You think business and society is carbon constrained . . . look at water. Future resource wars are inevitable without swift social response.

If the world's population continues to grow, if we continue to expand our economies, and if we continue to use our resources more quickly than natural processes can replenish them—then resource wars are inevitable. I say this because there simply are not enough resources, whether oil, gas, water, timber, fisheries, or agriculture land, that will available for us to continue our rate of consumption unabated. This is known. Yet we are slow to adopt strategies that can serve to mitigate the risk of future resource constraints and, worse yet, resource wars and catastrophic resouce failures.

Proclaimed the "Blue Planet," approximately 71% of the earth's surface is covered with water. This sounds promising until you consider that about 97.5% of the water on Earth is saline, while the remaining 2.5% is fresh water. And the majority of fresh water (68.7%) is currently in the form of ice. With a world population of 6.6 billion people and growing, the amount of fresh water for hydration, hygiene, agriculture, industrial production, and ecosystem health gets stretched thin quickly.

The Business for Social Responsibility (BSR) summarizes the challenging water issues society now faces in this new century. According to BSR, industry accounts for 23% of the total fresh water use worldwide. The United Nations estimates that more than 1.4 billion lack access to clean, fresh, and potable water.

With so much attention on climate change, clean energy, and alternative transportation fuels and technologies, often other significant environmental issues and social response actions taken by leading corporations are overlooked or understated. We focus on water in this blog because it is literally a life-line for all human existence and life on Earth. Water is a big-time resource issue in this new century. Companies like Pepsi, Coors Brewing, Coca-Cola, Diageo, and numerous others are taking very proactive measures to conserve, protect, and enhance the quality of water for their customers, the communities they serve, and future generations.

Water is something that we take for granted. It's probably more precious to human health, quality of life, and the sustainability of our planet and future generations than oil, yet we place tremendous economic value on oil, and very little on water. Water is essential to life, yet we pollute and waste it daily for products, services, and activities that on the surface provide economic utility, but in reality may be irrational choices we've made to earn a buck. If we continue to undervalue water and utilize it for wasteful products and processes, we will constrain future growth and ultimately impact global ecosystems and human health.

SOCIAL RESPONSE WATER LEADERS

Coca-Cola's corporate social responsibility efforts focus on numerous issues including, climate change, accountability, packaging, manufacturing processes, and water. Coca-Cola recognizes the value of water to its brand, reputation, and long-term longevity as a global beverage company. Coca-Cola has developed a Corporate Water Pledge that essentially state's that they will reduce, recycle, and replenish the water they use. First, they will reduce and recycle water from their manufacturing operations. Secondly, they will replenish water by developing watershed protection program, community water partnerships, and developing rainwater harvesting structures in regions that lack access to clean and potable water. Imagine if big oil reduced, recycled, and replenished?

In addition, Coca-Cola is working in partnership with the World Wildlife Fund (WWF) to conserve water in seven of the world's most critical eco-regions. The seven eco-regions in which Coca-Cola and WWF are collaborating include: the Yangtze River, the Rio Granda/Rio Bravo in the United States and Mexico, Southeastern U.S. Rivers and Streams, the Mesoamerican Reef, Mekong River on the Tibetan Plateau, Rivers and Lakes of Coastal East Africa, and the Danube River in Europe. Coca-Cola and WWF are addressing unique conservation and watershed issues in each of these seven eco-regions.

In Burkina Faso, one of the poorest countries in the world, Diageo worked to deliver its Water of Life initiative with NGO partner WaterAid. Together Diageo and WaterAid enhanced access to clean water, improved sanitation, and provided effective sanitation and hygiene education to local community organizations.

As global risks of depletion of water (price, availability, quality, conservation) impact consumers and communities, pressures will increase on corporations and governments to provide solutions. Whether delivered by corporations like Coca-Cola, NGOs like WaterAid or governments, the worlds growing population is thirsty for clean water, and is placing new demands on water for sanitation, agriculture, and industry. Examining, and addressing the life-cycle of water will be an essential responsibility of the Sustainability Generation.

Facing-Up to Our Entitled Sense of Self: The Ills and Promise of Social Networking

Since 2005 social networking has become a booming phenomenon. In 2010 Wikipedia referenced more than 100 social network web-sites ranging from Biip, a Norwegian community-based network with 13,000 registered users, to the infamous Facebook with 845 million active users and growing.[31] There are many well know social networking sites like Twitter, MySpace, LinkedIn, and Facebook that each allow registered users to customize information about themselves and network and learn about their friends, family, colleagues, and acquaintances. Complementary to the social networking bubble are websites like YouTube that allow society to post-and-play video, music, and images that reside on a continuum of educational to ludicrous and downright immoral and disgusting. At this time there does not seem to be any waning in the demand and thirst for social networking and immediate gratification these websites have enabled. What is amazing to me is the frequency and length of time that many users spend on social networking sites.

A great percentage of the "under-30s generation" who are known as the Echo Generation (also referred to as Generation Y, the Millennial Generation, or Generation Next or Net Generation) are registered users of multiple social networking web-sites. According to the February 2010 report *"Millennials: A Portrait of Generation Next,"* by the Pew Research Center, approximately three-quarters of the Millennial generation have created a profile on a social networking site (see Figure 2.2). In contrast only half of Generation Xers and a third of Baby Boomers have done so.[32]

Figure 2.2

Do You Have a Profile on a Social Networking Site?

% saying "yes"

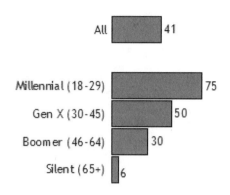

Source: Pew Research Center

The Echo Generation seems to feed its mind and spirit through daily discovery of what others are doing and telling their stories. The Pew Research Center report sums up the Millennial Generation experience stating, *". . . They [Millennial Generation] are history's first "always connected" generation. Steeped in digital technology and social media, they treat their multi-tasking hand-held gadgets almost like a body part—for better and worse. More than eight-in-ten say they sleep with a cell phone glowing by the bed, poised to disgorge texts, phone calls, emails, songs, news, videos, games and wake-up jingles. But sometimes convenience yields to temptation. Nearly two-thirds admit to texting while driving."*[33]

What is also interesting is that social networking is not necessarily generation-dominant, meaning there are millions of users that can be defined as Generation X, Baby Boomers, or older. The Internet and social networking has actually enabled generations to better communicate and keep in touch with one another. But from my perspective there is also a segment of society that social networking sites entice in a less productive sense. When I read many user posts on Facebook, or Twitter, or watch video clips on YouTube there is a strong sense of narcissism, "me—me—me" and "I—I—I" that is rampant in discussion threads showing people's desire for attention. This is tied to individual and generational "entitlement" in the sense that many people feel entitled to tell us their woes, their struggles, their

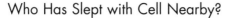

Figure 2.3
Who Has Slept with Cell Nearby?
*% who have placed their cell phone on
or right next to their bed while sleeping*

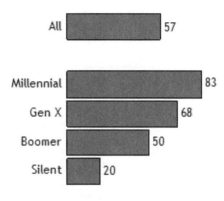

Source: Pew Research Center

happiness and challenges as if everyone has an interest or cares. This vanity is seen in how we interface with technology. For example, Figure 2.3 shows how 83% of Millennials have admitted that they sleep with their cell or smart phone right next to their bed, 68% of Gen Xers and half of Boomers have admitted this. It is as if we cannot be away from being accessible for even a good night sleep!

I don't mean this to sound completely critical since I do feel social networking is a useful medium to communicate with friends and family and useful for business and educational purposes. But the inner feelings of "entitlement" do emerge throughout the social networking medium and exacerbate this mentality that is so limiting for society's ability to coalesce toward more positive thinking and behavior. The names of many networks themselves feed the human ego for attention "MYSpace" and "Facebook" connote that everything is about "Me, Me, Me." There is nothing wrong with everyone wanting a little recognition, notoriety, and identity. HP had a huge marketing campaign in the 2003-08 timeframe that focused on this trend. The "You + HP" campaign which began in 2003 was a global consumer marketing campaign valued at $300 million, the largest in HP's corporate history.[34] The "You + HP" campaign focused on the company's expansion into digital photography and focused on enabling customers to capture "life moments" and share them with ease in the digitized world. It is interesting to reflect on how so many consumer brands like HP have focused in recent years on the individual, the "Me" or "You" in their marketing efforts. The digitized world seems at face value an incredible force in bringing us together, allowing data and information to be shared, and to result in greater collaboration. That is happening. But what has also happened is the formation of a new medium for the human ego to express itself, often without regard for the negative consequences that might result from sharing pictures, airing gossip from the office, or being dismissive of family members—openly and for the world to see.

Honestly, is this the right use of technology in the long run? Just a way for us to exercise or stroke or even damage each other's egos while yearning for identity in a highly-populated world? Thomas Friedman presented his case for a flat world enabled by our digitized society; yet it is not that flat at all. People have only lowered the grade of the hill we each climb in life, which is the pursuit of identity, who we are, what our purpose is, and how we communicate with others. It is by no means a level playing field or flat; just maybe less of an incline for some who choose to use the new dimension of the web to pontificate and boost their sense of self. This is not necessarily bad, just a reflection of what is happening.

It is interesting to note that in 2011, at the height of the social networking boom, Pope Benedict weighed in on society's infatuation with social networks, drawing questions of self-constraint, awareness, and the act of the individual being present to others in daily life. In January 2011 the Pope issued comments[35] under the title, "truth, proclamation and authenticity of life in the digital age," stating that social networks provide "a great opportunity." However he noted that ". . . it is important always to remember that virtual contact cannot and must not take the place of direct human contact with people at every level of our lives." The Pope asked "Who is my 'neighbor' in this new world?" as a way to have social networkers reflect upon how they spend their time, and whether an overuse of social networks can lead to alienation, self-indulgence, or depersonalization. In his comments prepared for the Catholic Church's World Day of Communications the Pope issued additional potential warnings about the over-reliance on social networking as a sole platform for communication; the Pope stated, ". . . entering cyberspace can be a sign of an authentic search for personal encounters with others, provided that attention is paid to avoiding dangers such as enclosing oneself in a sort of parallel existence, or excessive exposure to the virtual world . . . In the search for sharing, for 'friends,' there is the challenge to be authentic and faithful, and not give in to the illusion of constructing an artificial public profile for oneself." In his words the Pope went on to ask social networkers whether they were "less present to those whom we encounter in our everyday life."

So, the challenge is in how we as individuals and generations can use the good in social networking, from its ability to connect, educate, empower and enlighten people for greater advocacy of establishing the Sustainability Generation. The Echo Generation, Generation X, and Baby Boomers need to harness social networking toward a higher purpose, one that goes beyond a discussion board on all the evils of the world and a "poor me, look how bad my life is; I'm entitled to share my story with you" medium. The potential and power in social networking can be the ability to connect with and motivate, empower, and enlighten like-minded individuals toward a common purpose.

There are nuggets of promise in the social networking world toward this novel goal. On LinkedIn for example there are several networking groups that are making attempts to focus like-minded individuals toward a common purpose. Here are examples of the sub-groups that have emerged on LinkedIn:

- Corporate Social Responsibility
- Energy & Utilities Network
- Ethical Business Intelligence
- Global Sustainable Investment Forum
- Green
- Green & Sustainability Innovators & Innovation Network
- Clean Economy Network
- Green Collar Careers
- GreenBiz.com—Green Business Professionals
- Sustainability Professionals
- The Virtual Energy Forum

These and other LinkedIn groups host discussion boards, present news, post jobs and connect individuals together under a common purpose. I have not seen data on how these sub-groups of social networking sites have led to specific outcomes among the users, but my gut says some very unique and innovative relationships have been facilitated from these groups that did not exist prior to joining. For this reason social networking holds much promise for enabling the Sustainability Generation to develop and achieve a higher purpose in society.

Understanding the Underlying Causes of Entitlement

It is easy to point to entitlement as a root cause of unsustainable behavior, but to truly understand the underlying causes one has to ask what causes people to feel entitled or carry-out behaviors associated entitlement. There are five main categories of entitlement to consider:

Category 1: Resource Abundance

This category of entitlement can be given a short hand of "because it's available, we can and should consume it." When there is so much of something, such as a natural resource, human behavior can decouple itself from the logical views of consumption and overconsumption. When resources are vast it is difficult to determine whether they are being used inefficiently. However, when resources are consumed at a rate that is clearly outside the bounds of natural renewal and impacts of this can be seen, often behaviors will be curtailed. Resource abundance is a category of entitlement associated with our air, water, fisheries, and petroleum. In each case, many generations of people consumed these resources willingly and without fear of depletion. The abundance of these resources always appeared rich, vibrant, and renewable. However, as global population and consumption patterns for these resources have increased, there have been visible disruptions in the availability and quality of our natural resources. This has in turn led current generations to begin to assess and analyze our impact on the natural environment.

Category 2: Unknown Consequences

This category of entitlement can be given a short hand of "no known or perceived repercussions," so it's all right to consume without recourse. The fundamental issue with this category of entitlement is a lack of controls, policies, risk assessment, and mitigation of impacts. When people are unaware of consequences from their behaviors they often do not choose to act in the least risky way. Instead they take more risks. This logic holds true to resource consumption. If people knew, through sound science and risk assessment what the impacts of overfishing would have on marine ecosystems, people might reduce their consumption. Further, if fisheries were further protected by price controls that more aptly quantified their value not just in terms of human consumption, but in terms of ecosystem services, the financial/market controls would be in place to be a check and balance on human consumption.

Category 3: Lack of Governance and Oversight

This category of entitlement can be given a short-hand of "if I can get away with it, then why not?" When there is a lack of oversight, no one watches the till. Knowing that we now live in a resource- constrained world, we need to have assessment and enforcement over our extraction, conversion, and use of natural resources. Some politicians and those in the media have postulated that part of the underlying failures that led to the BP catastrophe in the Gulf of Mexico was lack of government oversight and inadequate controls of deep-water drilling. Some raised concerns that the Bush Administration stripped personnel from critical federal agencies like the Interior Department's Minerals Management Service to cut costs, leaving fewer government experts to provide the level of oversight and scrutiny needed for deploying riskier new technology for new deep-water drilling applications.

Category 4: Ill-Aligned Incentives

This category of entitlement can be given a short-hand of "spend now and pay later." Many of our natural resources are priced for today's needs and customers' willingness to pay. However, in the context of environmental damages, resource depletion and the unknown consequences of this to future generations, this model is inefficient and ultimately unsustainable. The issue is not so much the price customers pay, but the level at which government and industry subsidize many natural resources, from water to oil to fisheries, so that we can consume them in mass quantity. I love to eat salmon. Much of the salmon at the supermarket today is not a native species; rather it is farm-raised salmon, often grown in other regions or countries. The cost of getting that salmon to my stomach is subsidized heavily. There are transportation subsidies, farming and agriculture subsidies, tax subsidies for businesses, and so on. When combined together we can buy salmon, or oysters, or lobsters or tuna at lower costs. But when added up the bundling of subsidies lead to overharvesting, unsustainable agriculture, and perhaps a long-term degradation of our ecosystems and natural habitats.

Category 5: Generational Inheritance

This category of entitlement can be summed up as "join the crowd." When the masses are sharing a behavior, it is difficult to understand the reasons. There are underlying human emotions and elements such as social pressure, a lack of leadership, and a fear of standing out or being different, which keep people (and generations) in step with past generations. Generational inheritance is a form of entitlement that is accepted by the next generation and which compounds over time. Typically generations want to be different from those preceding them; however, there are elements of behavior that retain the status-quo, largely because entitlement issues remain unaddressed: such as a lack of governance and oversight of maintaining resources and no repercussions from their waste. If generations don't properly address these underlying causes of entitlement, these issues move forward to become the next generation's challenges to work through. And often the cycle repeats. Figure 2.4 summarizes the five categories of entitlement.

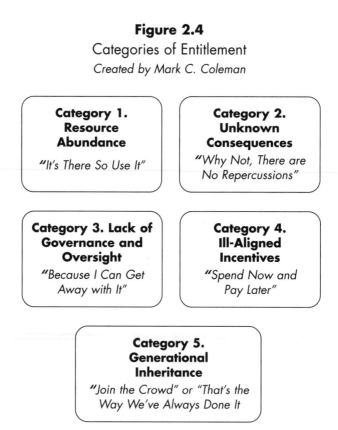

Figure 2.4
Categories of Entitlement
Created by Mark C. Coleman

Category 1.
Resource
Abundance
"It's There So Use It"

Category 2.
Unknown
Consequences
"Why Not, There are No Repercussions"

Category 3. Lack of
Governance and
Oversight
"Because I Can Get Away with It"

Category 4.
Ill-Aligned
Incentives
"Spend Now and Pay Later"

Category 5.
Generational
Inheritance
"Join the Crowd" or *"That's the Way We've Always Done It"*

A Generation in Transition

Modern society is at a fundamental crossroads in its evolution and future sustainment. The path marked by thoughtless overconsumption and greed that we've gone down has proven itself again and again as unsustainable and negligent about future generations. Only in retrospect do we see how individual and generational entitlement has negatively impacted human health and the environment. With this knowledge in hand, it is time to empower individuals and entire generations to think more critically about our consumptive choices and what we will leave behind as a legacy for our children and their children. A legacy of waste, greed, and damages to natural resources is not just unsustainable; it is immoral and irresponsible. We can figure out how to live a life with purpose with a high standard of living and in a sustainable way. This begins with empowerment and enlightenment as a new generation. As the new sustainability generation comes into being there will be questions to be addressed about consumption of natural resources: How much it too much? And, what are individual and generational responsibilities to human health and the environment today and in the future?

The Increasing Need for Collaboration and Innovation to Overcome Entitlement for Rare Resources

Sustainability and innovation go hand-in-hand. But a challenge for the Sustainability Generation is not only focused on innovation, it is also on collaboration and "getting to the collective WE." In coming years, global tensions may increasingly be centered on the availability of natural resources. To a certain degree, markets will help align and broker resource availability with demand. But, there is potential for economic, geo-political, defense, security and environmental risk whether competitive markets or governments rule the release of natural resources.

For example, in April 2010 the U.S. Government Accountability Office (GAO) issued a report that warned of an "impending rare earths crisis, especially as it relates to homeland security and national defense."[36] According to the GAO report:

- The United States relies heavily on Chinese sources of rare earth materials.

- China performs the majority of rare earth mineral and material processing, once dominated by the United States.

- Rebuilding of a competitive domestic supply chain could take up to fifteen years and will require significant capital and technology investments.[37]

- The United States Department of Defense (DOD) is assessing security and defense vulnerabilities to the new imbalance of rare earth mineral and materials availability and processing.

By the fall of 2010 the significance of China's stronghold on critical, rare earth materials began to be felt. In October 2010 China decided to reduce its supply of certain rare earth materials globally, and stop altogether the export of some materials to the United States. According to the European Commission, China holds more than half of the known global reserves of nine of fourteen of the most critical raw materials. For example, China is the leading producer of tungsten, which is an important material used in mobile phones (it enables phone vibration). China now controls 97% of these rare earth reserves as compiled from data from the European Commission.

From a sustainability context the availability of rare earth minerals and other natural resources is an enormous issue that is evolving. As the case of tungsten from China points out, governments and countries can control natural resources in a way that disrupts market prices, market availability, and potentially entire market sectors. Further, many natural resources and rare earth minerals are critical for the design, manufacture, production, distribution, and operation of new products and services that offer a better net environmental impact to society than alternative products or services.

For example, rare earth elements such as gallium (Ga), indium (In), graphite (G) and germanium (Ge) are in the largest reserves in China. These elements are used in products ranging from flat-screen and solar panels to fuel cells, batteries and other alternative energy technologies. Thus, constraints on the availability of rare earth materials globally can diminish the potential of certain sustainable technologies from being manufactured and put into good use.

As natural resources and rare earth materials are constrained, the Sustainability Generation will need to discover how to work with other nations to alleviate geo-political impasses and market tensions so that attaining sustainability in all regions of the world is not prevented by the limited availability of rare earth minerals, volatile commodity prices, or political tensions. In many cases, other nations may not intentionally mean ill-intentions when they restrict natural resources or rare minerals. They may simply want to reserve availability for their own development and domestic needs. According to a *Fast Company*[38] article *"Rare Earth"* published in November 2010 by Kate Rockwood, that intention had been articulated by Chinese Ministry of Commerce director general He Ning who noted rare earth restrictions were put into place to, "protect our (the Chinese) environment and preserve the minerals for future generations." That is an admirable goal and intention.

The challenge for a world with a global economy will be how to conduct trade and commerce with economic, national, and future legacy (sustainability) security in mind. Regardless of who controls natural resources and rare earth materials into the future, the

Sustainability Generation, characterized by all people of all nations, will need to do their part in reducing consumption, minimizing human and environmental impacts associated with the production and consumption of goods and services, and work collaboratively with the resources they have: human, economic, natural or rare earth toward a more sustainable earth.

Chapter Summary

- The individual's and society's sense of "entitlement" is one of the underlying root causes of persistent unsustainable behavior.

- Global indicators of ecosystem health and vitality based from years of science, policy, analysis and interpretation tell us that our global commons (air, water, and land) are struggling to support the diversity of life on earth they once did.

- Humans did not inherit the earth, although our ego and position at the top of the food chain would have us believe so. Our view that we inherited the earth exacerbates a sense of entitlement in our stewardship of natural resources and behaviors surrounding production and consumption.

- There are, in retrospect, humorous and entertaining examples of how we consume resource excessively. Going forward, the Sustainability Generation will need to embrace personal accountability and action toward its views and behaviors on resource consumption if it is going to continue to make an impact on the long-term sustainability of this and future generations.

- The current generation is comprised of individuals that have had experience with living in a world of frugality and abundance. As a generation we have the intellectual capacity and know-how to live a high quality of life within our means.

- Addressing individual and generational entitlement in the context of sustainability requires a look into who we are, what our values are, and how we choose to live. These questions are difficult because they force us to disregard the status-quo and understand our true sense of self and importance to our families, communities, and the world.

3

Personal Accountability:
Why Personal Accountability?
Why NOW? Why YOU?

*"Never doubt that a small group
of thoughtful, committed citizens
can change the world, Indeed,
it is the only thing that ever has."*

—Margaret Mead,
United States Anthropologist
(1901–1978)

This quotation from famed anthropologist Margaret Mead gets at the heart of the ideas expressed here. People can, through their behaviors and actions, make a difference in the world. And this notion is often lost as the world population increases and the complexity of social and environmental challenges intensify. "Personal accountability" is one of the most important, yet most challenging and undervalued quotients of the sustainability equation. Through personal accountability, individuals, and generations can transform the world around them, NOW.

The underlying opportunity and challenge for the Sustainability Generation is to conceptualize, design, and implement sustainability initiatives that are will be embraced, pursued, and accomplished. While individual notions of entitlement can lead to unsustainable behaviors, an individual accountability can be a force for empowering and enlightening generations to make a positive change in their lives NOW.

There are several reasons why accountability is essential NOW in society:

- The world's population is now 6.8 billion people and expected to reach 8–10 billion by 2050.

- Increases in global population have placed additional demands upon natural resources. Globally, the earth's natural resources are limited; and "ecosystem services" that support life-essential functions like cleaning our air or water are being diminished.

- Today 50% of the world's population is located in cities and 70% or 6 billion people are projected to live in urban areas by 2050, according to the United Nations.

- As the world's population moves toward urban environments, greater demands will be put on the human-built environment and infrastructure.

- Technology can enable us to meet future needs, but only with modification of human behavior. As the population grows and clusters in cities, consumer behaviors will need to correspond with the goals of technology to protect our natural resources and constrain our use of water, food and energy.

- A new breed of companies and technologies are now focused, as part of their value proposition to customers, on addressing human behavior as a key driver for achieving sustainable benefits (such as operational cost-savings and energy and greenhouse gas reductions). Consumer behavior can be a powerful tool for fostering sustainability goals. Achieving sustainability requires engaged consumers who understand their own behavior and the capacity of technology to serve their needs.

- By focusing on the "people and social" side of sustainability, governments and corporations can meet the needs of customers and their impact on society. By integrating technology and human behavior into total "systems solutions" that allow for tangible ways to measure, quantify, and incentivize consumer behavior, improvements can be made to our financial and environmental systems.

- At the heart of every social and environmental challenge, large or small, is a need for critical thinking, strong leadership, and an ability to make informed decisions. As individuals and society work toward more sustainable solutions, we will make mistakes. It is how we react to our mistakes, through personal accountability, that will make the difference about the possibility of a sustainable future. There will be visible behavior during the most public challenges of our time; and invisible behavior as we conduct ourselves and make decisions behind closed doors. Personal accountability is about doing the right thing when no one is watching, or when everyone is looking.

"No snowflake in an avalanche ever feels responsible."[39]
—Stanisław Jerzy Lec (1909–1966)

Personal Accountability Is Everyone's Responsibility

Unanticipated events happen daily. Whether they are man-made or natural disasters that are seemingly "acts of God," or something in between, these events sometimes turn out to be benign "non-events"; however, sometimes these events not only make the nightly news, but cause shifts in society's behavior forever. While it is uncertain exactly what the long-term societal impact of the BP Deepwater Horizon tragedy and oil spill will be in the Gulf of Mexico, this was a significant event of 2010 with broad social, political, environmental, and economic impacts.

On April 20, 2010 the BP Deepwater Horizon oil rig exploded in the Gulf of Mexico, 52 miles southeast of the Louisiana port of Venice. Eleven people lost their lives in this terrible industrial incident. And, for more than 100 days, oil bled into the Gulf of Mexico in what would become possibly the most catastrophic environmental disaster in a generation. Catastrophic events take a toll on all who are enveloped in them: the victims of the disaster, families of loved ones, first responders and rescue workers, emergency management and public officials, the general public, and corporate officers. On May 31, forty-one days into the disaster, BP CEO Tony Hayward made a choice. In an interview with Fox News the BP top officer stated, ***"We're sorry for the massive disruption it's caused their lives. There's no one who wants this over more than I do. I would like my life back."***

This brief statement, perhaps as honest and true as it may have been, represents a clear cut example of a leader not being or appearing personally accountable to a situation. This disaster would have obvious implications for BP shareholders, but more importantly, it affected families who lost loved ones in the disaster, and it would impact the greater culture of the Gulf of Mexico for decades. Coupled with Hayward's actions in the weeks following the disaster (including taking vacation time to go sailing with friends) this public remark was unacceptable to most people and caused an uproar in the media and social networks. Perhaps Tony Hayward was suffering from a lack of sleep; perhaps his level of stress during this event blurred his judgment. The reason was for his remarks do not matter. The point is that people have the power to make conscious decisions with regard to demonstrating their personal accountability in their personal and public lives. Tony Hayward chose a path of not showing accountability to his company, to the government, to the people of the Gulf, and to his employees. In the end, this lack of appearance of personal and corporate accountability in CEO Hayward led to his demise. By June 18 Hayward stepped down as the BP leader responsible for the oversight of activities in the Gulf, and by July 27 decisions were made to transition Hayward out of BP's chief executive role. Ultimately society expects or requires leaders to be or act accountable. Society is now requiring more from governments and corporations, beyond the public-facing leaders like Hayward. Society is thirsting and pushing for greater transparency of the leaders at the helm of large enterprises, and of all people that work for the enterprise. Ousting a non-accountable CEO may not change the culture of a company like BP overnight. Ultimately the practices, behaviors, and accountability of the entire enterprise have to be transparent if companies and governments are to continue to earn the trust of society.

Although the checks and balances and desired cleansing of unaccountable leadership may take more time than some would like, it can and does happen. The past five years have been littered with examples of ousted chairmen, CEOs, and financial advisors of fraudulent corporations, as well as disgraced politicians. Perhaps the one saving grace is our collective disdain for those that demonstrate incompetence and non-accountability in leadership positions. Often when society uncovers unaccountable leadership, they begin to see a wider pattern of lack of responsibility in the culture of the organization. In the case of BP, their actions pre-and-post the Deepwater Horizon oil incident was very costly to their reputation and with regard to social, environmental, and economic considerations for the people in the Gulf. In March 2012 BP agreed to pay $7.8 billion as part of a settlement to people and businesses that claimed they were impacted by the oil spill.[40] This was in addition to greater than $6 billion BP had paid under a separate settlement with the Gulf Coast Claims Facility.[41]

The BP example is an unfortunate illustration of how our generation will not only be judged by the innovations we bring to market, the monuments to capitalism that we build to the sky, or the policies put in place to ensure a vibrant economy. This generation and those that come after will be judged on what we do when faced with the most basic or complex of decisions. Again, what we do, and how we behave, as individuals and organizations in public, and behind closed doors, will be a testament to our ability to find balance with one another, and with living in harmony with the earth.

Accountability and Sustainability

In its most basic form, accountability is tied to how an individual interprets and chooses to live within the boundaries of values, beliefs, morals, and conscious behaviors we place upon ourselves and greater society. Having accountability is having a power over oneself in the context of how we live and engage with our peers, family, friends, workplace, institutions, and within society. This power comes in the form of knowledge and an ability to make conscious decisions that guide our behavior on a daily basis. As shown in Figure 3.1 , accountability in the context of sustainability can be summarized across three levels:

- Individual "Self" Accountability
- Societal Accountability
- Generational Accountability

Figure 3.1
3 Levels of Accountability: Magnification of Impact
Created by Mark C. Coleman

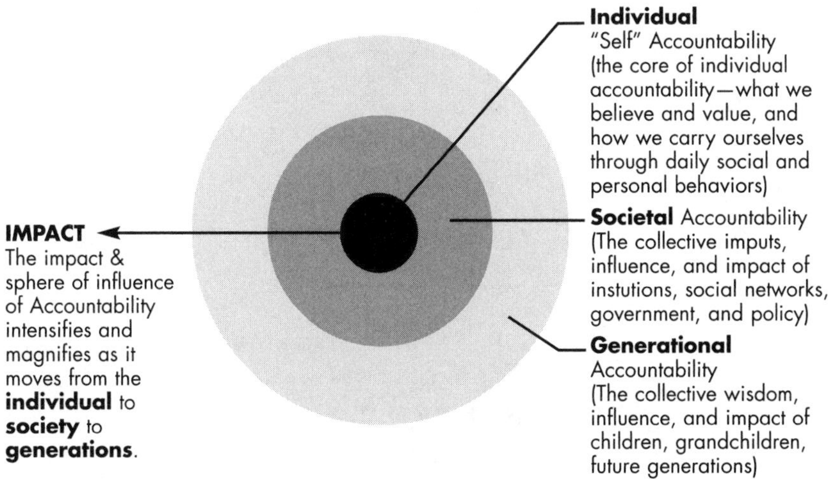

Individual
"Self" Accountability
(the core of individual accountability—what we believe and value, and how we carry ourselves through daily social and personal behaviors)

IMPACT ◄—
The impact & sphere of influence of Accountability intensifies and magnifies as it moves from the **individual** to **society** to **generations**.

Societal Accountability
(The collective imputs, influence, and impact of instutions, social networks, government, and policy)

Generational Accountability
(The collective wisdom, influence, and impact of children, grandchildren, future generations)

Each of these three levels influence one another (i.e., individuals influence society—society influences individuals—and generations influence both society and individuals). And, the impact and "sphere of influence" of the three levels of accountability intensifies and magnifies (compounds) as it moves from the individual to society to future generations. Individuals have the ability to take immediate and direct action in their lives that can influence society. As that magnifies within society to become a value or "norm," society has a broader impact on the behavior of the individuals, and as greater society chooses whether to adopt a new behavior, future generations are changed by the direct transfer or rejection of knowledge and belief systems. Figure 3.2 illustrates how the individual can be a critical element of magnifying their values, behaviors, and actions to influence the impact of the sustainability generation.

At the core is the individual or "self." As we conduct our lives we have a certain amount of accountability to ourselves and "self." That accountability can come in many forms depending upon your

Figure 3.2
How Accountability can Enable & Impact Sustainability NOW
Created by Mark C. Coleman

personal core values, but some examples include: an accountability to be healthy, educated, conscious of the world, empathetic to others, and of a well mind and spirit.

When individuals are accountable to themselves, and their core values and beliefs, they are being true to themselves and inner "self." In the context of sustainability, individuals must be accountable to themselves; otherwise they may not have an internal value-system to be understanding of the accountability requirements of society or generations.

Societal accountability is enveloped by the knowledge shared by society (generational knowledge). Society shapes the policies, rules, regulations and context in which we as individuals live within governed countries, and how we engage with the natural world. The rules are not arbitrary—they are defined by geography, cultural diversity, historical events, and other factors that specify how individuals perceive, behave in, and influence the world around them. At the heart of individual accountability is having a constant awareness of the world, and merging your awareness with the values of society, and generational knowledge to make responsible decisions.

The rules of nations, corporations, institutions, and families help dictate what our individual responsibility should be to ourselves and these entities. Yet, there are also more ubiquitous, overarching, and shared values and beliefs that also touch every culture and human being on the planet. Collectively, the values and beliefs guide humans globally. And the defined policies and "rules of society" defined by nations comprise the complex landscape of which individuals need to be aware and to which they are held accountable. While this landscape seems rigid, it is actually very fluid, constantly changing, and defined daily by everyone on earth who chooses to be accountable to themselves, their families and society NOW.

When sustainability is conceptually discussed it is often referred to as three interlocking circles. From a business context this is considered to be where people, profit, and the planet intersect. From a more societal focus it has been thought of as where environmental, economic, and social equity intersect. And there are other renditions of sustainable development, as shown in Figure 3.3.

In the past ten years I have participated in, facilitated and led, or designed dialog with industry, government, research, and academic leaders that have attempted to define sustainability, or at least attempt to understand it. In all cases the dialog revealed that sustainability is not necessarily something to have a definitive definition that fits all individuals, institutions, corporations, or generations.

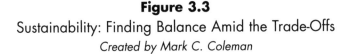

Figure 3.3

Sustainability: Finding Balance Amid the Trade-Offs

Created by Mark C. Coleman

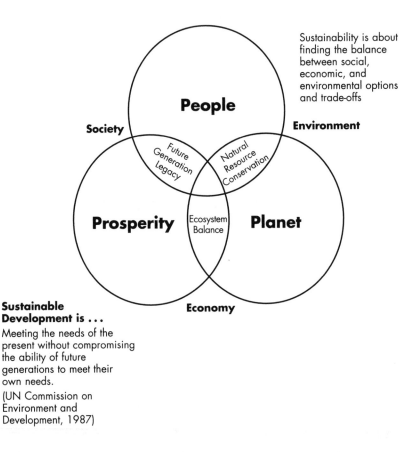

Sustainability is about finding the balance between social, economic, and environmental options and trade-offs

People

Society

Environment

Future Generation Legacy

Natural Resource Conservation

Prosperity

Ecosystem Balance

Planet

Sustainable Development is . . .

Meeting the needs of the present without compromising the ability of future generations to meet their own needs.

(UN Commission on Environment and Development, 1987)

Economy

Rather, sustainability is a process and philosophy that can foster a more conscious (aware) and strategic (critical thinking) approach to meeting the needs of society, both in the present and future. In this discovery, I have seen people's eyes, minds, and personalities light up. What they realize is that sustainability is not a huge undertaking that has to be achieved through a mad sprint in every direction, but a marathon that takes preparation, strategic planning, attentiveness, and most importantly, accountability.

Through accountability, the benefits of sustainability as a process and as a strategic approach in business, governance, and society can be realized. Humans have the power, individually and collectively, to project a future and conduct themselves in a way to achieve that future. The ability to follow a passion and vision with an aptitude to get things accomplished is what makes human beings a truly unique species on the planet.

In recent decades corporate and government executives have realized that sustainability is not just about future generations. In 1987 the UN Commission on Environment and Development (referred to as Brundtland Commission) did issue a report *"Our Common Future"*[42] that began to define sustainable development, summarized as "meeting the needs of the present without compromising the ability of future generations to meet their own needs." Part of the reason leaders in government and industry struggled in the 1990s and early 2000s with sustainability was the requirement to have a long-term focus. Government and business incentives and performance are on short, from two to five-year time-frames. Thus, sustainability had previously been viewed as a "good thing to have or be aware of," but never a strategic or political imperative.

The new millennium brought about some swift changes in business and the economy globally that began to realign the social-environmental context of business and government with notions of sustainability. The convergence of several global issues weighed heavily on industry and governments. Global financial market events ranged from government defaults to market failures from corporate greed. A string of global social-environmental issues included devastation from Hurricane Katrina and the earthquake in Haiti, as well as outbreaks of Avian Bird Flu and other escalating instances of disease, the price and supply volatility of oil and gas markets, global population growth, the inherent threats of global terrorism, and a growing recognition that many of the earth's natural resources and ecosystem services are constrained. There was a sense of urgency within government and industry to re-examine sustainability and sustainable development with open eyes. In doing so, the view of sustainability has been brought front and center with reflection not just about future generations, but about our responsibility and accountability as individuals, governments, and corporations to society NOW.

Much has been written on environmental impact assessment, or how to benefit financially from "going green." For example, in 2006 Dan Esty and Andrew Winston published the seminal *Green to Gold: How Smart Companies Use Environmental Strategy to Innovate, Create Value, and Build Competitive Advantage,*[43] which focused on the integration of environmental innovation to build financial results. To date there has been a lack of focus on social equity and the impact on, and influence of, people in sustainability dialog. There have been, however, advances in people's awareness of sustainability through the use of social media like Facebook and Twitter as well as You Tube and through other applications that have a very rapid influence on large masses of people. While dialog on sustainability has been heavily focused on environmental and economic considerations in the past, the social equity perspective is rapidly making its way into the conversation and practice. Greater inclusion of social equity will help balance and focus the dialog and decisions for the Sustainability Generation.

But while social media can have a broad impact, it remains under-utilized due to a lack of common goals to attain sustainability. Imagine if from day one of a person's life the value to have sustainability was directed toward that new born baby? Values and beliefs of society are shaped by past and current events and take time to become established and infiltrate into a common language and culture. But through individual and generational accountability a Sustainability Generation that begins NOW can advance an ethic of sustainability to impact the present and influence the values and culture of future generations.

From a societal point of view, accountability is made possible through values, beliefs, morals, ethics, empathy, and judgment. As society embraces these attributes it constructs governments, industries, and other institutions that have governing principles and rules of punishment and reward that come to bear on individuals' personal accountability to themselves and to greater society. This is why we as humans have control over our own destiny. Remembering that we are the ones who have created the governing structure of accountability in the world we live in is a key point in understanding how sustainability can be achieved through a generation of individuals having a greater responsibility to themselves and to society.

Another aspect of individual accountability comes in the form of how we behave within ourselves (our sense of self and how we individually interact with and experience the world) and also how we behave with our friends, family, peers, and others we engage with on a daily basis. Accountability is multi-faceted, layered, and complex. By understanding it, we can have a more full appreciation and understanding of how this simple concept, when put into action, can be a powerful and transformative agent for change.

The following three scenarios serve to further conceptualize this notion of accountability in individuals, generations, and greater society:

- *Individual Accountability* Jim works on a college campus. The campus has a "beautification" committee and goal in attempts to keep the environment looking clean, friendly, and safe. Jim sits on the committee and is well aware of the goals. Jim is leaving his office for the day and walks through a courtyard to his car. Jim notices a coffee cup littering the walkway. There are no trash cans nearby. Jim quickly assesses the situation, but chooses to leave the disposable cup in its place, feeling assured that the campus maintenance staff or grounds people will pick it up. Jim had a choice to exercise his accountability to himself, his committee, and to the broader community in his behavior. Why did Jim choose to not pick up the cup?

- **Generational Accountability** Lisa has been working as an environmental change-agent in the oil and gas and chemical industries for past thirty-five years. She began her career working for state and federal environmental regulators developing and enforcing environmental policy. She currently works for a Fortune 500 company as their chief sustainability officer focusing on business strategy, ethics, risk management, and innovation. Throughout her career Lisa has developed a unique skill set in stakeholder management, negotiation, current affairs, risk management, communication, and outreach. Lisa's professional network is very large with connections in government, industry, academia, research, and not-for-profit organizations domestically and internationally. Lisa intends to retire from her corporate position within two years to start her own small business. Lisa is passionate about sustainability and wants to leave a legacy of performance behind her; but more importantly, she wants to leave a team of individuals that have the same dedication, sense of urgency, capacity to lead, and understanding of the issues and challenges that she has. Lisa perceives a gap in leadership between what she believes to be her role, and skills of others in her organization. Lisa decides that she will take the next two years to personally train, mentor, and develop the skill set of three individuals in her organization to better prepare them to manage the complexity of issues she deals with successfully from her specialized knowledge and experience from her long career.

- **Generational/Societal Accountability** The greatest transfer of wealth in the United States will occur within this next decade as the Baby Boom generation retires and ultimately leave their wealth to their children, to charitable foundations, or other causes. This wealth was created on the backbone of generations of individuals that built the U.S. economy through an era of rapid industrialization. But, the creation of wealth in the United

States did not come without some externalities. The environmental impact of our industrialized society was, and continues to be, a core economic and societal challenge. Trillions of dollars have been reserved by the world's largest corporations and governments to address the clean-up of past environmental liabilities. Wealth creation in the future will be less about clean-up of past environmental liabilities and more about ensuring a balance between energy, environmental, economic, and societal needs. A cultural, economic, and generational shift is underway

Table 3.1

Level of Accountability: Individual	
Elements/Attributes/Influencers	Common Outcomes of Accountability
• Values/Beliefs/Morals • Family/Friends/Peer Groups • Love/Fear/Rejection/Punishment	• Moral and sound judgment for making decisions; healthy living; self-awareness and conscious decision-making
Level of Accountability: Societal	
Elements/Attributes/Influencers	Common Outcomes of Accountability
• Values/Beliefs/Morals • Policy/Regulation • Rules/Standards/Codes/Procedures • Fear/Rejection/Punishment • Incentives/Disincentives	• Ground rules for society, organizations, etc. • Recognition & promotion within community, industry, etc. (incentive) • Imprisonment or criminal behavior when societal values and rules are not abided by (disincentive)
Level of Accountability: Generational	
Elements/Attributes/Influencers	Common Outcomes of Accountability
• Family is an influence on the transfer of knowledge, values and beliefs • Society and history also influence knowledge transfer	• Values, beliefs, morals, knowledge, and intellect are carried forward to provide a re-birth (Cradle-to-Cradle) of accountability and ability for principles of sustainability that are grounded in the knowledge and attitudes of past generations.

where individual consumers and large corporations and governments are now choosing to embrace principles of sustainability as the new framework for conducting daily life. As the Baby Boom generation makes the largest transfer of financial wealth in history, the receiving generations are looking for ways to put that wealth toward the best possible uses.

So what makes up the components of individual and generational accountability? How can accountability catalyze the Sustainability Generation? In what ways does accountability take on influence among individuals and generations of people? Table 3.1 outlines some common elements and attributes that define the three levels of accountability. And the following sections of this chapter address these other pertinent questions.

Challenges and Opportunities in Personal Accountability

By accepting personal accountability in our individual lives, we can make real-time impact on our state of sustainability as well as the sustainability of future generations. The toughest challenge is realizing that we, as individuals, have the power within ourselves to actually make an impact. Once our inertia is overcome, the process of accepting change and personal accountability to ourselves and to our families and future generations becomes very easy, if not purely enjoyable. Most people want to make the right choices and do things for the right reasons.

Getting to Accountability, Overcoming Barriers

If we have the knowledge today that certain human activities are unbalanced from an economic, environmental, and social point of view, is it not our responsibility to take action NOW? Individually and collectively, we need to look at our state of knowledge and action regarding our potential to impact the natural world and society. We need to ask ourselves: Are we being personally accountable? Are we being negligent in our behaviors if we have knowledge of what is wrong and right? Do we have the collective intellect, know-how, and capacity to do something different?

Individuals and greater society now have the technology, tools, processes, skill set, and accumulated knowledge to identify and understand unsustainable behavior. These same attributes can enable us take action NOW on more sustainable solutions. The intermediary between what we know does not work and what we know is possible is simply our personal accountability to ourselves, our families, our communities and global society. In short, we have to get out of the way of own internal barriers that keep us from being held accountable on an individual and societal basis. A sample of the barriers that impact the ability to achieve individual, societal, and generational accountability is presented in Figure 3.4.

The barriers identified are also opportunities to enable more personal accountability. For example, a lack of information, knowledge, and awareness might cripple an individual's ability to make a decision reflecting personal accountability. However, the individual still has the power to seek out information, data, knowledge, and perspective to heighten awareness to prepare for taking responsibility. It is not enough to say that information does not exist. The responsibility to

Figure 3.4
Awareness and Action on Accountability
Created by Mark C. Coleman

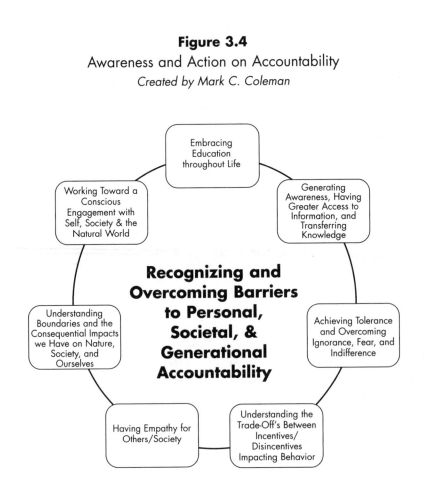

take action and be educated and informed resides with individuals themselves as best they can. As a species that has the ability to think, learn, react, and envision consequences, humans have no excuse, unfortunately, not to be personally accountable—even if that means taking ownership over what we know and don't know. The next section outlines an approach for how individuals and generations can move beyond the barriers we put in front of ourselves to keep us from taking ownership of our decisions and behavior and becoming truly accountable.

"Now" Characteristics of Personal Accountability

At a very foundational level, most people want to survive and thrive. Thus, when we peel back the onion to look at the social and environmental challenges of our time, we begin to see large and small things we can do as individuals, consumers, institutions, governments, industry, families, and society to begin a transformation to a more sustainable culture. There are many things we can do as individuals, society, or generations to help mitigate our impacts on the environment and to develop a more socially responsible society.

For example, we can pick up litter when we see it; we can recycle; we can use tap water instead of bottled water; we can work from home one day a week instead of commuting; we can give our used clothing or belongings to those in need; we can buy and prepare meals with organic and locally grown vegetables and meats; we can use less energy, produce less waste, and design better products. In my experience the plethora of books written on sustainability in the past decade have focused on the business opportunities associated with things we can do. These books have been a gift to society, helping all stakeholders better understand the options before us.

But personal accountability is a deeper and more humanistic approach to championing sustainability to enable better products and better living. Instead of making a laundry list of "go green" options for your review (and I am not likely to come up with anything better than what authors like Gil Friend, Dan Esty, or Thomas Friedman have promoted), I am going to outline what I believe are essential "NOW" characteristics of accountability that are more durable than any technology, more powerful than any policy, and have great capacity to result in impacts NOW and in the future, especially when they are directed toward a common global goal of sustainability. The "NOW" characteristics that can magnify the influence and impact of personal accountability include:

- ***Empathize*** Listen to, and understand yourself and those around you. By developing the skill to hear your inner self and the true needs of others, the potential for having a deeper sense of personal accountability can be heightened.

- ***Educate*** Educate yourself and return your knowledge to society. Education is multifaceted. People sometimes don't realize how much knowledge they have and how that knowledge can improve another person's life. By accepting that education is not just a formal degree that one earns, but a lifelong journey and commitment to continuously seek out knowledge for the sake of being a better citizen and more critical thinker, you can be better prepared to be personally accountable to yourself, and to society.

- ***Engage*** Get involved in something to improve yourself and engage with the world around you. Learning only through certain media (social media or television) is one-dimensional. People have a personal responsibility to themselves and to society to engage in the groups they belong to as a citizen, family member, employee, or in their spiritual pursuits. Increasing engagement in life helps to increase personal accountability to oneself while being aware of the world around you and reinforcing empathy among others. Engage others by sharing your passion and desire to get people involved in your personal accountability. By sharing what you do (recycling, gardening, practicing energy efficiency and conservation, and so forth) it fosters other "NOW" characteristics.

- ***Empower*** Having empowerment is much different from having a simple engagement of oneself in personal accountability. Empowerment is what we need to have to externally encourage others to achieve personal accountability. Associated with this is an empathy and ability to be supportive to other individuals when they do not agree with your values or your desire for immediate action. Encourage them by empowering them to think more critically and find common elements on which to base judgment and decisions. Through empowerment individuals can take a leadership role to extend their values and beliefs to help others to make informed decisions in ways that make them feel like they are part of a solution.

- ***Enlighten*** This is perhaps the most vague and misunderstood characteristic of personal accountability, yet very powerful. Enlightenment arises within one's consciousness (sense of self) that is connected with, yet also detached from, the physical form of our mind and body. Bestselling author Eckhart Tolle[44] has, in my view, done an outstanding job at capturing the essence of enlightenment and personal accountability in his works. *A New Earth: Awakening to Your Life's Purpose and The Power of Now: A Guide to Spiritual Enlightenment* conceptualize and define enlightenment and touch upon personal accountability within individuals as a method for tapping one's spirituality and better understanding your life's purpose. The wisdom of Eckhart Tolle provides a framework for guiding personal accountability in the context of a sustainable future. By tapping your inner-self and understanding what motivates you, you are better prepared to deal with ambiguity and the sometimes overwhelming unsettledness of life. It is the enlightened self that truly understands motivation and can therefore make decisions based not just on critical judgments from intellect and knowledge, but from decisions based on enlightened self-awareness and inner consciousness.

Developing these characteristics of personal accountability is essential to developing leaders to guide the Sustainability Generation.

Keeping the Silver Tsunami from Crushing the Green Wave of Innovation and Social Accountability[45]

In the past few years many leaders within industry and government have discussed and debated the potential impact of the "silver tsunami," as it has been cleverly named to describe the event of the and huge wave of American Baby Boomers born between 1946 and 1964 who will begin to turn 65 beginning in 2011. Along with the many concerns about having such a large population of seniors, this event also entails the projected loss of knowledge, leadership, and experience in the workforce with the mass exodus of millions of Baby Boomers at their time of retirement. For the past forty years many of these workers initiated and led the movement for environmental advocacy, protection, and innovation.

As these leaders leave their formal careers, will the United States lose the momentum of the "green tsunami" that has grown in breadth and consequence throughout government, industry, research, and innovation in the past few years? Baby Boomers have been thought-leaders, designers, and managers of pragmatic solutions to enable the

United States to move toward a more "green economy." Could the transition of Boomers to retirement crush efforts to move forward to a more sustainable economy? To remain competitive in a fast-paced global economy we need to be accountable to ourselves and to future generations by taking a hard look at bridging the knowledge gap that could result from this generational workforce transition.

Transfer of Wealth Should Be Grounded in Both Financial and Intellectual Resources

According to the Alliance for Aging Research,[46] beginning this year, 10,000 Baby Boomers will turn 65 every day, "and continue to do so for the next for 20 years." Further, "by 2030, almost one out of every five Americans—some 72 million people—will be 65 years or older. By 2050, the 65+ population is projected to be between 80 and 90 million, with those 85 and older close to 21 million."

The implications of the "silver tsunami" are vast. Future impacts of this on the workforce and the economy can be considerable:

- A knowledge-gap representing a chasm of lost information and experience is perceived to exist between the Baby Boomers leaving the workforce and those taking on new leadership roles within the current economy (Generations X and Y).

- If left unaddressed, the perceived knowledge-gap can lead to unnecessary financial, environmental, and human health and safety risks for industry, government, and greater society.

- In a global economy, "knowledge-gaps" brought on by generational transitions can also have an impact on industrial competitiveness. Knowledge-gaps within government and industry can exacerbate challenges the United States has to compete globally, both in terms of a talented and trained workforce and a workforce with the knowledge to sustain critical infrastructure.

The greatest transfer of wealth in the United States is also projected to occur within this next decade as the Baby Boom generation retires and leaves their wealth to their children and charitable foundations or other endeavors. This wealth was created on the backbone of generations of individuals that built the U.S. economy through an era of rapid industrialization. But the creation of wealth in the United States did not come without externalities. The environmental impact of our industrialized society was, and continues to be, a core economic and societal challenge.

Trillions of dollars have been reserved by the world's largest corporations and governments to address the clean-up of past environmental liabilities. Wealth creation in the future will be less about clean-up of past environmental liabilities and more about ensuring a balance between energy, environmental, economic, and societal needs. A cultural, economic, and generational shift is underway where individual consumers and large corporations and governments are now choosing to embrace principles of sustainability as the new framework for conducting daily life. As the Baby Boom generation makes the largest transfer of financial wealth in history, the receiving generations are looking for ways to put that wealth toward the best possible uses. And this new generation of leaders needs guidance!

The modern environmental movement has many trigger points and origins, but many mark April 22, 1970, the first "Earth Day" as a date of recognition. The Baby Boom generation influenced and became the leaders of the environmental movement in the United States and abroad. The Baby Boom generation brought the United States environmental and energy policy as we have it today. It was the generation that started environmental management systems (EMS) for corporations, established environmental risk assessments and models for decisions made by governments, and incorporated the principles of sustainable design and production into development of new products and services that reduce impacts of consumerism on energy and the environment.

Real or Perceived: The Knowledge Chasm Between Generations

In the past five years I have personally facilitated or attended several executive workshops involving leaders from Fortune 500 companies, government agencies, and not-for-profit organizations. One of the prevailing concerns about the future is the perceived gap in knowledge, technical understanding, and ability to manage projects in environmental issues that include the building blocks of the modern sustainability movement.

The chasm is defined and discussed anecdotally as many senior leaders in Fortune 500 companies or large federal agencies like the United States Environmental Protection Agency (EPA) share concerns about up to 75% of their staff nearing retirement age and a large gap of fundamental knowledge between the Baby Boom generation and those that will fill their shoes.

The gap in knowledge that exists between generations can lead to unnecessary financial, safety, and environmental risks. For example, in heavy industries like mining, energy, or transport, a lack of technical knowledge could lead to catastrophic failures in infrastructure or systems that support our modern economy. If the younger generation does not know the fundamentals of how energy is created, or does not have an interest in learning how to work with older infrastructure because it is not "sexy or cool," society has a fundamental challenge and huge risks going forward. And how can we ensure the infrastructures built decades or even a hundred years ago will continue to operate reliably and efficiently for societal needs? The Baby Boom generation built much of our modern infrastructure post-World War II. As Generations X and Y take the helm, it will be the responsibility of all generations of Boomers and X and Y to work together to close any voids of information, knowledge, or technology voids that could result in real risks to human health and safety and the environment.

The knowledge gap can also cause unnecessary financial risks and resource constraints. Retiring Baby Boomers leave behind decades of history of relationships and experiences of the progress in environmental issues among institutions in local communities, state and federal regulatory agencies, and companies. There is a critical memory in institutions on the history of how many environmental liability sites evolved and were later cleaned-up. This was established by working relationships, often decades in the making, between industry, government, local communities, and other stakeholders. If institutional memory for these events is lost, industry and government could see younger generations reliving or reinventing the wheel for agreements and progress already made. This resulting scenario could put constraints on personal and financial resources if Boomers are unsuccessful in grooming the next generation of leaders to take their place.

This knowledge-chasm is recognized in many industries, including chemical manufacturing, oil and gas, transportation, government services, mining and minerals, and environmental engineering. The gap is being addressed in a variety of ways: attraction of new talent; recruitment at top universities; internal leadership mentoring, development and coaching workshops; training days and academies for leveraging the institutional and technical knowledge of Baby Boomers for the benefit of the younger generation taking on new leadership roles.

Addressing "Green" Knowledge Gaps

But amid the concern over the knowledge-chasm, there is hope and opportunity. The younger generation may carry with it a curiosity and naiveté that allows for a new-era of open communication and dialog, engagement, and bright ideas. Generations X and Y have experienced and think about the world much differently from their parents and grandparents. While the younger generation may be lacking in some areas, they might make up for it in their approach to learning, decision-making, and problem-solving. The use of social media, for example, has proven to be an incredible force among members of Generation Y to communicate and innovate. While the benefits of social media may not address all of the knowledge-gap needs projected by Boomers, it is one element of how the younger generation can be engaged to learn and to take action.

Fortune 500 companies and governments are not alone in their efforts to close the knowledge gap. While institutional knowledge really needs to come from within a particular industry sector, fundamental and technical knowledge can be learned in other ways. For example, the Golisano Institute of Sustainability (GIS) at Rochester Institute of Technology (RIT) (see http://www.sustainability.rit.edu/) offers a multidisciplinary academic and research program leading to a Master of Architecture in Sustainable Architecture or a Master of Science or Ph.D. in Sustainable Production Systems. The GIS program at RIT has an applied an industrial focus to its programming, thereby growing a next generation of educated professionals that have a balance of both fundamental knowledge and pragmatic experience to come to bear on the social and industrial challenges of industry and government. Other colleges and academic degree and research programs at RIT have also integrated elements of sustainability into their programming, including the Colleges of Business, Engineering, Liberal Arts, and Computing Science.

Like RIT, many other universities across the nation have begun to focus directly on the knowledge-gap perceived and anticipated by industry and government (and broader society) and have revamped, or created entirely new, programs to address this need. As another example of a university taking a holistic approach toward sustainability, Arizona State University offers Bachelor of Arts and Science degrees in sustainability as well as Master of Arts, Master of Science, and Ph.D.

And other universities have targeted, industry-specific programs like nuclear engineering at Rensselaer Polytechnic Institute, environmental science and engineering at the Colorado School of Mines, or the University of Florida's graduate specializations in water resources planning and management. Social and environmental challenges have always been generational focuses. However, the impacts of these challenges are being felt and addressed by industry and government with greater intensity than in the past. As global population growth constrains natural resources, and as personal responsibility realigns with financial responsibility in the marketplace, there will be more need for workers that have strong foundational and institutional knowledge, but also tactical and technical experiences that can address these challenges. Colleges and Universities are taking on a piece of the knowledge gap by focusing on serving the needs of industry and society through their academic programming today, as well as in the future through basic and applied research and technological innovation.

The Sustainability Generation Is About Personal Accountability, Empowerment, and Taking Action Now

A "Sustainability Generation" that now exists in the United States and throughout the world is not just about Baby Boomers that led the environmental movement or Generation X and Yers that have taken social media to a new era of grass-roots action. There is also the recognition that the complexity of our modern society requires all generations to take responsibility for their actions, both today and tomorrow. The knowledge-gap between the generations in government and industry is an issue. However, by working together to understand how each other learns, communicates, and engages, Baby Boomers and Generations X and Y can transition the economy into a sustainable future without fear of financial, environmental, or human health and safety risks. Our transportation, communication, water, energy, security, and educational infrastructure are under a transition. The people (leadership) dictate how policies (governance and rules) and practices (daily actions) are developed and carried out.

Thus, it is no wonder many Boomers are concerned about those that will succeed them. Boomers want to ensure the infrastructures they created continue to operate successfully. The responsibility for ensuring a sustainable future is shared by all generations. The common denominator across all generations will need to be personal accountability, leadership, innovation, empowerment, and engagement. The responsibilities for enabling the transfer of their wealth of finances and knowledge do reside in the older generation. The Boomers also need to be a part of addressing the knowledge chasm in the next few years. By leveraging their experience and leadership, Boomers should take an active interest in transitioning organizations, people, resources, systems, knowledge, and finances to the younger generation.

And they need to do so in a way that engages and empowers the younger generation to take responsibility. The Boomers need to rest assured that whatever they transition to the next generation, whether it is capital or carbon, will be approached with resolve and the care, courage, and commitment that they would expect of themselves.

At the heart of every social and environmental challenge, large or small, is a need for critical thinking, strong leadership, and an ability to make informed decisions. The challenges of the "silver tsunami" are no different. As the "silver tsunami" advances in U.S. culture in 2011 and continues until 2020, the United States and all nations affected by this generational shift have an opportunity. The opportunity is to make both older and younger generations accountable to each other by asking the right questions to ensure the fears and risks associated with this transition are minimized and ensure the financial and knowledge resources are transferred.

Chapter Summary

- A knowledge-gap (chasm) has been said to exist between those leaving the workforce (Baby Boomers) and those taking on new leadership roles within the current economy (Generations X and Y).
- If left unaddressed, the perceived knowledge-gap can lead to unnecessary financial, environmental, human health and safety risks for industry, government, and greater society.
- In a global economy, "knowledge-gaps" brought on by generational transitions can also have an impact on industrial competitiveness. Knowledge-gaps within government and industry can exacerbate challenges the United States has to compete globally, in terms of needing a talented and trained workforce with the knowledge to sustain critical infrastructure.
- Colleges and universities have begun to realign, restructure, or develop entirely new academic, research, and technological innovation programs to address "knowledge-gaps" in society.
- To be accountable as a member of society means to be present, engaged, and aware. Accountable members of society do not accept the status quo as a general rule or social norm. Rather, they have the awareness to see when

change is necessary and the critical thinking and capacity to take action to enable positive change.

- Ultimately, the "Sustainability Generation" will require the culmination of all generations to be accountable for their behaviors and decisions, not just individual citizens that choose to be accountable. Being accountable individually and to society will require the Sustainability Generation to take responsibility for their actions, today and tomorrow. Baby Boomers and Generations X and Y can collaborate to transition the economy into a sustainable future without fear of unnecessary financial, environmental, or human health and safety risks.

- "Personal accountability" is one of the most important, yet most challenging and undervalued quotients of the sustainability equation. Through personal accountability, individuals and generations can transform the world around them, NOW.

- It is how we react to our mistakes, through personal accountability, that will make the difference in having a more or less sustainable future. How we conduct ourselves in public and how we make decisions alone behind closed doors alone when no one is watching are equally important. Personal accountability is about doing the right thing when no one, or when everyone is looking.

4

Empowerment and Enlightenment

Empowerment

There is something special that happens when people feel empowered. People communicate, collaborate, take responsible action, become more creative and innovative and adapt to change. Amazing results can be achieved when people feel empowered. The structural elements of empowerment include:

- Empathy and Understanding
- Communication
- Understanding boundaries
- Taking action
- Accepting responsibility and being accountable

Empowerment: Getting to "We"

Three years ago as I was preparing to facilitate thirty corporate environmental-remediation leaders at a private peer-to-peer benchmarking workshop, a senior corporate environmental leader in the auto industry told me that company cultures, particularly in the transportation industry, are seeing some dramatic change. And in his view this was for the better. He noted that corporate executives were more receptive to internal conversations about sustainability and how their products, operations, and people contribute to the long-term sustainability of their company and the mutual goals and needs of society. The auto industry was severely impacted by the global financial recession which began in late 2007 and continued through 2010. GM, which once stood as a pillar of capitalism and global growth, was essentially cut at its knees and entered into bankruptcy. (The senior leader I spoke with was not from GM, but another "top 3" U.S. automaker.) The U.S. government tried to jump start the industry through its "Cash for Clunkers" and other financial incentive programs. But as a family friend once noted, cars need three things to run: spark, fuel, and combustion. By the end of 2009 the auto industry had lost all three. The spark (auto innovation) was gone. Many of the products coming out of Detroit were the "same old thing." And the companies were still a few years away from production of models that might make a significant impact on consumer behaviors by having improved fuel efficiency, enhanced safety, and "lifestyle" features that fit who we are, how we spend our time, what we do. The fuel (consumer demand) had waned. And the combustion (financing) to get the deal made had dried up with the collapse of many lending institutions offering access to "easy" credit. Without incentives no one had the money or desire to buy something new. There were many signs on the wall that the auto industry was just one of many industrial sectors tied to consumer and generational entitlement that was in need of a makeover. And so a transformation began. Some might have wished it happened earlier, and with less distress to workers, communities, and the economy. But, the automobile industry is making a comeback powered by smart designs, new product innovations, and new management approaches. For example in February 2012 GM[47] reported a $7.2 billion pre-tax profit from North American operations, the highest in the company's 103 year history, recorded from fourth quarter 2011 results.

The senior environmental automotive leader also pointed that in many sectors of the economy, as well as government and academia, the human factor called the "ego" more often than not gets in the way of sound decision-making. He noted that in many critical decisions that impact human health, environment, and economy there are people that say "no" just because there is an opposition that says "yes." This is seen in partisan politics and on Wall Street. The auto industry environmental leader went on to say that in industry, government, and academia we need more "WE" decision makers who can find the middle ground between the "yes" and "no" and come to a decision based upon sound science and objective facts, not just "ego" based justifications. "WE" decisions require unique leaders who can get past individual egos and think about their decision-making in the context of societal needs. They need to find balance by weighing both the near-term appeal to their "ego" or organization with the long-term needs of society. As simple and logical as the idea of "WE" decision-making sounds, it is not widely practiced. The duality in this kind of decision making will require individuals who have incredible tact and communication and leadership skills. These leaders need to be empowered and empower those around them to find a way to get to "WE."

The concept of "WE" is not new. I met Jonathan Spector, Chief Executive Officer of The Conference Board,[48] a widely cited source of business intelligence based out of New York City, with my colleague Bruce Piasecki in the spring of 2010. Bruce and I had just presented to 22 CFOs at one of the Conference Board's "Council of CFO" meetings on the topic *"The Growing Relationships between Financial Controls, Sustainability and Climate Change."* Bruce and I were briefing Mr. Spector in his NYC office on how we felt the presentation went with the CFOs and discussed Bruce's latest book, *The Surprising Solutions: Creating Possibility in a Swift & Severe World.* I learned that Mr. Spector was an author himself, having co-authored the book *We are Smarter than Me* in 2007, which highlighted the ways in which businesses can harness the power of collective intelligence. In a few minutes he and Bruce covered an incredible amount of intellectual ground in lively conversation.

I left Mr. Spector's office that day thinking more about "WE" conceptually and more committed than ever to my concepts about entitlement and sustainability. Following our meeting with Mr. Spector that day I confirmed my realization that we cannot blame past generations for our current woes of social and environmental challenges. Past generations lived during a time when there was not enough science, technology, or as Mr. Spector wrote about, "collective intelligence" to assess future environmental risks related to industrial production. When signals and evidence of industrial and environmental disasters (rivers catching on fire, humans getting cancer, or facilities exploding) began to proliferate, we humans adjusted by learning from those experiences to shift our behavior and, hopefully, our values and beliefs. What needs to happen as we go forward is a more rapid assembly of the "collective knowledge and intelligence" that is contained in our institutions and individuals to leverage that "WE" toward more sustainable practices.

Empowering Sustainability 21st Century Style: GreenNurture

The GreenNurture mission is to provide the most revolutionary turn-key solution for organizations to achieve their sustainability goals by using the power of the web to unlock their most valuable resource—the collective intelligence of their people—to resolve the challenges in "going green"and realize positive yields in full-cost accounting.

GreenNurture engages and empowers the people that comprise a company to take environmental action to directly improve the environment and their company's bottom line.

We actively engage the participants by asking them what they think should be done in their job, department, and company to achieve greater sustainability. We provide the tool by which anyone in the company can make valuable suggestions . . . and be heard. Our system is centered on user-generated feedback. Plus, we track the results and provide in depth reports to back up the actions taken.

In addition, GreenNurture has developed a Green Action Index which uses a proprietary algorithm to provide a standardized method to gauge an organization's environmental actions. The GAI emblem sits on your organization's website and links to a public profile page that shows off your sustainability efforts. Source: http://www.greennurture.com/faq.aspx

Enabling "We" Thinking in Corporations:GreenNurture

An example of the sustainability generation using the potential of empowerment is through the Tempe, Arizona based GreenNurture, http://www.greennurture.com/about.aspx.

GreenNurture markets itself as "the premier turn-key corporate sustainability program focused on engaging the human resources of an organization and empowering them to take environmental action." GreenNurture's approach provides employee engagement, knowledge, rewards, brand value, assessment and reporting as the critical elements of how an organization can motivate, reinforce, and empower its human talent toward optimizing the sustainable development and realization of the company. Like GreenNurture, a number of proactive social-media organizations launched with a fury in the past three to five years helpings government, corporate, and not-for-profit clients better align with shifting customer preferences and needs. These companies providing a value proposition focused on attaining sustainability seek to remain relevant through their innovation and creativity and will continue to sprout up and evolve. Many of these organizations are supporting, and making it possible for the social equity perspective of sustainability to gain greater prominence with decision makers.

Enlightenment

When people are empowered, their enthusiasm for what they do can be infectious. When individuals are empowered, they become advocates for what they believe in and stand for. Empowered leaders become the glue that keeps things together and the conduits by which new ideas are exchanged. Empowered leaders lead others to be enlightened through their ability to communicate, take action, and accept responsibility. Enlightenment is transformational. It is the means by which individuals and organizations not only understand that change is imminent, but also see how they can effect change for the good and be a part of making a difference.

For the members of Sustainability Generation to be effective in addressing the imminent changes in climate, natural resources, and technology, they must be empowered to take responsibility for their actions and decisions while enlightened to be awake to the surrounding world. Understanding and respecting that the world is constrained by limits, yet also vast in its endless opportunities, is a challenge for anyone. The limits are physical and biological and the opportunity lies in the endless possibilities of innovation from human intellect that can make limitless what is seemingly limited. Enlightenment can lead to the elimination of the mindset of entitlement in our society. Through a more enlightened society, choices about the constraints of our physical natural resources can be made with sound judgment and a sense of equity for existing and future generations.

The Enlightened Leader

There are too few enlightened people walking the earth! You know them when you find them because they carry an aura of high potential, limitless opportunity, and an open mindedness that is unparalleled. Enlightened leaders are not necessarily "yes" people or "no" people. They are "WE" people as previously defined.

The enlightened leader may be decisive, but don't let their decisiveness fool you. Their decisiveness is simply the ability, some may call it a "sixth sense," to quickly assess an opportunity or situation and make a rational and balanced decision. The enlightened leader has a decision-making capability, with the only the bias of being less restrictive than others. In short, the enlightened leader weighs decisions with greater balance and more clarity as to the needs of society when others may weigh decisions only on the basis of their financial or other personal motivations.

Now, the idea of the enlightened leader seems noble enough. But keep in mind that enlightened leaders are human. What they seek is to be humane in their actions. But they too make mistakes and are not "above us" mortals struggling with tempering our egos. Many enlightened leaders struggle with the same temptations that others do, but they have learned to quiet their ego enough to think more holistically and less selfishly. Enlightened leaders essentially remove entitlement from their vocabulary and mindset and think more about how they can help, rather than how others can help them. It is the differentiator to explain how and why many "enlightened leaders" have started and successfully grown some very interesting new-age companies driven by social and environmental sustainability.

The Buzz about Enlightenment

When I first met Bob Stiller I knew he was a special kind of leader. While he may not formally view himself as or designate himself as an "enlightened leader," I would like to create the case that he is. And here is why. Bob Stiller is the founder and Chairman of the Board of Green Mountain Coffee Roasters (NASDAQ: GMCR). Mr. Stiller also served as President and CEO for most of the company's existence (from its inception in July 1981 to May of 2007). I met Mr. Stiller in January 2007 when he was a speaker at a private corporate industry workshop in Phoenix, Arizona sponsored by the AHC Group, Inc. Mr. Stiller's presence, articulation of his business strategy, and personal reflections on growing a small specialty coffee roaster were, in a word, "enlightened." Perhaps it was because in 2007 so many companies continued to wrestle with the idea of corporate social responsibility, or perhaps it was just how convincing Mr. Stiller was as a passionate speaker. But in every word and action he the concept of an "enlightened leader" shined.

Green Mountain Coffee Roasters was founded by Bob Stiller in 1981. In the years between 1998 and 2008 the company grew by more than 20% annually year over year. Throughout its corporate history Bob Stiller has instilled a corporate ethic of social responsibility within the company's people, policies, and practices. As the leader of ship navigating its way through the burgeoning specialty coffee market, Bob Stiller was able to maintain and even grow GMCR's corporate social responsibility initiatives. At face value, that seems counterintuitive to financial performance and growth. How can a company, as it grows and sells more products, simultaneously increase its efforts to curtail its impact on human health and environment as it focuses on the social responsibility elements of procuring coffee beans from sensitive ecosystems and low-income countries?

The answer to that question resides it GMCR's ability to strip any notion of entitlement from its business by finding ways to give back more than it takes. Through his passion for excellence Bob Stiller has been able to empower his employees to make "WE" decisions that affect not just the company bottom line, but also a societal bottom line. GMCR is one of the rare companies that sees its existence today and into the future in the context of a "societal license to do business." The idea of a "societal license to do business" has both shareholder and stakeholder implications. GMCR has realized, largely through the vision and passion of its founder, Bob Stiller, that building a sustainable enterprise requires a focus on today and tomorrow, not just how much financial benefit one can reap today from entitlement to natural resources and sale of commodities like coffee.

GMCR has taken interesting steps toward social responsible business growth. The GMCR web-site states, ". . . for 25 years, we have been on a deliberate journey to create and sustain a values-driven company that views profit as a means to achieve a higher purpose. . . ."[49]

Examples of how GMCR's, has through its goal of "enlightened leadership" to achieve a higher purpose has been making progress for more than a quarter of a century are summarized here.

Making the Manufacturing Supply Chain Accountable

In 2008 GMCR began measuring compliance with their **Set of Vendor Expectations**,[50] a set of guidelines that outline GMCR's expectations of their vendors toward legal compliance, labor conditions (including child labor, wages and benefits, hours of work, freedom of association, discrimination and abuse, and health and safety), and environmental responsibility. In essence, GMCR's **Set of Vendor Expectations**, and ability to measure compliance, is a form of corporate accountability that has infiltrated their supply chain. To aid in the measurement of compliance, GMCR "created a set of tools, including self-assessments, surveys, on-site assessments by GMCR staff, and commissioned audits of vendor facilities."

PARTNERING WITH SUPPLY-CHAIN COMMUNITIES

GMCR's coffee supply chain goal is stated as: "to help the people in coffee-producing communities lead healthier and more prosperous lives." To help achieve this goal, GMCR provides two levels of outreach:

- First, they "provide on-the-ground assistance by helping suppliers improve their ability to deliver high-quality specialty coffee to the marketplace." GMCR provides "advice on cultivation techniques, training on cupping skills or connecting suppliers with industry resources to help them strengthen and grow their business."
- Second, GMCR's provides "financial grants to nonprofits that have both the technical skills and the on-the-ground connections to help coffee-growing communities chart their own course towards a more sustainable future."
- To further their accountability toward their supply chain goal, GMCR created and publishes a **"Partnering with Supply-Chain Communities Scorecard."**[51] The scorecard includes data on GMCR grant-making efforts in coffee communities, pricing of fair trace certified and other coffee sources, and total commodity purchases from organic, nonorganic, Fair Trade Certified, or other conventional sources.

PROTECTING THE ENVIRONMENT

In the energy realm the company installed an electricity cogeneration system at its Waterbury, VT facility to reduce demand and reliance on the electric grid.

The company also purchases 100% of its electricity from renewable energy credits making them greenhouse gas neutral. The company sets an annual goal to reduce energy use by 5% per a certain unit of sales. In 2006 the company reduced its natural gas usage by 15% from the previous year.

The company has been active in conducting energy audits of its facilities and offices and retrofitting equipment where possible to foster energy efficiency improvements. The company is also greening its fleet of vehicles and encourages conservation of energy among its employees.

BUILDING DEMAND FOR SUSTAINABLE PRODUCTS

GMCR's is using the power of their purchasing power and coffee community supply chain relationships to bring more environmentally preferable and sustainable products to mainstream markets. For example, GMCR's is focused on stimulating demand for, and brining more Certified Fair Trade Coffees to market. With the theme of remaining accountable toward their goals, GMCR's also publishes the **"Building Demand for Sustainable Products Scorecard"**[52] which summarizes over a three year period, the Fair Trade coffees shipped by the company.

The company has also led efforts to bring sustainable products toward its industry. For example, as early as 1989 GMCR developed Earth-Friendly Coffee Filters which were Oxygen-whitened and dioxin-free. In 1996 GMCR developed the industry's first biodegradable bag for bulk coffee purchases. And, in 2006 GMCR's "developed an eco-friendly hot paper cup, and introduced cold beverage cups and lids made from renewable resources."[53]

WORKING TOGETHER FOR CHANGE

At the heart of GMCR's corporate behavior is accountability through partnership, collaboration, engagement and empowerment. The company is committed toward what they define as "working together for change" by bringing together all stakeholders within their product and service offerings. The company strongly believes that creating awareness and educating suppliers and consumers about sustainability challenges and opportunities will help the company achieve profitability, while continually working toward improving its sustainable performance.

The 2009 GMCR Corporate Social Responsibility Report[54] states, *"Consumers have an enormously powerful role to play in encouraging businesses to move towards sustainability, both in how they operate and the products and services they provide. By engaging consumers with our mutual sustainability challenges, increasing their awareness of the issues we face, and boosting consumer demand for more sustainable products, we contribute to the global conversation on corporate social responsibility and deepen its strategic integration into our business model."*

CREATING A GREAT PLACE TO WORK

GMCR's focus on employees is another attribute demonstrating "enlightened leadership" and corporate accountability. The company's **"Purpose and Principles"**[55] outlines and defines fifteen core principles by which the company strives to operate. Within the fifteen principles is an underlying human element of personal accountability. For example, GMCR's core principles that include good communication to appreciate differences, continual learning and support of a high standard of ethics, leadership and personal excellence within a vibrant workplace, are elements of accountability that are carried out in the daily actions of GMCR employees.

And, as they have done with other CSR goals, GMCR has put specific measures in place to track just how they are "creating a great place to work" for their employees. The GMCR "Creating a Great Place to Work Scorecard"[56] summarizes employee metrics such as: compensation and benefits, hiring and development, safety, and retention and satisfaction.

Innovation through Enlightened Sustainability: Small Companies, Strong Leaders, and Big Impact

Small Business Has Big Impact

The amount of data and information that has been publicly reported regarding the sustainability of large corporations has increased dramatically in the past few years. This information is wanted by external rating agencies, customers, investors, social investment funds, government regulators, NGOs, and other stakeholders. These stakeholders have influenced large Fortune 500 corporations' disclosure through their company's sustainability reports, annual financial statements and, in particular, the reports for publicly-traded companies.

The efforts, as summarized in the external sustainability and corporate social responsibility (CSR) reports of Wal-Mart, Google, Intel, McDonald's, Coca-Cola, Shell, DuPont, Toyota, Starbucks, and other large industries, have influenced all of us. As these companies report out on their sustainability progress, and as they introduce more sustainable products, services, and programs to the market, we feel a momentum building within society. The Sustainability Generation has legs. The transformation is underway before our very eyes. A lot of unanswered questions remain, and there is a huge need for independent validation of the sustainability, environmental, CSR, and other claims for the products, services, operational improvements, and other sustainability initiatives reported by small and large companies. But there is a general sense that there is a shift toward a culture of accepting and even embracing sustainability as a core value in business, government, academia, and other institutions.

As this shift increases in intensity and impact, small businesses form an enormous backbone of influence. Small businesses attribute to the vast majority of economic activity, jobs, and infrastructure in the United States and throughout the world. Further, small businesses are the engines that support large corporations and governments as those institutions align their strategies to enhance their sustainability.

According to the non-profit association SCORE:[57]

There are an estimated 29.6 million small businesses in the United States which:

- Employ just over half of the country's private sector workforce
- Hire 40 percent of high tech workers, such as scientists, engineers and computer workers
- Include 52 percent home-based businesses and two percent franchises
- Represent 97.3 percent of all the exporters of goods
- Represent 99.7 percent of all employer firms
- Generate a majority of the innovations that come from United States companies[58]

As the facts on from SCORE[59] point out, small businesses play a significant role in U.S. private-sector employment, exportation of goods, and innovation. While the economic and environmental footprint of large industrial giants like Boeing is much larger than a small privately-owned machine shop in Chicago, the impact of hundreds of suppliers to machining and tooling of a Boeing 787 is significant.

The effort of small businesses to enhance their sustainability often goes untold and unnoticed. While the challenges and opportunities of embracing sustainability are similar for small and large businesses, there are large differences in the amount of resources, talent, and impact small businesses can have compared to larger organizations. Thus, small businesses often have to be very innovative, creative, and engaged to achieve impacts that align economic and environmental priorities. Large companies like Wal-Mart can issue sustainability goals to suppliers and allow the open market to come up with solutions.

The innovation toward sustainable products and services does not lie with the company that sets the goal of sustainable products (i.e., Wal-Mart) as much as it does with the suppliers that need to discover and provide the additional dimension of designing products to meet customer needs and expectations. Smaller businesses are discovering that to remain competitive in this fast-moving world where large industries are now frequently pursuing and demanding sustainable supplies, they must innovate rapidly and learn quickly to create sustainable products and services that remain cost-competitive and deliver high-quality performance and reliability.

In summary, the Sustainability Generation operates in a complex ecosystem of stakeholders including government, large corporations, NGOs, colleges and universities, applied technology and research organizations, builders and developers, architects and engineers, and those that maintain critical infrastructure of hospitals, telecommunications, energy, transport, information, and food and housing. Small businesses account for a great deal of the economic activity, employment, and future growth among these stakeholders. It is important and necessary for the Sustainability Generation to recognize and assess how small businesses can be an important catalyst in creating a more resilient and sustainable planet.

Harbec Plastics: Innovation & Sustainability through Enlightened Leadership

Harbec Plastics is an example of how small businesses can have an impact to be empowering and enlightening for a new Sustainable Generation. The injection-molding company in upstate New York proves that when it comes to enhancing sustainability, it is not only Fortune 500 companies that are taking action.

Founded in 1977 by its President, Bob Bechtold, Harbec Plastics is a leading manufacturer of prototypes high-tolerance tooling, machined components, and quality injection-molded parts. While there are many attributes that define the success of a sustainable company or organization, the Harbec mission, vision, and corporate value statements[60] reinforce the following characteristics of success evident in its people, culture, and policies:

- enlightened, passionate, and visionary leadership
- empowerment of employees
- Edisonian approach to innovation
- strong strategic planning and management disciplines
- care, compassion and urgency about the future

Mission

HARBEC's mission is to provide tightly toleranced prototypes, tooling, machined components and quality injection molded parts in a sustainable manner with a social conscience. We provide superior customer service, satisfaction and timely delivery of custom engineered solutions. We proudly foster an atmosphere of encouragement and respect for the health and prosperity of our customers, employees, and the global community.

Our Core Beliefs

EMPLOYEES ARE OUR #1 ASSET

We cannot accomplish anything without you. We value your contribution and active involvement. In return, we promise competitive compensation and the best possible work environment. When you thrive, we thrive.

ENVIRONMENTAL CONSCIOUSNESS AND RESPONSIBILITY

HARBEC will meet today's needs without compromising those of future generations. We invest responsibly to stand behind this commitment. We take the welfare of our global community seriously.

APPLYING ADVANCED TECHNOLOGY TO ENSURE BUSINESS SUSTAINABILITY

Technology is our future and our competitive advantage. We promise to give our customers the level of performance they're seeking, or better, through innovation and advanced applications. We will not compromise.

CONTINUOUS IMPROVEMENT

HARBEC is not the same company today as it was yesterday—and we will work together to be a better company tomorrow. This translates to recognition and reward for collaboration, ideas, solutions and action. Status quo is not an option.

QUALITY IN EVERYTHING WE DO

We don't just tell our customers, "We can do that." We ask ourselves how to make it better. From front-end design to finished goods, shipping and delivery, striving for excellence is a top priority. Our customers depend on it.

INNOVATIVE, FULL-SERVICE, COST-EFFECTIVE SOLUTIONS

HARBEC's Vision is to be a recognized leader in providing innovative, full-service, cost-effective solutions to our valued customers. We will:

- Provide greater value to our customers
  Value-added services
  Engineering-intensive solutions
  Better processes (i.e., manufacturing, quality, service)
  Resource availability (i.e., cross-training, equipment)
- Demonstrate our environmentally sustainable best practices to the world
  Be the "go to" company for environmentally responsible solutions (i.e., waste stream, renewable origin materials)
  Become carbon and water neutral
- Provide superior tooling solutions (i.e., lower price, quick delivery, higher lifetime value)
- Become the industry leader in Direct Metal Molding and provide significant benefits to our customers
- Become an employer of choice by providing our employees with a challenging, rewarding and safe work environment
- Maximize the return on assets while delivering profitability
- We will do this in a way that enables managed growth and long-term business viability for our company.

Harbec continues to maintain and grow employment in New York State despite a global recession and challenging business environment. The story of Harbec and its ability to "compete for sustainability" is an excellent example for other organizations, large or small, of what attributes enable sustainability to be envisioned and implemented.

Upstate New York has traditionally been heavily dependent on its manufacturing sector for higher paying jobs and a baseline level of economic activity. The Finger Lakes and Greater Rochester regions of New York have, like many areas of the U.S., relied upon its small businesses and manufacturing base as significant elements of their regional economies. Unfortunately, in the Finger Lakes Region alone, 28.3% of its manufacturing workforce was shed from 2000 to 2007, a loss of nearly 32,000 jobs. This trend continued through 2009 as an additional 7,200 manufacturing jobs were lost (an additional 8.5%). In the past decade from October 2000–October 2010 the Greater Rochester region alone lost more than 42,500 manufacturing jobs, representing 41.6% of the manufacturing employment in the region.[61] This was largely caused by major manufacturers restructuring regional operations and shifting work from regional to global suppliers. Stagnant wages, higher unemployment and underemployment, and flat population growth resulted from the shifting economy and exodus of manufacturing jobs.

Given the outflow of manufacturing employment and activity from New York State between 2000 and 2010, Harbec's ability to remain competitive in the state during that decade is an exception. Harbec's ability to remain a viable employer in New York and choice supplier to several industries including biomedical, automotive, aerospace/defense, electronics, telecom, and sporting goods is attributed to innovation, leadership, passion, and hard work.

My interest in the story of Harbec's success begins with a memory I have when I worked for the New York State Energy Research and Development Authority (NYSERDA). I recall a senior leader at NYSERDA and some of the staff referring to Harbec's visionary and passionate founder Bob Bechtold as being "way out there," as if to suggest being innovative and visionary was a negative attribute. As a young state worker at the time, I thought my superiors were passing negative judgment on someone because of his passion for embracing a different way of thinking or doing business. It became common knowledge that Bob was passionate about sustainability, and someone who was not afraid to show it. A decade ago this was perceived as extreme. In retrospect, Bob was a visionary and enlightened leader simply sharing his enthusiasm in the right place, but wrong time. Ten years later Bob reflected that he was superbly emphatic about sustainability, conceptually, but had to learn the hard way that most of the market, including customers, government agencies, economic developers and others did not know or understand the language or meaning of sustainability.

Back then many conservatives in business and industry looked at sustainability as a leftist value to further push environmental goals exclusively. Bob once noted that it was not until he adjusted his communication style to express the need to balance energy, economic, and environmental goals that others began to take note. Bob once told me that when others saw there was an "eco-economic value" and good business reasons for what he was preaching, "they became much more open minded" to learn more about how this could be accomplished. And in this change in himself, along with his passion and aptitude for understanding the concerns and beliefs of others, I believe he became more enlightened and was able to begin a process of true transformation, both within himself and toward those around him.

A decade after being viewed by some as a man with a crazy passion for the environment, Bob Bechtold is now viewed as a sustainability thought-leader—recognized by his peers as a visionary and someone who represents the future of business, manufacturing, and innovation in America. Bob is sought after by many organizations, trade associations and business groups to speak about how he has made great strides toward making Harbec Plastics a sustainable enterprise, and also about his personal journey and discovery of how to empower and enlighten others about sustainability as a concept not to be feared, but to be revered as one approach to a more balanced economy.

When I first met Bob it was years after I had first heard his name when working at NYSERDA. I recall having a perception that he would be more of a "tree hugger and granola" persona. But I found in Bob someone much different. Sure, Bob was passionate about environmental awareness, conservation, and protection. But he carried something else with him, this light in his eyes, whenever he spoke about leading his company to be innovative with a new way of doing business that could balance economic, environmental, society, and energy goals. Bob's passion for the environment was transparent, but it did not overshadow his overall passion for creating a sustainable enterprise by positioning his company to be a supplier of choice. He embraced innovation and creativity to enable the production of sustainable goods and services, and all the while delivering on the traditional bottom line of business: to earn a profit.

Bob's passion for sustainability, innovation, and business success has had a transparent and tangible impact on Harbec's customers, employees, and community in which it operates. Harbec has been recognized by Dow Chemical for its Innovative Molders Program. From an operational perspective, the company is leading the way in its peer group. Harbec has reduced its energy consumption through efficiency measures while also incorporating on-site renewable and distributed power generation to shield itself from energy price volatility. The company has reduced long-term energy costs, business risk associated with climate change, which enabled them to gain competitive advantage as a preferable "green" supplier. The company has a 100% green transportation fleet; they have purchased and deployed more energy-efficient electric presses; up to 350,000 kWh's of the company's electricity comes from a 250 kW wind turbine on site; and the company takes advantage of combined heat and power (CHP) efficiencies through 25 (30 kW) cleaner burning natural gas turbines they deployed nine years ago.[62] Real-time information on Harbec's energy management and on-site clean energy generation initiatives, including CHP and wind, is available through: http://www.harbec.com/sustainability/energy-management-solution/.

And, as the company transitions toward a more sustainable enterprise, it has taken a leadership role to influence other businesses to embrace sustainable business practices. On its website Harbec asks its suppliers and customers to join in its passion for sustainable growth:

We Want to Tell Your Story[53]

As HARBEC continues to become firmly entrenched in a significant and growing environmental market niche, there are a few things we want from you:

- Recognition as a socially and environmentally responsible company
- Identification as an industry leader (i.e., the nation's premier "green molder")
- We want to tell your story!

HARBEC would love to partner with a firm who is embracing our environmental values as strongly as we are and work together to garner significant press about our collective efforts in environmental sustainability. We believe it's a win-win situation.

Examples of firms with whom we want to write the book:

- Energy Star® qualified manufacturers
  Consumers love your Energy Star products: why not take them to the next level with e-friendly parts inside? Partner with HARBEC to manufacture "green parts" in order to complement, and more strongly market, your Energy Star claims.
- Manufacturers who are ISO 14000 certified
  We have an action item for you: Ensure your suppliers are also environmentally compliant. Take even greater responsibility for your manufacturing practices through sustainability throughout your supply chain. By partnering with HARBEC, you can add (and fulfill) two new measures: "impact on environment" and "impact on bottom line."
- Manufacturers who are currently buying green power
  If using green power is important to you, please ask yourself, "Why aren't we buying parts from someone who is doing the same?" We share your passion.

In addition to its "call to action" Harbec provides on-line tools for potential customers to use to determine the environmental and carbon impact they can achieve if they choose Harbec as a supplier. Harbec's carbon calculator, available at http://www.harbec.com/environmentalimpact.html enables users to input the number of plastic parts they intend to order to quantify "the positive environmental advantage of choosing HARBEC."

Today when I meet people regionally and outside of New York, I am often asked if I know of Bob Bechtold and Harbec Plastics. Bob's vision and passion have exuded from him and his company like lightening. Similar to how enlightened leaders have been perceived at Patagonia (founder Yvon Chouinard), Stonyfield Farms (founder Gary Hirshberg), Green Mountain Coffee (founder Bob Stiller), Tom's of Maine (founder Tom Chappell) and Ben and Jerry's (founders Ben Cohen and Jerry Greenfield), Bob is now looked at by his peers, customers, and competitors as a standard of innovation to aspire toward.

Like many visionaries, Bob is also an endless thinker and tinkerer. He is constantly "tweaking" his sustainability strategy and company. Bob is also seemingly tireless and fearless, and constantly in pursuit of improvement of himself, his employees, and his company. For example, on the Harbec web pages they state clearly how they are **"working and striving to be a carbon-neutral company by 2013"** (see, http://www.harbec.com/sustainability/green-molder/). The company has made great strides toward that goal through their combination of on-site energy efficiency and management and clean energy generation initiatives. Harbec actively brands and communicates its Carbon Neutral by 2013 goal with employees and customers using a crossed out foot with CO2 printed on it as a form of self-imposed accountability. Harbec has also taken a similar stance on water neutrality and has committed to be a water neutral company by 2015 (see Harbec CO2 and Water logo images). Bob Bechtold's passion and aptitude combined into an intriguing leader: a person who defines, in my view, the difference between doing business as usual and reinventing businesses for the better.

As an example of "self-imposed accountability, Harbec Plastics has adopted this logo to communicate (and brand) their Carbon Neutral by 2013 goal with customers, employees, and other stakeholders.

By 2015

Another example of self-imposed accountability, Harbec Plastics has adopted this logo to communicate (and brand) their Water Neutral by 2015 goal with customers, employees, and other stakeholders.

We all hear of visionary and enlightened leaders like Tom Chappell of Tom's of Maine, or Jack Welch of GE. When you experience them first-hand, you begin to get a sense of the gravity they bring to the world by their ability to visualize a better future, and inspire and empower those all around them to take action. It is an impressive, awe inspiring process that is infectious. Bob has influenced the formation, development, and sustainment of a number of other businesses: Northern Biodiesel, Northern Development, Sustainable Energy Developments, Inc. a not-for-profit organization called B9 Plastics, Inc. (www.b9plastics.org); and an eco-industrial sustainability park: the Wayne Industrial Sustainability Park (WISP).

ENLIGHTENED, PASSIONATE, AND VISIONARY LEADERSHIP

Since its founding in 1977, Harbec Plastics, a small manufacturer in upstate New York, has through the leadership and vision of its founder, Bob Bechtold, understood that opportunities existed in that market for innovative solutions and problem solving. The vision and leadership of Bob has navigated the company through three decades of growth and competitiveness. Now, into its fourth decade, Harbec is has reinvented itself through enlightened leadership to be a sustainable enterprise, striving to be carbon neutral by 2013.

EMPOWERMENT OF EMPLOYEES

Harbec recognizes employees as its #1 asset. Company founder Bob Bechtold has continuously empowered employees to help be a part of the success of the enterprise, by challenging assumptions on growth, innovation, and sustainability. In the process, employees have "made sustainability their own," often coming up with cost-effective solutions to challenges in manufacturing, logistics, sourcing, and facility operations. And, the company invests back into its employees.

EDISONIAN APPROACH TO SUSTAINABLE INNOVATION

One of the pillars of Harbec's corporate values and success is embracing everything they do. That includes the process of innovation. Harbec's approach is to partner with their customers through all stages of the product lifecycle, from product design through prototyping and manufacturing. The company also makes use of the most advanced technologies to meet or exceed customers' requirements. Harbec's team is strategic and tactical. But they have built a certain amount of trial and error into new product innovation through the creativity and passion of their employees.

The company and employees embrace a degree of ambiguity in their work related to sustainability, opting to take some risks where other companies may not be as tolerant. This approach enables the company to "learn/fail/succeed quickly" and enables them to leverage their internal knowledge for the benefit of customer needs and requirements. The passion for innovation at Harbec is evident in their investment in people and new technologies such as selective Laser Sintering including their next generation 3-D Systems capabilities which allow them to "grow" functional plastic and metal parts in one day, and their mastery of engineered resins.

STRONG STRATEGIC PLANNING AND MANAGEMENT DISCIPLINES

Amid the passion from their founder, and a creative core of Edisonian Innovators, the company stays focused and grounded in core business planning and management. Harbec is managed toward its mission, values, and vision in a way to maximize the return on assets while delivering ever-increasing profitability. The company states, ". . . we will do this in a way that enables managed growth and long-term business viability for our company. HARBEC is committed to the future well-being of our employees and our customers."

CARE, COMPASSION AND URGENCY TOWARD THE FUTURE

Harbec continuously focuses on its people, the planet and profitability. In this equation, the company attempts to balance the eco-economic drivers and benefits associated with bringing sustainability to life at this small manufacturer. A value-system of care, compassion and sense of urgency keep this company grounded toward its business model, mission, values and vision. An example is how the company has created a "biopolymer information center" on its web-pages to educate its customers, suppliers, and others about the evolving options available to encourage the use of biodegradable biomaterials for injection molded products.

Getting Religion on Climate Change and Personal Behaviors Affecting the State of Our Economy

Transitioning society out of unsustainable practices through personal and generational accountability is very challenging. Being accountable by being present and in the right frame of mind for sound decision-making is essential for (1) recognizing our behavior; (2) understanding the impact of our behavior on economy, environment, and society; and, (3) being able to take action through personal accountability to modify behavior to effect change.

Pope Benedict XVI has used his influence to begin to create an awareness of a moral obligation to have personal accountability to reduce human-induced impacts on climate change. If the Catholic Church is ringing its bell on climate and sustainability, individual awareness and accountability might just begin to take a stronger hold throughout society.

As one of the oldest institutions, the Catholic Church is struggling with controversy about sexual abuse and a declining base of parishioners in the United States and globally. With history as one of its measures, the Catholic Church is also extremely resilient and influential. Today there are more than one billion people worldwide that identify themselves as Catholics, making them the largest sect of Christianity.

In 2007 Pope Benedict XVI made a request to the world to have a faith and moral obligation to reduce human impacts on global climate change. The Pope's appeal for more sustainable development throughout the world had a wider message that more sustainable consumption of resources would lead to greater prospects for peace and prosperity in many countries. A large portion of Catholics live in developing nations where poverty, health, and environmental challenges impact the quality of life and basic needs of millions of people. In Brazil alone there are more than 130 million people who identify themselves as Catholic.

In a speech in Northern Italy in 2008 Pope Benedict XVI stated, *"God entrusted man with the responsibility of creation."* The Pope suggested that environmental destruction is directly tied to a materialistic society where *"God is denied."* Pope Benedict stated, *". . . In a world closed in on its materialism . . . it is easier for the human being to make himself the dictator of all other creatures and of nature."*[64]

In separate speeches Pope Benedict commented, *". . . Perhaps reluctantly we come to acknowledge that there are also scars which mark the surface of our earth: erosion, deforestation, the squandering of the world's mineral and ocean resources in order to fuel an insatiable consumption."* And the Pope has in recent years introduced excessive wealth and the creation of poverty amongst the new seven sins.

In 2011 the Pope took his message and extended it to the broader economy. In August 2011[65] on a trip to the Catholic Church's World Youth Day in Madrid, Spain, Pope Benedict issued the following remarks to reporters onboard the papal plane regarding a need to have greater ethics in economic affairs, *"... The economy doesn't function with market self-regulation, but needs an ethical rationale to work for mankind ... Man must be at the center of the economy, and the economy cannot be measured only by maximization of profit but rather according to the common good."*

What's significant is that all major institutions of society—industry, government, religion, and academia—are now talking a similar talk regarding climate change and natural resource degradation—with a self-effacing call for greater ethics, accountability, and reform. What is most interesting about Pope Benedict's position and direct language on the subject is that he focuses the issue on "people" and our inability to manage our consumptive behaviors, and a need to maximize the "common good" of society, not just the economy. There are also undertones of "entitlement" in the Pope's remarks suggesting that society has become ambivalent about our relationship with the natural world, choosing to be a "dictator" over nature and reaping the reward of the riches the world has to offer, but unconcerned with the ecological impacts of our behaviors.

With more than one billion Catholics listening to the Pope's call for a "moral obligation" to curtail our consumptive behaviors and its impacts on climate and the natural world, the Catholic Church's stance on climate and consciousness of our behavior could be transformational. The Pope is choosing to use his position of power and influence to empower and enlighten those that will listen. As demonstrated through this example of enlightened leadership, the Sustainability Generation is well at work in every facet of society.

Chapter Summary

- Small companies play a significant role in advancing innovation and sustainability within their supply chain and within the broader context of society. The Sustainability Generation needs to work on sustainability for big government and big companies, but just as importantly, for small businesses and local communities that comprise the backbone of the American economy.

- Sustainability cannot be defined as a one-sized fits all strategy for every organization. It has to be tailored to the culture, strategic focus, people, and aspirations of each organization.

- Sustainability is also not just about optimization of resources, or creating more efficient "smart products and processes." Sustainability is a process, much like the quality revolution, that requires continual monitoring and improvement. At the center of sustainability are people, policies, and practices for ensuring the process endures.

  Enlightened leaders don't always start out as being viewed by society as such. They achieve success and foster empowerment in others through self reflection and a process of empathy, personal growth, and discovery.

- There are no limits to what the Sustainability Generation can achieve when it aligns care, commitment, courage, and compassion with a common value system toward improving the future.

5

Equity for a New Generation

Building a Culture of Ecologic and Economic Equity

To be successful in addressing the imminent changes that are underway, the Sustainability Generation needs to define and apply a new social, environmental, and capitalistic equity for current and future generations. In simple terms, the extraction, production, and consumption of natural resources are not equitable. This is partly due to the availability of resources like clean water where the demand for this is located. For example, the Great Lakes hold eighteen percent of the potable clean water on Earth. Other regions of the United States, including the southwest (Arizona in particular) and southeast (the State of Georgia in recent years), are starved for water resources for drinking water, agriculture, and industrial uses as increased development has contributed to increased demand for water. The availability of water for the existing infrastructure is constrained or incapable of meeting all of the water needs of many regions where population is growing. This is a challenge not only in the United States, but throughout the world. Global demand for clean water, particularly in China, India, countries in Africa, and throughout Europe and the other Americas is increasing with population growth as demand for products in water-intensive industries (i.e., agriculture, oil and gas, chemical, and semiconductor production) also increases.

In the past decade there have been a great many political, financial, governance, and environmental events with consequences that the

Sustainability Generation can learn from and try not to replicate in the future. The global financial meltdown of 2007–2010 brought on in part by greedy investors and criminals like Bernie Madoff, along with unexpected bankruptcies like that of Lehman Brothers, are just a few examples of what caused the wake of financial disaster for unsuspecting victims. The following section identifies options and "ground rules" to guide how the Sustainability Generation can build a more equitable future while considering the current constraints on global natural resources, our desire for individual wealth creation, and need for greater social responsibility.

Greater Transparency in Financial Dealings, Money Management, and Wealth Distribution is Needed

Whether dealing with federal stimulus dollars and initiatives like "cash for clunkers" or "cash for caulkers "or hidden credit card fees and the hard-to-understand practices of rating agencies and hedge fund managers, we have learned that more information and transparency is needed for regulators and consumers to make better, more informed money and investment decisions. We may never completely strip greed from our behavior, but we can begin to reduce future risk by building more transparency into our financial dealings, particularly where we have had direct experience to educate us about what works and what doesn't. Wall Street can be a magical institution, and how that magic is performed might be left to the magicians in many ways. But when this magic benefits only the magicians and is destructive to investors, something is very wrong. Building wealth should not be a game played by a select few who make the rules and build castles on façades of false numbers. Building wealth should be grounded in something more tangible, something that is consequential to human health and environment and return on capital investment.

Greater Moral Judgment and Leadership are Needed on Natural Resources and Consumption

We live in a resource constrained world. The world's population is exceeding seven billion and projections through 2050 project population exceeding 10 or 12 billion people. As global population expands, so do our need for common resources like clean air, water, food and shelter. And as developing countries become "developed" and their middle class citizens begin to crave consumption, perhaps erroneously as we have in the United States, the strain on natural resources will only be magnified. Perhaps one of the most defining natural resource

Figure 5.1

Oil Price Volatility: 10-Year Perspective on
the Price of Crude Oil per Barrel

Created by Mark C. Coleman

Price/Barrel	Date		Price Increase (%)
• $10 — December 28, 1998			
• $27 — September 10, 2011	3 Yr $ ↑		**170%**
• $40 — December 29, 2004	6 Yr $ ↑		**300%**
• $101 — February 19, 2008	9 Yr $ ↑		**910%**
• $143 — July 2, 2008	10 Yr $ ↑		**1,330%**

This *upward* trend in oil prices is not economically sustainable—for businesses or consumers. A new 21st Century focus on energy innovation, conservation and efficiency and development is needed to prepare the Sustainability Generation for curtailing future energy price volatility while remaining vigilant on environmental protection and global competitiveness.

issues of the past decade has been the global thirst for oil. From strictly a price perspective, oil was highly volatile in the past ten years. In 1998 the price of crude had hit a low of $10/barrel. By 2008 the price had escalated more than 1400% to more than $140/barrel. Figure 5.1 shows the past decade's ramp-up in oil prices more visually.

The issue of oil consumption is not just price-sensitive. According to LMI Government Consulting,[66] the United States consumes approximately twenty-five percent of the world's oil. Half of this can be attributed to the country's continued demand for transportation fuels for automobiles and trucks to support our economy and standard of living. And fifty-eight percent of the oil consumed by the United States is imported. And consistent with the worldwide trends in energy demands, it is projected that by 2025 the United States will have to import some sixty-eight percent of its oil. This level of economic dependence on politically unstable energy sources such as Venezuela, Nigeria, and the Middle East creates concerns over our future security posture and vulnerability.

BP's deep water oil well continued to gush and spew tens of thousands of barrels of oil into the Gulf of Mexico daily. Millions of gallons of oil polluted the Gulf of Mexico and flowed landward and seaward to create ecologic and economic destruction. As oil gushed and days turn into weeks and months, there was a sense of hopelessness regarding the BP oil crisis. President Obama said that he would "find whose ass to kick" regarding the spill and said that he would have fired BP CEO Tony Hayward. BP lost more than 40% of its market value as investors' dumped BP stock and as the United States launched civil and criminal investigations of the company whose catch-phrase of the new millennium was "Beyond Petroleum."

What will be interesting to see in the aftermath of the BP crisis is if a world "beyond petroleum" actually results from the loss of human life, the extreme wastefulness from loss of oil, and from the incredible ecosystem damages of this disaster. While most people want to focus on BP as the antagonist of the unfortunate situation the Gulf absorbed, we need to take a step back as a generation and look at this as an opportunity to change our collective behaviors, and become more accountable as citizens, and consumers. The U.S. government may find BP at fault, perhaps negligent in the oil rig failures. There will be huge fines and settlements to be paid by BP. But there are no winners or losers in situations like this. The people and communities of the Gulf lose. BP loses. The U.S. government loses. The American people and all people of the world, lose. This situation could have easily been off the coast of Brazil, China, or Russia. While finger pointing and blame is centered on BP and its leadership, we need to realize that our relationship, our thirst for oil, as individuals and as a society has gone too far. We are also to blame and need to take responsibility for the crisis in the Gulf of Mexico.

Operating in a competitive economy BP, like many of its peers, will push limits to discover, extract, and distribute new sources of oil. As our thirst for petrochemicals has increased in the 20th Century we have consumed much of the easily accessible, shallow water or land-based oil reservoirs. Companies like BP have had to move further out on the continental shelf and beyond this where oil exploration and extraction carries greater financial, human, and environmental risk. Greater risks have been accepted as the price of oil has escalated in recent years. While the continued push for finding and extracting new oil at any expense and risk may seem greedy to many, it is actually the result of a functioning capitalistic society. BP, like its peers, responds to consumer demand for its products. As more oil is needed, companies like BP do what they do best: they find it and they extract it and they refine it into higher-value petrochemical products. BP may have gotten greedy, perhaps lackadaisical, and too focused on saving a buck by doing things as quickly as possible.

There are shortcomings and inefficiencies of our competitive economy that sometimes result in devastation, as is the case with BP and the Gulf of Mexico. At the crux of this is our entitlement for oil and the perceived freedom oil provides us as a transportation fuel. The U.S. government will investigate the BP disaster and derive new operating rules and procedures for deep water oil drilling. This will be a necessity. But it is only a postpartum band aid approach to the larger issue—the world is largely a one-fuel town and in a precarious position when it comes to the future of mobility and the impact we have on climate, water, and land from our use, waste and emissions of petrochemicals. I hope we can wake-up from this BP disaster to become more informed, enlightened, and empowered individuals, using our intellect to truly move beyond petroleum to develop new, less polluting fuels for transportation and our other energy needs. The Sustainability Generation will not be successful if it only seeks out "whose ass to kick" to place blame or find only short-term policies and corrections for situations like BP in the Gulf.

The Sustainability Generation needs to rise above the contaminated water and see the situation for what it is. We live in a world of erroneous consumption that has gone too far. Oil and other polluting resources have been extremely helpful in affording us our current quality of life. Yet these resources are dwindling, and as they do our behaviors to extract new value from them become more costly to human health and the environment. In basic terms, they are more risky to continue to pursue than other alternatives. Our entitlement and self-indulgence for oil is at the heart of the BP crisis. When I saw the oil gushing out of the BP subsurface oil well I immediately thought of an artery in a heart being critically injured, gushing blood. Since the 1970s oil availability crisis the world has experienced several oil price and supply hangovers. We have also had the petrochemical flu in the past (Exxon Valdez). But the BP oil spill in the Gulf of Mexico situation is more critical than a seasonal flu or hangover. It is the beginning of a cardiac arrest for the earth, induced by societies own behaviors and lack of individual restraints.

Our reliance on petroleum is akin to consuming too many foods high in fat, cholesterol, sugar, and non-nutritious additives. These foods may give us quick energy or an "emotional fix," but they leave us feeling fatigued. We know that if we over-consume these foods for too long we will alter our health, suffer from heart disease or, worse yet die of a heart attack. Our relationship with oil (or any over-consumed natural resource) is no different than the body's relationship with exercise and good nutrition. Oil has given us quick and relatively low-cost energy. We got hooked and addicted on the freedom easy oil provided us. But we have abused our earth too much from our petrochemical addiction. Waterways and river systems have been contaminated. Our air quality has declined in many metropolitan regions. Smog in Los Angeles has become a joke. Climate change is happening. Most scientists agree we can trace the shift in climate to increasing levels of greenhouse gases like carbon dioxide in the atmosphere as a result of human's consumption of oil. The Sustainability Generation needs to recognize that we are out of time. The earth's critical ecosystems are showing signs of stress and fatigue. Are these early symptoms of a more systemic illness? One thing is for certain: regardless of how bad or severe the "earth illness" is, if we don't shift our consumption behaviors and move beyond our sense of entitlement to overuse natural resources that sustain life, eventually humans will flat-line our ability to reap the benefits of our bountiful Earth.

There are direct geopolitical, financial, and environmental issues at stake that all tie to the generational entitlement for oil that we have built as a society, Addressing our entitlement for oil might just be the number one pressing issue and opportunity for the Sustainability Generation. At stake is the health and vitality of our ecosystems ability to continue to provide life essential services including clean water, abundant fisheries and food supplies, and the abundance of ecologic diversity necessary for discovering life-saving medicines in the future. By addressing our relationship with oil we will also address our relationship with many of the other social, health, economic, and environmental challenges impacting us today.

Education Earns Dividends

I have highlighted the entitlement to have unlimited use natural resources as one of the root causes of erroneous consumption and unsustainable behavior. This kind of entitlement inhibits our and future generation's ability to continue to meet our basic needs, let alone our desire for higher standards of living. When people talk about sustainability and sustainable development, many often begin with a Venn diagram with three overlapping circles that represent Economy, Environment, and Society. Others may use nomenclature such as Profit, Planet, and People. Education and knowledge transfer are fundamental building blocks, often overlooked or underemphasized, when people try to define sustainability. The idea that individuals and generations continue to be generally unconscious of (and unaccountable to) their consumptive behaviors (and continue to demonstrate a sense of domination and entitlement over natural resources) is due in part to a lack of education and knowledge transfer.

The Sustainability Generation needs to embrace education and the development and transfer of technology and knowledge as a cornerstone for creating more responsible consumer behaviors. Imagine what the intergovernmental panel investigating the BP crisis will learn. That knowledge will be transferred throughout the oil industry to try to alleviate future accidents. But that is business as usual with the focus on traditional natural resources like oil. The Sustainability Generation needs to acquire more experience, information, and knowledge for deployment of clean energy technologies like solar, wind, geothermal, combined heat and power, micro-turbines, fuel cells, biofuels, anaerobic digesters, and smart grid technologies. There are a myriad of other tools, processes, products, and services that can help society diversify its energy requirements, to reduce demand on petrochemicals and minimize adverse human health and environmental impacts. Clean technologies will also enable a future that can integrate environmental protection, clean-up, restoration, and enhancement. The bundling of ecologic services is something the Sustainability Generation will need to address in years to come. No longer will we be simply solving one problem singularly. We need to use our collective knowledge to prevent future ecologic calamity while simultaneously cleaning-up environmental damages of the past. An educated and knowledgeable Sustainability Generation will have the data, information, tools, and skills required to be more proactive, innovative, and collaborative—all necessary traits for enabling sustainable development.

> *"Passion rebuilds the world for the youth. It makes all things alive and significant."*[67]
>
> —Ralph Waldo Emerson

Engaging Youth

The Sustainability Generation is representative of all generations of people living on Earth here and now. Those in Generation Y and those even younger are, however, critical forces for enabling the Sustainability Generation to take action to define and pursue a more equitable future. Given the complexity of social, environmental, and economic challenges before the current generation, we need to spend the time and resources necessary to ensure that our youth have the day-to-day critical thinking skills, training, and experiences to be entrepreneurs, problem-solvers, innovators, and change-agents. The passion and altruism of youth are special gifts in life. The young don't see challenges the same way adults do. They are not encumbered by the overlay of institutional thinking, societal rules and norms, and behaviors that define prior generations. Youth's minds are still relatively free of obstruction, perhaps making them the most ideal at creative solutions to complex challenges, if only their attention can be dedicated to such pursuits. And the young are the future employees, managers, politicians, technologists, philosophers, writers and musicians, teachers, doctors, and business owners that will one-day take our place in the marketplace. Understanding our younger generation and enabling them to be empowered and engaged is one requirement for the Sustainability Generation. We need to provide them resources for having the best minds—the structure to make them a generation interested in learning, asking questions, discovering themselves and the world around them, and pursuing their life aspirations with purpose and passion.

Engaging our youth as key contributors to the Sustainability Generation is essential. Boomers and Generation X need to take action to encourage our nation's youth to contribute to society in a substantial way, so they are not just bodies in a classroom waiting for direction. To accomplish this will require fundamental changes in the design and delivery of education in the United States. But it also requires action and accountability from the citizenry, and those that represent small and large businesses, government, local communities, parents and guardians, to teach, guide, reinforce, and empower our youth. Now is the time for an "all hands on deck" approach to engaging the Sustainability Generation as we enlist the support from all sectors of society to focus resources on the younger generation.

"There's a radical—and wonderful—new idea here ... that all children could and should be inventors of their own theories, critics of other people's ideas, analyzers of evidence, and makers of their own personal marks on the world. It's an idea with revolutionary implications. If we take it seriously."[68]

—Deborah Meier, Author and Education Leader

There are signals that suggest the younger generation has a strong interest in sustainability and that future opportunities await them. For example, a 2008 study by the Higher Education Research

Institute sampling 240,580 first-time, full-time students at 340 of the nation's baccalaureate colleges and universities found, "Almost a third of entering freshmen (29.5 percent) reported feeling it is "essential" or "very important" to help clean up the environment, an increase from 26.7 percent in 2007 and 22.2 percent in 2006. Close to half (45.3 percent) believe it is "very important" or "essential" to adopt green practices to protect the environment, while 74.3 percent believe "addressing global warming should be a federal priority."[69]

In a 2011 article by Rachel Farrell of CareerBuilder.com, "Sustainability Officer" was listed as one of the "10 Jobs of the Future."[70] The article stated, *"Sustainability has become a concern around the world and also among businesses. Since the executive suite may not have time to learn all there is to know, organizations are hiring eco-savvy individuals as sustainability officers. These folks will find, research, and implement eco-friendly policies to benefit the organization."* Other "top 10" jobs of the future cited by the article included: Cyber Security Specialist (#1), Organic Food Farmer (#3), Medical Records Administrator (#4), Social Media Manager (#8), Stem Cell Researcher (#9). Sustainability officer was listed as #10.

And, research on the hiring preferences of small-large companies have validated the emergence of "Sustainability Officers," not just as a legitimate job title, but a key skill set and academic grooming they seek out in new hires. In 2011 Kevin Dooley of the W.P. Carey School of Business at Arizona State University reported, based from a research study of 200 hiring managers representing small-and-large companies, that employers are looking for, and giving strong weighting to, job candidates with sustainability pedigree. The Dooley study concluded:[71]

- 65 percent of small-company respondents said they would consider a sustainability concentration when making a hiring decision;
- 87 percent of the large-firm respondents agreed;
- A whopping 97.5 percent of the large-firm executives said they would value the concentration.

Kevin Dooley's research also revealed that "certain sustainability-related topics should be taught to all managers and executives" particularly in the areas of "corporate social responsibility, sustainability strategy, measuring sustainability, sustainability-related product and process improvement, and environmental and health policy and business." This suggests that while an academic background including a focus on sustainability is important, having professional experience and training in areas that emphasize sustainability skills is very important. In summary of his study, Dooley[72] pointed out, *"Right now, sustainability jobs in business are linked to existing organizational structures ... you're probably not going to find a sustainability department in many companies, but employees with skills and interest in sustainability will get assigned to related projects and move up the ladder. Job candidates with both sustainability skills and a solid professional background in a field like business or engineering are receiving job offers that far exceed what's warranted in the current market, and that's because there aren't many of them."*

The demand in the marketplace for talented "systems thinkers," "problem-solvers," and "sustainability strategists" is growing. Creating new academic programs within colleges and universities to meet the growing demand of the marketplace is one dimension of enabling the Sustainability Generation. However, there remains a fundamental, almost instinctual need for creating cultural and social change so that the citizenry incorporate characteristics and values of sustainable behavior into their everyday lifestyles. This goes beyond buying a green car, recycling, composting, or many of the tangible (and often materialistic) actions people associate with sustainability.

A philosophical mind-shift needs to happen as far as how people make decisions about their consumptive lifestyles, how they choose to spend their time, and what pursuits they dedicate their life to. Youth can think critically, but there is so much distraction and distancing between their physical "here and now" self and their inner self. The ego of youth is pumped up by social media, gaming, and a myriad of different ways to distract and distort the mind from having to focus on what the person is on the inside. By focusing their attention externally, both youth and adults can get lost in the chatter and noise of the moment, subduing the inner-self from discovering who it is or what its true potential can really be. The younger generation is not the only one to fall victim to the pull of media, social networking, and other outlets for bolstering the ego. However, together the Boomers, Generation X, and Generation Y can work with modern technology to express themselves in ways that are more creative and purposeful. Everyone needs "down time" and a certain amount of escapism. But if we focus more attention on shared morals, values, and goals, we can awaken our inner-selves to realize our potential as individuals and as an entire generation to make a significant impact on our current state of social, economic, and environmental affairs, and those of our children.

Building Equity for a Sustainable Generation

When I think of companies like Patagonia, Green Mountain Coffee Roasters, Tom's of Maine, Timberland, McDonald's, and Coca-Cola, I think of them as established or emerging sustainability leaders. These small and large companies seek to compete for the long-term in a way that addresses the sustainment of the natural resources they transform into valuable consumer products, from outdoor clothing to freshly brewed coffee and toothpaste. Even with sustainability goals, strategy, and programs in place, each company has been able to remain competitive, grow revenue, and achieve top-and bottom-line results for their investors. A new ethic has emerged for many business leaders and subsequently in the businesses they operate. A social responsibility and sustainability ethic is embraced more and more by businesses every day. This ethic focuses business strategy on individual, social, and generational responsibility toward improving people and the planet, not just on reaping profits at the expense of others or ecosystems.

The idea and ethic that we as individuals and as a generation "know our limits" is only beginning to take hold throughout society. To move beyond a world of unsustainable erroneous consumption the Sustainability Generation will need to redefine its notion of money, wealth creation, happiness, and sense of self. In many ways our greatest adversary is our own ego. We have to move beyond keeping up with the Joneses and focus on keeping up with our own goals, established at our pace, within our own personal definition of success and what brings us joy and happiness. Too often we look next door or over the fence for the answer, to see how others are living and to assess what they have compared to us. When we see what they have, we feel unfulfilled, envious, and angry. We ask ourselves, "How do they afford that?" This battle with our ego brings nothing but frustration and disappointment. So the transition to a more sustainable culture has to begin within ourselves and expands by empowering and enlightening others.

Taking a "Cradle-to-Cradle" to Lifestyle (not just products)

In the 2002 book *Cradle to Cradle,* sustainability pioneer William McDonough and German chemist Michael Braungart summarize a new way of thinking about industrial design that seeks to integrate our use of products and their subsequent retirement and rebirth with the knowledge of how this affects our living earth. Since then the "Cradle-to-Cradle" concept has been a primary reference in the context of the design of products and services. Now a decade old in mainstream sustainability thinking, this was an innovative approach that required product designers to think more critically about the full life-cycle of our products, including their impact on the environment.

I have begun to think about "Cradle to Cradle" more in the context of people, and less as a focus on products. Conceptually this can also be extended to our own life-cycle as humans to discover our personal impact on the environment, economy, and society.

There is great merit in thinking about our life-span and our impact on Earth while we are living and working and finding enjoyment and satisfaction on our planet Earth. By taking a Cradle-to-Cradle approach to how we live our life, we can more fully understand where we as individuals and as generations have the greatest impact on natural resources or the ability for our children and their children to meet their desired needs.

As individuals making up larger society, we have a responsibility to the current and the next generation. That responsibility shown in McDonough and Braungart's Cradle-to-Cradle philosophy can be applied inwardly toward our own individual lifestyles, and externally in our ability to educate, empower, and enlighten each successive generation so that they have the collective knowledge to take pragmatic steps to embrace sustainability principles.

The current generation of Baby Boomers, alongside Generations X and Y, has advocates for sustainability, including L. Hunter Lovins, Bob Bechtold, and Bob Stiller who are working to influence the adoption of sustainable behaviors, whether demonstrated in farming communities in rural America, manufacturing floors in Detroit, or in the production of products and services we consume. In the future, as these concepts evolve in industrial design and our daily lifestyles, advocates and consumers will become united. This is to suggest that this kind of thinking will become inherent in the social fabric of the next generation born into the world, and part of the very value and belief system in which they will live.

At the core of sustainability is our need to sustain life on our earth. Thus, prioritizing the conservation, protection, and enhancement of those things that sustain life on Earth is a critical mission for the Sustainability Generation.

Redefining Wealth in Terms of Financial and Ecological Capital

Money is a man-made instrument to represent wealth. The value of the dollar is upheld in part by commodities like gold, silver, and platinum, and tangible assets like natural resources. If you go upstream far enough, the man-made instrument of money is actually backed by the earth and its natural resources. We really own nothing. But we place value on our ability to transform natural resources into "value-added" products and services that society needs and wants. Through entitlement we give ourselves the right to take resources from the earth to convert into a value that we monetize. Money is earned as resources are converted into useable goods and services that consumers are willing to pay for. While many of the earth's resources are renewable (if given a long enough time-schedule), society is consuming most resources more quickly than the earth can replenish its reserves. This results in a long-term negative balance sheet for the earth, and for the entitled society. Society's short-term focus on accumulating wealth in the form of money and material goods is unsustainable in our self-defined model of entitlement. Eventually, as global population grows, and without dramatic changes in our consumptive behaviors, we will constrain our man-made definition of wealth creation. There is no "leveraged buyout" opportunity from a corporate suitor or Uncle Sam to come to our aid if the ecosystem services that clean our water, provide biodiversity, and support the well functioning of fisheries and agriculture systems, are diminished beyond repair.

One of the greatest struggles for environmentalists and economists in the past thirty years has been finding reasonable and correct market mechanisms to place financial value on ecosystem services. The challenge is placing an agreed upon reasonable financial value that accurately reflects the worth of ecosystems. For example, is timber from a rain forest more valuable as a hardwood floor in a multi-million dollar home or as a living organism in the rain forest? Is a forest that is "sustainably managed" more valuable harvested for creating building materials to be used in new low-income housing, or for its inherent carbon sequestering potential? Who decides these values and how are they derived and used? This is a challenging aspect of wealth creation that the Sustainability Generation will need to better understand and address in years to come.

To move forward, the Sustainability Generation needs to find balance between the instrument of wealth creation and protection of ecologic assets that provide wealth to our current and to future generations. If we consume ecologic assets today, are we simply devouring the wealth of future generations? People say a dollar is worth more today than it is ten years from now because it can be invested today and be put to work. That notion applies to ecological assets as well. On one hand, timber, fisheries, oil, minerals and ores can be put to work today for the betterment of society. But we need to account for the loss of biodiversity and the environmental damages (losses that include the innate ability of ecosystems to do their natural processes to keep a balanced environment, like the way wetlands clean water and the way coral reefs provide critical habitat for ocean life.) The value of ecosystem services is determined by whether those assets are consumed today or tomorrow. We may be making a more sound investment if we choose to conserve natural resources, as opposed to harvesting them only for short-term economic gain based upon a one-dimensional view of their value: earning money now. The Sustainability Generation needs to redefine societies views on money and wealth so that protecting strands of hardwoods is just as valuable as harvesting them for human consumption. In this model we will have more equitable choices before us. If we conserve, it pays.

Ecosystem services are being examined as the next economic opportunity for entrepreneurs, investors and major corporations as they evaluate how to address erroneous consumption and the need for sustainable development.

Looking for the Next Economic Boom: Put Your Greenbacks into Companies that Enhance Ecosystem Services

Ecosystem services sustain all life on planet Earth. They are the critical gears, valves, filters, pumps, batteries and buffers that accomplish essential earth functions. They are moderating weather, storing carbon, mitigating droughts and floods, cycling nutrients, cleaning the air and water, protecting against erosion, regulating the diffusion of disease, maintaining biodiversity, pollinating plants, decomposing wastes, rejuvenating soil, and regulating climate. Ecosystem services have really only begun to be understood by humans, including how essential they are to life and to the long-term sustainment and quality of life we've established.

Ecosystem services represent the processes that produce and sustain life, many of which we have taken for granted for decades. The "commons," as some ecologic services are now known, are becoming less common. The availability of clean water, old growth forests and timber, habitat for fisheries, and the pollination of flowers and agriculture commodities are examples of ecosystem services, each of which is undergoing stress from overproduction, overconsumption, and degradation placed upon them from a burgeoning global population of 6.5 billion people.

The Ecological Society of America, U.S. Forest Service, Millennium Ecosystem Assessment, The World Conservation Union, and The Katoomba Group's Ecosystem Marketplace are each useful references for defining ecosystem services as well as organizations that have committed resources to understanding the science, economics, and social aspects of how ecosystem services impact the future of capitalism.

For example, The Katoomba Group's Ecosystem Marketplace seeks "to become the world's leading source of information on markets and payment schemes for ecosystem services: services such as water quality, carbon sequestration, and biodiversity." The Ecosystem Marketplace provides "solid and trust-worthy information on prices, regulation, science, and other market-relevant issues, and markets for ecosystem services" in hopes that they "will one day become a fundamental part of our economic and environmental system, helping give value to environmental services that have, for too long, been taken for granted."

The future of capitalism is intimately linked with ecosystem services. It always has been. The key difference between the first 100 years of industrialization and the next century is the realization that there is just as much value in preserving, protecting, and enhancing ecosystem services as there is in extracting the value through consumption and degradation, marked by our behavior with ecosystem services in the last 100 years.

Gary Luck, Associate Professor in Ecology and Environmental Management and Principal Researcher in the Institute for Land, Water and Society at Charles Sturt University, has written: "... I am unaware of any scientist who argues that the ecosystem-service approach should replace traditional strategies for protecting nature. However, it offers great promise as a value-adding tactic to secure conservation gains in regions dominated by humans. It is especially powerful in arguing for the importance of nature conservation in the spheres of society where moral and ethical responsibilities are sidelined—and money talks ... The concept of ecosystem services offers a fantastic opportunity to link research and land management agendas across disciplines, as it can incorporate ecological assessment of service-providing organisms, economic and social valuation, and cost-benefit trade-offs of different land management strategies for both the landholder and society."

U.S. policy makers are now taking a serious look at ecosystem services for future policy and market based mechanisms for conserving natural resources, cleaning and protecting the environment. For example, The Food, Conservation, and Energy Act of 2008 seeks to establish a procedure, protocol, and register for measuring, reporting and collecting/maintaining information on environmental (ecosystem) services within the United States.

With 100 years of industrialization and environmental damages under our belt it's refreshing to see that we're now taking a more proactive, interdisciplinary and bipartisan approach to environmental economics and valuating the building blocks of life, environmental services. In the next 50 years there will be greater market, shareholder and public attention/emphasis on companies that conserve, protect and enhance ecosystem services—perhaps more than was ever placed on those that purely exploited resources. As we further our understanding about the full extent of "human services" embedded in ecosystems, perhaps we will finally give the environment its true market valuation.

Watch firms like ARCADIS, Dow, DuPont, IBM, Geosyntec, Akzo Nobel, Syngenta, BC Hydro and others in years to come as they identify new business opportunities around ecosystem services. The World Resources Institute March 2008 publication, "The Corporate Ecosystem Services Review" is a useful on-line guide outlining and summarizing the emerging business opportunities to address human induced changes in our ecosystems.

Creating Equity for the Next Generation: A Conversation with the CEO of Enolia Ventus

I first met Stelios Voyiatzis in 2007. Stelios and his colleague, Konstantinos Mitropoulos were participants in an AHC Group executive workshop[73] with 80 other global leaders. Both from Greece, Stelios and Konstantinos participated in the AHC Group sessions to learn from other business leaders, and to create awareness of their clean energy business, Enolia Energy.

Enolia Energy was created in 2007 to serve regional needs of the South Eastern European renewable energy market. Enolia develops and operates solar (photovoltaic and concentrated solar power), wind farms, and other clean and renewable energy developments (including combined heat and power systems.) Today Enolia Energy is part of the Enolia Group, a growing conglomerate of high value companies delivering competitive financial and environmental returns to their investors, and through the delivery of select innovative clean and renewable energy technologies that also benefit the communities within Greece and Southeast Europe.

The four principle companies that comprise the Enolia Group include Enolia Energy, which is the umbrella of the Enolia Group of companies; Enolia Premium Capital, which is a private equity investment fund supporting select renewable energy technologies and developments; Enolia Solar Systems, which is the company's development arm for photovoltaic and concentrated solar systems; and Enolia Ventus, a conventional developer of wind farms and an emerging player in hybrid wind/storage developments.

The following story demonstrates that The Sustainability Generation has taken root. But it will only succeed by its members learning from one another, leveraging best practices and good ideas, and building new relationships, even those that might be separated by oceans.

When Stelios and Konstantinos were in New York in 2007 I invited them to meet Bob Bechtold, president and founder of Harbec Plastics, At the time, Bob was working to license the know-how and technology to manufacture multi-megawatt wind turbines in the United States from one of the last privately-owned German wind manufacturers. Further, Bob represented and continues to represent ingenuity in U.S. manufacturing. Bob fully understands that equity is something that is built over time, and redefined and refreshed as the enterprise grows. For decades Bob has brought new innovation and systems thinking to his manufacturing operation in Ontario, New York. Through the design, deployment, and operation of clean and renewable energy systems, Bob Bechtold has enabled his Harbec Plastics to be a model of how smart technology and innovative processes can achieve operational efficiency, cost reduction, and higher quality.

Stelios and Konstantinos were so intrigued by Bob's integrated systems that Stelios made a trip to visit Bob and tour his facility in Ontario, New York. Konstantinos's family had operated several successful manufacturing enterprises in Greece, and I believe his interest in Bob and Harbec stemmed from a shared understanding and passion for manufacturing.

It surprised me that Stelios took the initiative to visit Bob and have exploratory discussions regarding wind technologies and developments. But as I watched Stelios and Bob interact, and have gotten to know Stelios since that time, it is no longer surprising. One of the qualities of leaders is having a thirst for learning and for engaging with other leaders.

Today Stelios is the Risk Officer of Enolia Premium Capital and the CEO of Enolia Ventus. He is an economist and a certified project management practitioner by training and has had experiences ranging from being the chief information officer at a pension fund to being a manager in management consulting services at PriceWaterhouse-Coopers, a Senior Manager in Business Consulting, and strategy advisor to railroad construction company, ERGOSE. Stelios is also very entrepreneurial. In 2006, he founded the energy consulting firm, Metron Navitas S.A. Serial entrepreneurs and leaders seek out individuals to learn from who are often like-minded and sometimes have polar opposites from their personalities. In Freidman's "flat world" it is fascinating that Stelios and Bob connected in-person, not just electronically. While no business transaction may have resulted from their time together, the fact that they shared knowledge, from Greece to New York, signifies how the Sustainability Generation continues to evolve, in part due to a common curiosity and desire to build new models of business that create financial, social, and environmental value. It has been a pleasure knowing and learning from Stelios and Bob over the years.

One of the reasons I have chosen to profile Enolia Energy and its wind operating company, Enolia Ventus, is for its corporate philosophy and behavior as it relates to the consumption of natural resources. The accountability for ensuring that the existing generation meets its needs in the context of its current values and global affairs while also considering future generations in our decision-making is someone's responsibility. Enolia Energy and Enolia Ventus have deliberately defined their vision and goals toward sustainable growth and created a model by which people are accountable for their behaviors to align with the corporate vision. The Enolia Ventus[74] website states:

"Enolia Ventus believes that natural resources can be developed and utilized in a manner consistent to the preservation of environment. We fully recognize the fact that all activities associated with the development of electricity production units impact the environment, therefore our projects are designed and managed to minimize both risk and negative impacts to the environment."

To achieve that vision, the company closely models its behaviors according to the World Energy Council (W.E.C.) that established "3 A's" toward Millennium development goals:

1. Accessibility to modern, affordable energy for all;
2. Availability in terms of continuity of supply and quality and reliability of service;
3. Acceptability in terms of social and environmental goals.

Enolia Ventus and its employees conduct their operations in support of achieving these sustainability objectives. In the process,

Enolia Ventus communicates their business actions and practices of energy production to the communities in which they work to emphasize the constraints necessary in existing generations to help future generations.

Profiles in Sustainability Generation Leadership: a Q&A with Enolia Ventus' CEO, Stelios Voyiatzis

Because of Enolia's strong commitment to sustainable growth, in the fall of 2011 I got back in touch with Stelios to ask him some questions that I thought might inform this book, and that related to Enolia Energy, the current financial situation in Greece, and the future of clean and renewable energy development as an option for creating sustainable value. The question and answer (Q&A) conversation with Stelios is significant as he offers global perspective, drawing from his knowledge and strong career, as well as personal perspective on the evolving Sustainability Generation. The Q&A below summarizes our interaction in October 2011 and highlights Stelios' unique perspective:

Question 1. Do you feel the existing generation (in the U.S., Greece, or generalize globally) is personally accountable for their behaviors related to sustainability (i.e., consumption, production, education, etc.) In what ways are they accountable?

Personal accountability should be unconditional when it comes to sustainability matters. On the other hand, it is a natural human tendency to seek accountability (and/or responsibility) in others. In this way, tackling efficiently our sustainability issues raises first of all an ethical challenge: to overcome a blame-pattern, to overcome the questioning of "how-and-why" and take direct responsibility for remedial actions. Our generation is in front of unprecedented environmental challenges. The risk is simply not acceptable for not acting immediately and in many directions at the same time. Our current model of economic growth is driving the system we rely upon for our present and future prosperity over the edge.

We need a global economy paradigm-shift. Carbon based capitalism should move towards a "sustainable environment, sustainable results" operational mode. Not tomorrow, not when we think it can be afforded, not when other pressing issues are resolved. It has to be done today—and this means "Change." Change has an inherent revolutionary sense. The bigger the change, the bigger the revolution. Change has to be realized on both personal and communal level.

On a personal level, we need to work mainly on behavioral patterns that determine consumption habits, lifestyle habits, and norms that until now were almost without any serious sustainability concern, if any. Education will play a key role towards building a sustainability aware conscience. On the communal level, we need to apply appropriate legislation, regulation, and proper incentives in order to build a solid basis for a massive and quick shift towards sustainable ways of manufacturing products, power production, and energy saving.

Question 2. Do you feel "entitlement" plays a role in unsustainable behaviors (i.e., societal "entitlement of natural resources" or "sense of entitlement" for certain services or products?

Entitlement, in the false sense, always creates disastrous effects as it gives a completely wrong "right" to the current "owners" to behave as if there is no one else to follow. In this sense, entitlement played a key role for the last 250 years both on exploiting earth's resources in an exhaustive manner and destroying environment during the processing of these resources.

Question 3. How have the financial challenges in the U.S., Greece, and globally impacted Enolia Energy's ability to deliver its business strategy in photovoltaic's, wind, or other clean and renewable energy technology developments? Has Enolia Energy been able to generate competitive returns in this challenging economy?

Global financial context provides the womb where renewable energy (RE) technology flourishes. It can't be done otherwise. RE technology is still a part of a global investment portfolio which includes a vast spectrum of competing investments. As a general rule, social sensitivity is not a prerequisite. Profitability reigns supreme, when at the same time we need RE funding in a world were billions of people are living desperate lives in appalling poverty. In light of these conditions, renewable energy, and power production in particular, is in need of what I call the "two-and-a-half support mechanism":

1. A secure debt providing mechanism for large RE investments

2. A robust Power Purchase Agreement (PPA) framework for RE based electricity production

3. Subsidies when and if needed (the "half" part, as subsidies should have a limited time presence)

Though Greece in particular is facing an unprecedented financial crisis that has driven the country to an unemployment rate similar to

1950, and the country's GDP annual decrease is about 5%, RE still holds strong as it was chosen by the country, along with tourism, shipping and bio-agriculture, to provide a stepping stone towards getting out of the crisis.

Having still in place factor 2 and factor 3, the impact on our business is heavy but not decisive. Enolia develops power generation projects based on a twenty-year power purchase agreement (PPA) which becomes valid as soon as the project (wind or solar) is connected to the national grid. As this procedure does not involve any kind of sales and customers, the only visible risk is that the national grid operator is not able to pay for the energy produced. A risk which is otherwise very distant, but under current circumstances, it is well above zero.

Question 4. The word "equity" assumes a sense of balance or fairness. Is it important for businesses to consider not just financial returns, but an overall economic, societal, and environmental equity in their business strategy, products, services, and orientation in the competitive marketplace? How does Enolia Energy address this sense of balance?

The road from "exceptional financial equity returns" to a kind of overall equilibrium between economic, societal, and environmental results is still long and winding. There is still a huge gap between investor's welfare and societal welfare. We can refer to the example of wind energy and its potential for combating long-term environmental concerns such as global warming. UNEP (1998) suggested a real societal discount rate of 3% (or 4%–6% according to latest data from developed countries) for analyzing climate change mitigation projects. The Stern Review, http://en.wikipedia.org/wiki/Stern_Review, on the Economics of Climate Change argues for zero discounting of future generations. In contrast, the corresponding rate demanded by private investors in wind energy can be well over 15%. It is self-evident that projects that appear to be more viable from a societal perspective may not find the actual equity that will make them happen. Obviously there is no "one-size-fits-all" solution. It is still a pending quest whether we can quantify societal needs appropriately.

At Enolia we address societal needs on case-by-case scenario. Project development costs typically include road works that improve school access to students at mountainous areas, PV installation to municipal rooftops and improvement of sports facilities, to mention a few. It is important also to refer that the Greek Renewable Energy law obligates wind energy producers to return at local communities 3% of their turnover.

Question 5. What are your thoughts on the risks and opportunities in clean tech within Greece or globally in the next 3 to 5 years? How can investors, government, business leaders, band others work together to mitigate and minimize risks and maximize opportunities?

The Renewable energy sector will continue its dependency on financial and geopolitical fluctuations. In spite of this ever-changing environment, technology will continue to improve dramatically, lowering capital cost and increasing investment performance. Investors, policy makers and, generally speaking, every renewable stakeholder should work in tandem towards:

- Improving and streamlining regulation
- Providing an adequately controlled project finance basis for RE power production
- Improve and maintain a high level of renewable energy awareness and responsiveness: Environmental illiteracy is just not an option.

Question 6. Do you personally see a change in how the current generation (the generation alive here and now) thinks about and takes action on "sustainability" related challenges and opportunities? What has been in your view the impetus for a change in behavior? What's needed for the current generation to advance its ability to have an "equitable" impact for today, and the future?

I think that the first question about accountability answers very much this question, too. In any case, the main impetus is the understanding that we cannot continue our existing carbon based model of living as the consequences of a "do-nothing" strategy will be way worse than the "act-today" strategy. Actions, as shown above, are to be taken on both personal and societal level leading to a genuinely sustainable future.

The main challenge on the personal level is and will be behavioral. I am afraid that until we build a sustainable strategy on sustainability, incentives have to be financial at a large extent (such as subsidies of any kind) so as to smooth the necessary transition to the new economy model.

Interview with Stelios Voyiatzis
CEO, Enolia Ventus SA
October 3, 2011
www.enoliaventus.com

Chapter Summary

- The consequences of the current generation doing nothing, whether out of fear or a lack of information and education, will be severe.

- There remains a gap between how the current generation values social and economic impacts and the resource needs for future generational needs. However, the gap may be closing, not becoming further apart.

- Change is required, and is actively happening, as the current generation of business and government leaders and everyday citizens embrace their accountability for generating more sustainable wealth and having a greater impact.

- The Sustainability Generation will be supported by financial incentives and pushed by regulatory requirements. However, the greatest impact will be achieved through behavioral changes at an individual and personal level. Having citizens who take action to be accountable in their role to develop a new culture focused on sustainable development remains a complex challenge, but this can be accomplished with more education and awareness.

6

Taking Action on Personal Accountability by Simplifying Sustainability for the NOW Generation

Taking Action on Personal Accountability

For the Sustainability Generation to succeed and have great impact we must, as individuals and as generations, move beyond our "ego" and sense of entitlement and work toward empowering and enlightening ourselves and those around us to think more critically as we seek to be more accountable in our daily lives. We must also dismiss any perceived or justifiable blame about the current slew of social and environmental challenges inherited from past generations. Thirty years ago there simply was not the range of awareness about the sensitivity of ecosystems and interrelatedness of ecosystems and economic systems to persuade prior generations to think differently about their behavior. The reason society is at this critical crossroads is due to multiple converging issues: global natural resource consumption, the state of the global economy, the transparency of health and environmental impacts, and an emerging awareness that our fixed resource base of planet Earth cannot replenish itself as quickly as we have been consuming its resources.

A fundamental reason we have greater transparency and knowledge about the world around us is because of the "Information Age." In less than two decades, it has afforded us incredible capabilities in communication technologies to enable a more connected and "flat" world. As the Sustainability Generation assumes greater prominence it will be critical to continue to empower people throughout the world to communicate, share ideas, collaborate, and innovate a new paradigm in how we consume, live, work, and play.

135

More than any time in history, a fundamental disconnect between humans and our natural world exists. We are reliant on our natural resources and ecosystems more than ever, and yet we still have not figured out how to fully protect, conserve, or sustain what feeds, clothes, and sustains us. Without an intervention in how "WE" humans connect with one another and the natural world, we simply will not survive for many more generations without some catastrophic collapses in our food, water, energy, communication, health, education or political systems. While dooms-day thinking makes blockbuster movies and evokes anxiety (and sometimes action), the reality is that we have the capability in our human condition to adapt and make changes to our present and future. When a billion people inhabited the earth in the late 1800s the world still seemed small. With a burgeoning population of seven billion and growing, the world seems smaller each day.

The human impact of natural disasters like tsunamis, earthquakes, and tornados seems to be growing as population centers push into regions more prone to these natural events. The human impact of disease and health outbreaks like H1N1 and Avian Flu are creating a new anxiety about the world's enhanced connections through travel and commerce. More education, training, empowerment, and enlightenment are needed if we are to make swift changes toward a more sustainable lifestyle. For example, we need our children to know where electricity comes from and how it is generated. We need to know what is in our foods, where they are produced, and the ecologic footprint of producing them. We need to understand the environmental and economic life-cycle impacts of operating a new car versus riding a bicycle to work. It is not enough to continue to say "I don't know" or "I don't care" in our information-driven, well-connected society. The era of "thoughtless consumption" is coming to an end. We need to move beyond thoughts of entitlement and "ego" and work on how "WE" as a society can find middle ground toward common goals that curb the creation and passage of social and environmental challenges to future generations.

The Sustainability Generation cannot solve all of the world's woes. And it is likely that many mistakes and unintended consequences may result from what appear to be balanced efforts today. However, the Sustainability Generation will be the ground breakers of new science, technology, and innovation that will solve some of the most pressing and critical challenges of our time, including the need for clean water, clean and renewable energy, and smart and sustainable products. Mobilization of the Sustainability Generation is underway thanks to the actions of leading-edge corporations, not-for-profit organizations, foundations, governments, and social networks. Humans are resilient in part through adaptation to our environment, and in part through ingenuity and innovation. By addressing issues of entitlement in our individual behaviors we can change our impact on human health, social, and environmental challenges. But change cannot happen without buy-in and support from an entire generation. The "WE" decision model needs to be adopted and pursued in all facets of government, industry, academia, and society. Establishing consensus and compromise can be a powerful way of empowering a generation toward enlightenment and toward sustainability. The following ideas are offered as opportunities for enabling the sustainability generation and mobilizing them toward empowerment, enlightenment and action:

- **Get to "We"** This is the sustainability generation's equivalent of Nike's famous "Just do It"! And it will also be the "Intel Inside" of the sustainability generation's ability to comprehend, analyze and make decisions on complex social and environmental challenges. To "get to WE" take note of and learn from social entrepreneurs and enlightened leaders that have the unique ability to get to "WE." Examples like Bill Shireman's Future 500, Bob Stiller's passionate Green Mountain Coffee Roasters, and the new-age corporate empowerment builder GreenNurture each have elements of how collaboration and empowerment can yield resolutions in environmental disputes or innovation through a well defined sense of urgency toward common goals. Getting to "WE" requires removal of the "ego" from most situations and achieving enlightenment as Eckert Tolle would conceive of it. Not everyone has to be enlightened to make the Sustainability Generation form and grow. But, working toward the collective "WE" is needed more than ever for society to address our "tragedy in the commons" and our current unsustainable behaviors in consumption.

- **Work with Past Generations** Past generations may or may not have left the current and future generations with a better place than they started with. We know that our consumptive habits are not sustainable and we know that our thinking and behaviors need to shift if we are to reduce our negative impact on human health and environment. But past generations have not only created environmental problems. They have also acted as good stewards of the environment and have empowered and enlightened many through the advancement of business, commerce, science, technology, and innovation. The current generation can learn a great deal from the Baby Boomer and older generations, both what has worked (the successes of innovation, for example) and what has not worked (from the problems of lack of information or inability to collaborate to avoid negative consequences). In the Sustainability Generation not just the youngest in society will lead the way to, as Green Mountain Coffee puts it, "a Higher Purpose." The current mix of young and old need to work together to achieve a higher purpose. There is no advantage in blaming past generations for wanting more or for younger generations for being too bold or confident. Advancements can be made, however, in removing barriers to inter-generational dialog and communication that can lead to a shared view on what sustainability means, and how generations can collaborate together toward a common vision and goals.

- *Focus on the "Commons" and Social Needs* There are fundamental building blocks to human health and our long-term viability as a species on the planet. Of course we need shelter, clothing, education, healthcare, and a myriad of other societal or public resources that we have come to depend upon, such as energy (electric transmission and distribution) systems, the Internet, and satellite networks that enable everything from remote imaging to telecommunications and global transport. There is a higher order or prioritization of needs, however. We need clean air, water, and food. These life-critical systems are interconnected. Many ecosystems contribute to the health and vitality of these vital elements. The intricacies of ecosystems are being understood more and more. But human population growth and consumption have expanded so quickly and with such tremendous impact on fragile ecosystems that we are sometimes unable to curtail our behaviors before crisis moments occur. Moving forward, the sustainability generation will need to focus more time and attention on the conservation, protection, sustainment, and enhancement of our "commons"—those things that every human should be entitled to: clean air, clean water, and land for agriculture. We can no longer afford to be passive onlookers as crisis moments arise. We need to utilize our public and private resources to study, analyze, and predict critical ecosystem failures before they occur so that real-time decisions can be made.

- *Work with Enlightened Leaders* Enlightened leaders are a conduit for positive change. They have a heightened ability to align moral beliefs and values with the needs of both business and society while making legitimate economic and societal progress. There are too few enlightened leaders in our government, industry, academia, and not-for-profits. We need to find a way to foster the development of this new kind of leader that can advance the sustainability generation through their passion, intellect, and empowerment.

- ***Place Emplasis on Action Through People, Policies and Practices*** The philosophy and concept of sustainability continues to evolve. As a concept, sustainability equates to a "goal" or "future state" to be pursued and achieved. As a reality, sustainability has very challenging implications as it spans theoretical discussions, basic science research, direct technology application, and consideration of energy, environmental, economic, and societal interests. In most instances where organizations are finding success in sustainability, those organizations have operated on the premise that "sustainability is a journey"; and "sustainability is defined by the culture of the organization, its leadership and the stakeholders that interact within that sphere." Because sustainability can be overwhelmingly broad, it is a challenge for large institutions to reach consensus on "what sustainability is," "what the journey entails," and "how to even begin the journey," let alone "measure success."

Based upon a review of organizations and institutions that are "Living Sustainability" with a sense of urgency, direction, purpose, and impact, the following framework is summarized. There are, at a minimum, three pillars to the initiation, capitalization, and implementation of sustainability programs/initiatives/strategies:

- ***"People"*** represent the "heart and mind" of sustainability, enabling the evolution of an institution-wide guiding vision and mission that includes the definition of operational goals and objectives. "People" represent the leadership by which sustainability policies and practices (including processes) are designed, developed, and carried out. Without "people," sustainability is held together only by "policies" and is rarely effective since "practices" are often singular events with less opportunity to have broader impact.

- ***"Policies"*** are the governing rules that guide the vision and mission of "people." "Policies" unto themselves (in the absence of "people") are just words on a page. "People" are needed to not only create "policies" but also to ensure "policies" are implemented, remain relevant, and are monitored for effectiveness. "Policies" are critical to the success of sustainability because they help create guidance, structure, and general "operating rules" for carrying out sustainability "practices" and toward a common vision.

- **"*Practices*"** are the tangible, measureable, and practical strategies by which "people" can carry out actionable strategies (deployment of technology, enacting a process, measuring outcomes) toward sustainability goals and objectives. "Practices" are defined by "people" and "policies." But most importantly, "practices" are carried out by "people" by direct implementation, short-and-long term monitoring and measurement, and quantification of results and impacts toward sustainability objectives, goals, and broader mission.

- ***Make Entitlement Positive*** In this book I have talked about "entitlement" outside of a legal definition to indicate a pejorative connotation when illustrating how many global environmental and societal challenges can be linked to a human "sense of entitlement." This idea that individuals believe they are deserving of some particular reward, benefit, special privilege or similar benefit has been defined in this book as a negative force against sustainability. Entitlement can be positive, however. If the individual and generations of individuals choose to feel "entitled" to greater protection of our natural resources and better conservation, perhaps we can make a generational shift in the direction of sustainability. This will require a change in our behaviors: how we think about and engage with our natural environment; how, what, and how much we consume; how and what we learn and in turn disseminate knowledge; and who and how we empower one another to take action toward sustainable goals in everyday living.

Simplifying Sustainability: The Sustainability Generation Tool-Kit for Industry, Academia, Government, and Not-for-Profits

Begin by Articulating, Framing, and "Owning" Your Goals and Meaning of "Sustainability"

The concept of sustainability has been poorly communicated. Part of poor communication is due to lack of a grounding and understanding of the definition of just what sustainability is and what it means for individuals and organizations. Many view sustainability as a utopia, a state of being and living where humans live in harmony and balance with the natural (some might add "the spiritual") world. A utopian state of living may be ideal and a path worth pursuing, but when defined and communicated this way many people become frustrated and see sustainability only as an oasis or just a mirage in the sand.

The definition of sustainability from a government, corporate, NGO or "common citizen" point-of-view, is likely to be dramatically different. There is a need to simplify the concept of sustainability to have action-oriented goals that people can understand and feel as if they can achieve in their own lives. An Environment, Health and Safety (EHS) leader at Hewlett Packard (HP) once told me, "... general citizens tend to align themselves and understand recycling or the idea of Earth Day more than they do the concept of sustainability." And in this sense the individual is correct. Do a Google search for "Sustainability Definition" and more than 19.4 million options are available.

I once heard Rick Walker, who was at the time a Senior National Manager–Environmental Solutions at Siemens Building Technologies, present to eighty corporate leaders his personal and his company's thoughts on corporate sustainability. The talk lasted forty-five minutes. In that time I had one of those "a–ha" moments that are powerful in shaping my thinking. Rick talked about sustainability as a journey, not a destination, and the idea that sustainability may never truly be achieved, but is an ideal that we as citizens, corporations, and governments should strive and work toward.

This basic premise of the idea that sustainability is not a destination, but a journey, was at the time very novel to me. At the time of Rick's presentation in Phoenix, Arizona in 2007, I had been hearing perspectives from corporate environmental sustainability and strategy officers I worked with for more than a decade. Typically companies either had very definitive statements about sustainability or would dismiss the concept all together on the basis that it did not hold value for top-line growth or bottom-line financial performance. But Rick's message was different. It was enlightening to hear someone with a practical and more realistic orientation toward corporate sustainability. Rick noted that not every challenge will be solved, nor should companies deal with every sustainability issue. Every company will have a different journey in the pursuit of sustainability. Some will be leading, other laggards. Some companies will innovate; others will die a slow death.

The natural evolution of humans, governments, capitalism, corporations, and many man-made institutions is, quite literally, a journey. It begins at a certain point, with certain beliefs and values in place. However, the final destination is never really known. The baton is handed to future generations to keep pushing, striving for something better and more balanced, more sustainable. This is perhaps a key breakthrough in my personal understanding of sustainability. When a challenge seems insurmountable people lose enthusiasm and capacity to try and overcome it. However, if the challenge can be restructured and realigned with one's strengths, people are then more apt to take some form of ownership and control to address the challenge. We as humans won't have all the right answers during our lifetime. The best we can do is to try and be empathetic to the needs of future generations.

We must at a minimum know our limits (the carrying capacity of our community, our natural resources, and the earth) and what our basic needs truly are. If our needs are 50 grams of protein a day, do we need two larger burgers from a fast food restaurant that get us to 100? Of course not. Reevaluating our needs with our wants and desires is part of individual and generational restraint that we need to think about and hopefully instill within ourselves. This restraint can make healthier people and a healthier planet. And it is one of the most cost-effective and immediate steps we can make toward sustainability that has impact on today and tomorrow.

Table 6.1 lays out a rudimental approach to think about sustainability. It defines the basic elements of sustainability in their raw form—something that I believe is lost in many mainstream discussions of sustainability, innovation, and creativity. Typically I hear about technology, science, product design, and innovation as core elements of sustainability. These attributes have been proven to improve the health and vitality of our planet while offering opportunity for economic growth. Some of the most leading-edge companies now "compete on sustainability" in the ways they have traditionally competed on the price, quality, and performance of their products and services. But technology, science, and innovation represent only one dimension or lens to evaluate sustainability.

If the basic building blocks highlighted in Table 6.1 are not present in the design, use, or afterlife of new technology, there is high potential that the new technology may lead to unsustainable outcomes. The unintended consequences of "going green" too quickly and without a balanced review of the energy, environmental, social, educational, and economic impacts can be severe. While a new technology may solve one challenge (i.e., the need for renewable power) it may create new challenges (i.e., increased water consumption and creation of new hazardous waste from the production of silicon into photovoltaic cells). Some points-of-view I have collected over the past few years after hearing hundreds of talks on sustainability from leaders like Rick Walker help us to see the scope of sustainability:

- Sustainability is not just about the environment. While a great amount of public discussion pertains to environmental concerns, sustainability is also about human health, fiscal responsibility, natural resource management and conservation, addressing social needs, and the nature of spirituality. In a business context, sustainability has been linked to competitive advantage, optimization of corporate resources, and access to new markets as major drivers.

- Sustainability is a journey, not a discrete destination where we arrive all at once. To be effective as an organizational, individual or generational strategy, sustainability needs to be defined by your goals, resources, and risk tolerance in financial terms and with evolving financial tools. Sustainability is something whose pursuit is marked by growth, development, metrics, measurement, and refinement and improvement across time.

- Sustainability is an ideal, not just an end-state to be achieved and reported upon. This is an important distinction. When the environmental movement began in the late 1960s and early 1970s it was in reaction to many seemingly blatant and negligent human behaviors and impacts on the natural world. In retrospect it seems ridiculous that people would dump trichloroethylene or other nasty solvents "out back" behind the factory. However, a few decades ago people didn't necessarily know any better. Thirty years ago there simply was not the amount of scientific research on environmental and human health impacts of chemicals as there are today. A lack of knowledge and information does not make polluting justified. But without a clear understanding of the human health and environmental impacts associated with chemical dumping, there were no policies or practices to guide people's decisions otherwise. In the absence of clear policies and practices and strong leadership, people will inherently cut corners, take shortcuts, and make mistakes. The Sustainability Generation has been an evolution in our social history. We need to be patient with ourselves as we learn and engage on sustainability issues. But we need to also act with a sense of urgency when we have enough information and critical thinking to substantiate a common goal.

- Sustainability for our generation has begun with an incredible journey to change our consumptive behaviors. We have started to adopt cleaner technologies like more fuel efficient transportation, distributed renewable energy resources, and more efficient means of producing and consuming a variety of consumer products. We have and will still yet, make mistakes. What we believe is "clean and green" today may turn out to be just as harmful to human health and environment a decade or two from now. But one thing should be for certain: the environmental legacies of our past shall not be replicated into our future. For the Sustainability Generation to succeed it must learn from past mistakes, move beyond blame, and work toward a more holistic and integrated approach to minimizing future human health and environmental risks. This can only be achieved through the use of more information, data, sound science, and strong leadership to make decisions that are balanced.

- Sustainability is inherently interdisciplinary requiring expertise from multiple stakeholders and long-term collaboration. Change is occurring within the world's largest industries, organizations, and institutions. Organizations need to re-think supply chain, products, and policies for greater transparency, more efficient use of natural and financial resources, and greater accountability for human health and environmental concerns.

Table 6.1
The Sustainability Continuum

People
Rating: POOR:
Traditional behaviors that focus on entitlement, greed and poorly-designed financial incentive structures. This is a negative feedback element that promotes unsustainable short-term thinking and short-term profit; often at the detriment of human health and environment.
Rating: GOOD:
Organizations that invest in their people to become more aware of sustainable practices and which can empower their workforce to take action.
Rating: GREAT:
Organizations that have created, deployed, and measured active sustainability policies and programs and encourage sustainable behaviors through properly designed incentive structures.
Rating: INNOVATIVE & TRANSFORMATIONAL:
"Enlightened" organizations that understand competitive posturing, but are also educators and advocates for creating more sustainable enterprises throughout their industry and throughout their communities.

Table 6.1 (continued)

The Sustainability Continuum

Policies

Rating: POOR:
Policies that don't take into consideration the human health and environmental implications of their impact.

Rating: GOOD:
Policies that conserve natural resources and protect human health and environment (i.e., Clean Air Act, Clean Water Act, Sustainable Fisheries Act.)

Rating: GREAT:
Policies created to sustain natural resources not only through regulation, but through market incentive programs that curtail the use of natural resources.

Rating: INNOVATIVE & TRANSFORMATIONAL:
Policies that encourage sustainable development and break down unsustainable institutional and policy barriers to sustainable growth. Policies that encourage the protection and enhancement of natural resources and support the stewardship of ecosystem services.

Processes and Products

Rating: POOR:
Traditional product development that focuses exclusively on product price, performance and quality—without stronger weighting/consideration of sustainability indicators/metrics including human health and environmental impact.

Rating: GOOD:
Considering long-term impacts of products and services on human health and environment.

Rating: GREAT:
Designing, manufacturing and controlling the end-of-life disposition of products to that they have no negative human health or environmental impact.

Rating: INNOVATIVE & TRANSFORMATIONAL:
Designing, manufacture and use of products that actually enhance human health and environment. These products would go beyond "zero waste" goals and would actually enable the self-healing of sensitive ecosystems.

Communicating Sustainability

According to a 2008 survey by KPMG, annual reports on Corporate Social Responsibility (CSR) are on the rise, ". . . Corporate responsibility reporting has gone mainstream—nearly 80 percent of the largest 250 companies worldwide issued reports, up from about 50 percent in 2005."[75] The reputational value surrounding disclosure on corporate ethics and economics were among the top drivers referenced by KPMG that are influencing more and more companies to publicly report out on key CSR indicators. In the mad rush to publish CSR content, how effective are companies at communicating themselves to stakeholders effectively? How do they differentiate sustainability as a business and societal directive? How do they communicate clarity when there is conjecture about the future?

Communicating and Empowering the Sustainability Generation at Green Mountain Coffee Roasters (GMCR)

In 2005 GMCR's published its Corporate Social Responsibility report, *"From Understanding to Action."* The report achieves "10 principles" of communicating sustainability. For example, the first words in the report state, *"For 25 years, we have been on a deliberate journey to create and sustain a values-driven company that views profit as a means to achieve a higher purpose."*

Like Patagonia, GMCR has a foundation with a passionate and articulate executive. Bob Stiller, founder and President of GMCR says *"Understanding the realities of people's lives and the conditions of our shared world motivates us and helps guide our decisions. When people understand underlying issues, I believe they will take action. That is why we have sent more than 20% of our full-time employees on trips to coffee-farming communities. Whenever I visit with coffee farmers, I am touched by their hard work, perseverance and pride in producing high-quality coffee. Seeing first-hand some of the challenges and complexities integral to the specialty coffee industry inspires us to move toward a vision of long-term sustainability for everyone in our supply chain."*

GMCR's sustainability and social responsibility efforts are critical to their success as a company. GMCR's views its suppliers not as commodity providers, but as an integral part of the company's future and vice versa. This humanistic and emotional connection to their products and the communities in which they source products from enables GMCR to have a realistic notion of their business present and future.

The eloquence in which President-elect Barack Obama spoke of his vision for our nation was one of the defining and winning elements of his 2008 presidential campaign. Trying to communicate such vision to 100 million registered voters, through nothing more than the delivery of words, is an incredible skill and nothing shy of amazing. President Obama's victory speech exemplified how and why words matter.

There are some basic principles and key lessons in communication that we can draw from President Obama's ability to communicate complicated and often unresolved issues to diverse audiences. These key lessons on are valuable for communicating complex information like a corporate sustainability strategy, which is often not well defined, not yet rooted, and in most cases, a vision or framework for business strategy and governance.

Key Lessons for Communicating Your Sustainability Strategy:

1. Create Trust by Giving Praise
2. Be Articulate and Succinct
3. Be Visionary yet Grounded in Tangible Example and Application
4. Show Emphasis but not Exaggeration
5. Transcend All Stakeholders with Common Themes and Examples
6. Be Realistic on the Present and Future
7. Demonstrate Force and Grace Simultaneously
8. Don't Overwhelm Your Audience
9. Create Enthusiasm
10. Leave a Door Open for Others to Join

I am sure there are other basic principles one can draw from President Obama's oratory and speech writing skills. However, these ten principles are directly applicable to corporate communications and disclosure on sustainability.

As I think about some of the more successful communicators of business sustainability I see these ten principles in their blogs, annual reports, speeches and presentations, and press releases. The ten principles are often tied together to tell a story, one that is rooted in both the emotional-and-tactical side of business. I often see sustainability communications that are so mechanical that the essence and richness of what is communicated is lost in a sea of data and numbers, non-descript and non-personal quotes, or language that is unrealistic for the ideas communicated. There is a certain bravado that garners attention from investors and the media, but too much can send many analysts running for the hills.

Go Beyond "Random Acts of Greenness"

Developing an Enterprise-Wide Sustainability Strategy through Internal and External Alignment of Corporate Goals is Essential to the Long-Term Performance and Success of Your "Going Green" Efforts

Going green is great, but if it is not aligned within an enterprise wide strategy, going green is just a random act. Taking "random acts of greenness" and building enterprise sustainability strategy is not a trivial matter. It requires commitment and alignment from all levels of the corporation.

The year 2008 has left a huge wake on all facets of the economy and in every industrial sector. The housing, credit, and financial markets have dramatically impacted many corporations. In late 2008 and throughout 2009 and into 2012, companies have been continuing to cut costs amid financial worries and uncertainties in the marketplace. While the financial crisis continues to impact most corporations, there is still a need to push forward through these trying economic periods. And often, new growth and opportunity is uncovered during times of constraint.

In trying economic times it becomes a priority to optimize efficiency, reduce unnecessary expenditures, and cut non-critical programs. Challenging times are also a time to rebuild strength in operations, brand, products and personnel. There is no doubt that industry is on the cusp of a profound transformation. The "go green" movement of 2008 is continuing to advance, and President Obama has outlined his key priorities for economic recovery and growth which include, among other initiatives, increasing renewable energy production, decreasing the nation's use of foreign oil, and rebuilding the nation's highway and education infrastructure.

Market indicators and signals continue to show that consumers are seeking "more green" products and services, albeit at competitive prices and continued high quality and service. Existing and emerging policy and regulatory indicators show that government is advancing clean technologies, renewable energy, and also focusing on "going green" through its own operations and practices. From a corporate perspective we see many companies taking the time to define what "green" and "sustainable" means to them in the context of business strategy and growth. For many companies "going green" remains synonymous with corporate communications and branding.

Communicating corporate sustainability efforts is essential. However, it needs to be grounded to measureable initiatives that are centered on an enterprise-wide corporate strategy to have the greatest impact on financial performance, and recognition as legitimate claims from the external world. Too often corporations are "going green" so quickly that they don't fully define their goals and objectives, leading to "random acts of greenness." These random acts get attention, and sometimes make great headlines and sound bites, but ultimately they are short-lived exposures that fail to build better brands, stronger reputations, or long-term shareholder value. And, in worst-case scenarios, random acts of greenness backfire on the corporation as stakeholders see through the green glitter and glam only to find a shell of substance and true commitment toward "going green" or business sustainability.

The following seven questions can inform and enhance your organization's sustainability efforts:

1. ***Do You Have Reactive or Proactive Strategy Development?***

   Would you characterize your firm's corporate sustainability efforts as "Random Acts of Greenness?" superficial "go green" activities caught-up or trapped in the moment (or in reaction to market conditions), but also not tied to any type of corporate strategy to yield long-term value, reputational enhancement, or shareholder value? Proactive strategy development that involves senior leaders and those in charge of profit-and-loss of business units and line operators is required for moving beyond Random Acts of Greenness toward a comprehensive and unified sustainability strategy. The simultaneous top-down and bottom-up approach yields internal buy-in, elevation of bright ideas, and often uncovers inefficiencies.

2. ***Does Your Firm Exemplify Strategic Alignment or Turf Warfare?***

   Who owns sustainability in your firm? Is that an issue? Turf battles over new growth initiatives often emerge and can be the detriment of a well orchestrated strategy. The reality is sustainability is a goal, objective, future state, a journey, and a business principle. It is not something that should lend itself to turf disputes within the corporation. To help move beyond turf disputes, engage others in questions and discussions with questions like: Have we established corporate sustainability principles, values, and goals? Are the sustainability principles, values, and goals communicated and understood at an enterprise level? What are the internal and external integration challenges and issues associated with our sustainability principles, values, and goals?

3. ***Do You Have Performance Measurement or Data Collection Jitters?***

Are there existing tools to monitor sustainability performance, track performance, and report-out through the use of corporate sustainability metrics?

4. ***Are Your Green Efforts Focused on Telling a Story or Storytelling?***

No enterprise-wide strategy for sustainable business growth is going to be 100% on the mark right out of the gate. It will require proper conditioning, support from senior management, line operators, suppliers, vendors, and customers. Temper the urge to appeal to all stakeholders through "storytelling." Internal and external stakeholders will ultimately see through the fiction from the non-fiction. Instead, focus on building the story, its characters, its theme and storyline, and then acting it out across time. Given everyone a tangible role. This will result in the ability to tell your story based upon real personal actions versus the perception that you are only storytelling via green washing or random acts of greenness. Questions to consider: Has any one person or team been assigned to conduct performance monitoring, tracking, and reporting across the organization? How is performance being measured and communicated? What tools and processes are in place to ensure continuous improvement occurs over time?

5. ***Are You Undergoing a Cultural Transformation or in Denial?***

Taking on new business principles and values cannot exist superficially. It has to transcend the corporate culture and day-to-day corporate behavior of all employees. Questions to consider: Has your firm established a mechanism (i.e., use of performance metrics, business unit performance goals, establishment of an executive or operating unit guiding coalition/council, or other means) to facilitate a cultural and operational integration of sustainability principles, values, and goals? What can you do to facilitate cultural integration of sustainability principles, values, and goals?

6. ***Is Your Firm Navigating a Course of Action or Afraid to Explore Unchartered Territory?***

New journeys are overwhelming. And, achieving business sustainability is definitely an overwhelming journey. Spending the necessary time and resources to properly plan for your journey will enable a safer, less risky, and more enjoyable experience. Questions to consider: Has your firm mapped out its journey with key strategic goals, tactical objectives, and achievable milestones across time? How is this roadmap diffused throughout the organization? Do all essential employees know their role in the journey? Is the roadmap oriented and aligned toward other business goals, or are they divergent?

7. ***Do You Benefit From Competitive Posturing or Still in the Dark?***

Experience tells us that the smartest and most effective companies know the playing field. They benchmark with their peers and accept humility when they are not the leader and pride when they demonstrate strength. This ebb-and-flow of business performance and benchmarking is critical to building a strong sustainability initiative within your firm. Don't catch yourself in the dark when it comes to what others are doing on business sustainability. Seek-out opportunities to learn from other leaders. And don't be afraid to engage as a participant in corporate sustainability benchmarking. What you will find is a room of collegial peers that are experiencing the same thing as you; but also a support group and network that can convey incredible business insight and experience that can shape the design, or improve the execution of, your corporate sustainability strategy. Questions to consider: Has your firm benchmarked your enterprise sustainability strategy with corporate peers to understand what they are doing? How they are doing it? And, what is the value others derive from their efforts?

A Stimulus for a Better World: Give Them Sustainability Without Compromise

Sustainability sounded good when money was flowing in. But now that the economy is broken, business sustainability is taking a back seat to business survival. However, now more than ever this is a time to advance your business case for sustainability as a top-line and bottom-line strategy for not just survival, but long-term growth and profitability.

The triple bottom line is alive and well in this broken economy. Smart corporations are embracing principles of business sustainability and positioning their business units, products, and services for new growth. There are early-adopters, a late-majority and laggards in every distribution of companies that choose to introduce new business strategy and processes to their organizations. In the case of sustainability, it is more of a corporate value that needs to be accepted and injected into the very culture of the corporation for it to become operational and of value. That point is lost on many corporations that simply seek to overlay some sustainability principles on a few of their facilities or products and wait for positive financial returns. A passive speed-dating approach to corporate sustainability will not work.

To be successful, a corporation has to proactively adopt sustainability principles, make them their own, align them across business units, and devise clear goals for operational excellence, corporate responsibility, and product strategy. This can only be accomplished through complete senior level buy-in and support. Additionally the business units have to align themselves with the new corporate value for sustainability, develop their own goals and performance indicators toward the new value, and make it relevant to their employees, customers and stakeholders.

Developing, implementing, monitoring and adjusting corporate sustainability for continuous improvement is not an easy task. Corporate sustainability embodies values, vision, goals, actions and improvements. It is as much a process as it is a tangible product or service. To reap the full benefits of sustainability, companies have to be prepared for a cultural change, a process that takes time, and a new way of doing business that is more complex, but ultimately more profitable.

Survival of the Fittest ... Darwin Says Sustainability is Evolution

This all sounds reasonable, right? And you are going to tell me that the economy is broken and your company is in survival mode. You don't have the time, resources or support to think about business sustainability. And this sounds very logical to me—except that you are compromising the future success of your corporation with survival tactics, not with sound business strategy. Darwin's mantra "survival of the fittest" holds true to business, but it is not just solid financials, or cutting costs, or restructuring in tough markets that lead to survivors. Two decades from now the companies that will still be alive and thriving will have evolved. On one hand they will have superior products and leaders that know the fundamentals of operating a strong business. On another hand they will have transformed to adopt principles of sustainability that allow them to evolve their business, products, and operations. They will be fit enough to survive energy price volatility, natural resource and commodity constraints, shifting customer preferences for greener products, and new regulatory or market requirements.

What I mean by this is that the financial and business landscape is transforming. Business as usual may sustain your operations for a few months or years; but ultimately government, business, and consumers are asking for more. And the "more" that is being requested is not necessarily more money. It is a smarter, better run, less risky and ultimately more profitable business that views the world through the lens of sustainability. That lens views the world more holistically, with people, planet and profit as a more balanced screen. Twenty and thirty years ago the screen of sustainability was not only foreign to corporations; it was rejected and defied all principles of capitalism and why businesses existed. Today however, the evolution of business sustainability is bringing new life to modern corporations that better understand their relationship with the natural, physical and human world, and knowing that for their survival they need to become more sustainable enterprises. That means reducing waste, reducing water and energy consumption, reducing greenhouse gas emissions, designing better products, minimizing their transportation footprint and doing all this while still making a profit.

For those companies that have embraced business sustainability and proactively pursued sustainable business strategies, the following benefits are most frequently cited (1) lower operating costs; (2) a license to operate; (3) enhanced corporate reputation; (4) more efficient and responsible use of commodities and natural resources; (5) more competitively priced products and higher margins; (6) a realignment of products that meet customer expectations for price, performance and quality, but also for addressing specific social needs like clean water, more sustainable transport or cleaner energy; (7) product and service differentiation among competitive landscape; (8) attraction of new customers in competitive markets; (9) gain in market share; (10) new revenue toward top-line growth and greater earnings toward profit and bottom-line growth.

A Case Example for Sustainability Without Compromise: Crafty Solutions at Kraft Foods

With revenue topping $37 billion in 2007 Kraft Foods is the United States' #1 food company and is #2 in the world (behind Nestlé). Its North America unit makes the world's largest cheese brand (Kraft), owns the cookie and cracker business (Nabisco) and is the maker of the childhood favorite, Oreos. The company has more than 103,000 employees worldwide. In addition the company operates 187 manufacturing and processing facilities, including 51 in the US, 13 in

Canada, and 123 in 44 other countries. Wal-Mart accounts for some 15% of Kraft's sales. Like all companies, Kraft Foods is feeling the economic crunch. But this market leader is not just looking to survive, they are seeking to thrive. So, Kraft has begun to infuse a culture of sustainability throughout its business units, operations and people. To "make sustainability its own," Kraft has designated Six Sustainability Focus Areas:

1. Transportation & Distribution
2. Agricultural Commodities
3. Packaging
4. Energy
5. Water
6. Waste

Kraft chose to focus on these six priority areas because they felt that is where they could have the greatest impact on their business. And Kraft's focus on these six areas is paying off. If fact from a baseline year of 2001 Kraft has monitored performance toward key performance indicators (KPIs) and demonstrated continuous improvement. For example, since 2001 Kraft has decreased its global water consumption by 34%, energy use by 25%, carbon dioxide emissions by 30%, and solid waste by 16%.

Operational Excellence

But performance on KPIs is just one indication of how a sustainability strategy is performing. Kraft has also adopted a triple bottom-line business sustainability culture and it is beginning to show in their operations, products and performance. For example, in 2007 Kraft Foods adopted anaerobic digester technology at their Lowville, New York facility that processes cheese. The Kraft facility produces whey as a byproduct waste of cheese processing. The waste whey is consumed by bacteria in the anaerobic digester at the Lowville facility and methane gas is produced during the process. The methane gas is then used by Kraft to offset 25–30% of the on-site energy needs. Kraft's use of anaerobic digester technology not only reduces the amount of waste they have to either process or transport offsite (whey waste), it produces onsite energy to minimize Kraft's operational expenditure.

Another example at Kraft Foods is their underground storage facility that is built into a reclaimed limestone mine in Springfield, Missouri. The facility is Kraft's largest refrigerated warehouse and a strategic distribution center for the company. Because the facility is built into a limestone mine that is thirty meters below ground, a constant temperature of 15.5 degrees Celsius is maintained year round. The constant temperature translates into significant energy savings for Kraft Foods. In fact the company estimates that the Springfield warehouse uses 65 percent less energy than comparable above-ground facilities.

Superior Products and Supply Chains

And, as one of the world's larger food and beverage companies Kraft Foods is using its market size to influence its suppliers while providing the scale necessary to introduce more sustainable products to market. Case in point is Kraft's commitment to buy coffee beans certified by the Rainforest Alliance, an independent NGO that works to conserve biodiversity and ensure sustainable livelihoods by transforming land-use practices, business practices and consumer behavior. Kraft Foods is now the world's biggest buyer of Rainforest Alliance certified coffees. Kraft's commitment to the Rainforest Alliance and sustainable agriculture practices in coffee communities has not gone unnoticed. In 2007 McDonald's UK decided to switch 100% of their coffee to Kraft Foods Kenco Brand which is Rainforest Alliance certified. The switch by McDonald's happened in part due to changing customer preferences for more sustainable products. The McDonald's decision to purchase Kraft's coffee opened an entire new account and added market share to Kraft's coffee line.

Sustainable Packaging

Recognizing that the shipment of its products from manufacturing facilities has an environmental impact in the form of greenhouse gas emissions, namely CO_2, Kraft has made efforts to minimize the amount of packaging materials it uses for shipping and it has redesigned some product packaging so that shipping containers weigh less. For example, Kraft has redesigned some salad dressing bottles so that they use less material, resulting in less waste, and a 19% decrease in unit weight, and less fuel required to transport the product to market.

Social Responsibility

Kraft recognizes that the packaging of its products carries a large ecologic footprint; that is why Kraft has also partnered with TerraCycle Inc. on a packaging-reclamation program for "unrecyclable" items in which the packaging is "upcycled" into new consumer products available at retail stores. TerraCycle Inc. "upcycles" Kraft products like used Capri-Sun drink pouch containers, reclaims, cleans, and uses them in new products such as tote bags. The TerraCycle Inc. and Kraft Foods partnership is raising awareness about sustainability; product reclamation, reuse and recycle; and using Kraft's scale and TerraCycle's creativity to divert waste from landfills. Kraft is working with TerraCycle Inc. on creating a broader national network of collection points, often in partnership with local schools. In fact, Kraft donates two cents to participating schools and other groups for every Capri-Sun pouch collected as incentive for working with TerraCycle in this program.

The Most Fit are Sustainable

During a financial crisis it is reasonable and necessary to go into "survival mode." But what does that really mean? For some companies survival mode means getting rid of unnecessary expenditures and underperforming business units and people and tightening cost controls. This is necessary in many cases. But survival is also about adaptation and transformation. We know the financial markets are changing. We see a shift in consumer behavior and also a new era of reform in government and business. The adoption of sustainability principles into a corporate culture may be, for the right corporations, a necessary tool for survival. Kraft Foods demonstrates one large corporation's decision to "get more fit" through the adoption of sustainability principles and values into its corporate culture, and ultimately into its products. And as seen in Kraft's operational efficiency at its facilities and success in accessing new markets with more sustainable product options, those that are "sustainability fit" can thrive.

Simplifying Sustainability: A Guide for Action and Results

How can people be empowered and enlightened to take action? How can the collective "we" take responsibility for their actions today and feel accountable for future generations? Sustainable development can be achieved through a process of self-discovery and innovation that allows generations to "Get to We," that is, the collective way we can engage toward mutual sustainable development goals.

Trying to define sustainability can be very overwhelming. It is essential to work on tangible strategies to take action at an individual level. It is also important for society to simplify sustainability so that it is not so unwieldy that we choose to do nothing as individuals or as a generation. We may not succeed in every facet of sustainability. But we cannot run the risk of being afraid to ask the right questions of ourselves, our society, our economy or governments and corporations that are part of this broad ecosystem of decision makers. To this end, I have enjoyed providing this quote by Director James Cameron when I give talks on sustainability:

> *"Curiosity is the most powerful thing you own . . . Don't put limitations on yourself. Other people will do that for you . . . failure has to be an option in art and exploration because it's a leap of faith . . . In whatever you're doing, failure is an option, but fear is not."*[76]
>
> —James Cameron
> *Creator and Director Avatar*
> *February 13, 2010*

The topic and pursuit of sustainability can be overwhelming; clear headed decisions that balance human, financial and natural resources can be clouded in uncertainties involving technology, processes, markets, and trends. Much like making ambitious New Year's resolutions to cut debt, lose weight, or live a more balanced life, pursuing sustainability goals without a clear vision, strategy, and discipline often falls flat.

This guide for action and results has been developed because far too often I have witnessed small and large companies, governments, and not-for-profit organizations struggle with defining sustainability in the context of their organizational strategy and goals. In this challenging process, many fall short of winning true sustainability. When sustainability is not defined as a measurable strategy, it loses its intended purpose and effectiveness.

Even worse, financial, human, and natural resources are not optimized toward achieving sustainability. They are often deployed blindly, with right intentions, but ineffectively and inefficiently. This happens because individuals and organizations chase sustainability to catch up with their peers (keeping up with the proverbial Joneses/Kardashians) or for the appearance of taking action.

Individuals and organizations that "compete on sustainability" do so to achieve a balance in how they grow and enhance their revenue, reputation, and ability to report to their stakeholders a measurable progress toward sustainability goals. The process can be quite simple and effective when it is defined as an organizational or corporate strategy, not just as an "add-on" initiative. Simplifying sustainability is about linking leadership with the shifting values of society in a way that leverages innovation.

The framework summarized within the following pages was developed primarily for business and organizational development, but it is just as transferrable to the adoption of sustainability in your personal life. The framework is based upon more than ten years of knowledge and direct application working with small and large companies and governments to understand their sustainability challenges, goals, opportunities, and competitive advantage. The best strategies and plans begin with asking the right questions. Taking action on sustainability requires self-reflection, assessment of your values and beliefs, and having the ability to define your purpose and desired outcomes.

Embrace the Generational Intelligence Shift

The Sustainability Generation represents a major societal shift forty years in the making. It began out of necessity and through the force and intellect of early thought-leaders. Over the years reluctant risk-takers began to take action and realize there was genuine benefit to "doing business differently." In the past decade, the Sustainability Generation has been supported by the "chic change-agents." Familiar politicians, Hollywood stars, musicians, and sports heroes have touted their green living, eco-homes, and hybrid cars. These "chic change-agents" have served to mainstream some of the modern environmental movement, but more importantly, they have also shown that sustainability is about balance and trade-offs, and that changes we can make to our lifestyles do make a difference. Slowly but steadily, a generational intelligence about sustainability has taken root in America and throughout the world.

This new generational intelligence is demonstrated by individuals taking greater responsibility and accountability for their consumptive behaviors with the types of lifestyles they choose to lead. Like an "S-shaped" curve of innovation, the Sustainability Generation is ready to climb the steep incline of greater influence and impact, through the power of innovation in products and people, ultimately wielding a greater collective societal/generational intelligence for humans (see Figure 6.1.) That intelligence will leverage our knowledge, past experiences, and shared intellect. But that intelligence is marginalized if we do not use it responsibly and proactively. For example, should we sit idle, as a people and as a nation, while other countries pollute the air, water, and land? If we know of a more balanced solution that could curb their waste or emissions (that do impact us half a world away), is it not our responsibility, in part, to try to engage, empower, and enlighten others to take action and be accountable to their impacts?

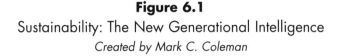

Figure 6.1

Sustainability: The New Generational Intelligence

Created by Mark C. Coleman

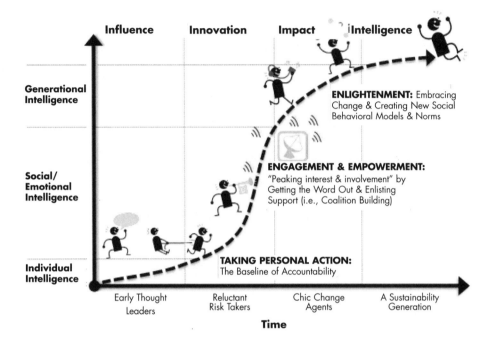

Customizing Sustainability to Your Life

The advent of citizens taking action to customize their sustainability is the next major advancement toward becoming a more sustainable culture. As a fundamental societal shift, sustainability has made strides from the regulations and policies created by government to oversee the products and services now being offered by business. Yet much remains to be accomplished. Sustainability is not a new zoning ordinance prohibiting oil and gas drilling or a more fuel-efficient vehicle. These are policy and technical outcomes of a sustainability generation in action. Rather, sustainability is much like the word "bespoke." It is a way of being, a customization of values, beliefs, and actions around the context in which people are living their lives.

Sustainability is not static; it changes as people grow, as life changes, and as humans interact with the natural world and our human-built environment. Business sustainability, led by companies including Green Mountain Coffee Roasters, Harbec, Inc., and GE, are bringing the world new, exciting innovations in products and services that provide greater choice for consumers to make informed and wise decisions regarding their consumption of goods. But living a balanced life that takes into account many trade-offs requires many more options than those enveloped in just one product or service. For example, there is a greater choice of alternative fueled vehicles, energy-efficient home appliances, and fair-trade and organically grown coffees. These product offerings are addressing critical natural resource and social challenges involving energy, water, materials availability, and fair wages. The value of these new innovations and options to society should not be understated. Individually, these new product options represent a few aspects of lifestyle: transport, entertainment, cooking, eating, and relaxation. Living a sustainable lifestyle goes beyond the here-and-now turn-key options pushing us to buy more product to consume less resources.

A sustainable lifestyle requires a long-term commitment from oneself: to continuously monitor, assess, and take action according to your values, beliefs, and behaviors as they relate to the goals you have for incorporating sustainability within your life. This includes the pursuit of balance, meaning, and happiness. Buying more things, whether they are more-or-less efficient, still means buying more stuff. The building blocks of everything we consume comes from nature. Too often we are removed from that point. Some resources are renewable, others are not. Exercising wise-use and restraint in our consumptive behaviors, and making the most logical choices that align with our personal values, is part of our personal accountability to this and future generations. Figure 6.2 helps visualize the opportunity for customizing sustainability to your life.

Sustainability is also represented by our ability to be adaptable, resilient, forgiving, and accepting. These traits allow us to change ourselves, and be accepting when others change around us. They are essential traits to master for living a life of balance and resolve. Sustainability also requires critical thinking, innovation, and enlightenment. These traits are fostered best by subduing the ego-driven mind so that the subconscious "self" can have room to breathe, reflect, and emerge. Sustainability is self-defined and then magnified and played out in greater society. It is a personal reflection of values and ideals put to action by left-and-right brain thought, and anchored by an ability to be present and conscious of our behaviors and when making decisions.

Figure 6.2

The Sustainability Generation: Customizing Sustainability to Master a Life of Balance and Resolve

Created by Mark C. Coleman

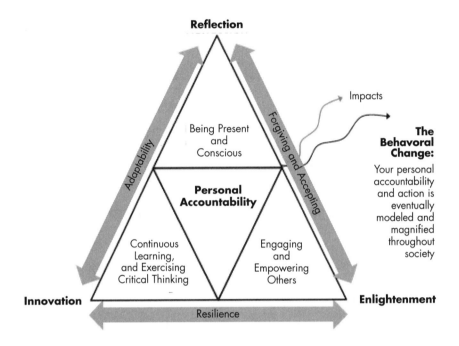

I am often asked about the role of "Chief Sustainability Officers," "Vice Presidents of Sustainability and Corporate Responsibility," and other similar organizational titles. What I get asked most often is: "What do people with these positions do? and "How they do it?" A common underlying trait I see in many organizational leaders with "Sustainability" and "Accountability or Responsibility" titles is that they really are "Chief Logic Officers," "Chief Innovation Officers," and "Directors of Ambiguity and Risk." The dashboard of sustainability issues and stakeholders for any corporation is very dynamic and complex. Those working to understand, define, and create strategy around sustainability objectives for a corporation, are screening millions of data points and weighing that against an underlying moral code and a value and belief system that defines and governs how the organization sees and operates in the world.

Day-to-day Chief Sustainability Officers are working to find that balance, and in the long-term they will provide the company and society with tangible value through innovation, impact, and intelligence. The influence of sustainability professionals as strategists who are helping to define the future state of business and government is growing tremendously, and in large part because of their ability to accept and work with a great deal of ambiguity, and analyze and manage risk. And ultimately they work collaboratively with internal-and-external stakeholders to define what is logical for operational efficiency and smart growth through innovation and the integration of multiple intelligences.

Become the Chief Logic Officer and Architect of Your Sustainable Future

The earth is a dynamic living system. Not that it needs more stress, but add seven billion people to the equation and the planet feels less vast. When it comes to environmental affairs, social justice, and the pursuit of a well balanced, healthy, and happy life, we are our own worst enemies.

To achieve sustainability throughout society we must do many things extremely well. We need to transform our educational system, we need to be more innovative, we need to be more conscious and present, and we need to be accountable to our actions and inactions. We are imperfect, but we have the capacity to learn, improve, and ultimately perfect.

As the global context in which we live changes, many challenges and opportunities will confront us. We can only postulate and forecast what the world will be like forty years from now. It is estimated that more than three million people move from rural areas to urban centers per week worldwide. Further, it is estimated that 70% of the world's population will live in cities by 2050, as compared to less than 30% in 1950. And, the global population is anticipated to reach nine billion people by 2050, two billion more than today. There are researchers that believe population will peak around 2050, and trends suggest population growth is declining, although there are dramatic regional differences in growth rates.

Regardless, more people will be competing for a fixed supply of natural resources across the next four decades. Factor in the findings of the Millennium Ecosystem Assessment regarding the challenges that exist in life-essential critical ecosystems, and a myriad of indicators of socio-economic, geo-political changes, as well as climate change, natural disasters, and natural resource shortages, and the future begins to look very challenging. Let's not sugarcoat it: the problems of the future seem overwhelming. We recognize now that there are natural limits and constraints to unfettered and unsustainable growth. Forecasts and predictions by world-class research organizations, corporations, governments, and individual scientists and researchers are beginning to coalesce. A convergence is happening in society, business, government, politics, and among the citizenry of the world. This convergence reflects the idea that to address the challenges of the next generation, this generation needs to be more collaborative, integrated, innovative, and accountable. The Occupy Wall Street and other global protests of the past year are signals of a generation trying to find its balance and voice. The convergence can seem convoluted at times, as ideas and passion collide with fear and constraint.

But take a step back, and at the center of the chaotic swirling storm there is calm. The calm comes from a variety of hopeful and ambitious leaders and from everyday citizens choosing to accept change and work toward creating a more sustainable world. What will result in a more balanced, fulfilling, and sustainable lifestyle for this generation is ... us—we, the people, and our direct actions, behaviors, and accountability. Too often we look to external sources of fault as we reason our way through the chaos. But eventually this is fleeting and destructive. Change begins with us, as consumers, parents, working professionals, and citizens. The gift we have is life in and of itself. What and how we choose to use that gift is our ultimate challenge to reconcile within and among ourselves.

Assess Your Role as an Engaged Citizen

This book advocates for individuals to take responsibility and action toward creating a better world through innovation, technology and collaboration. Part of this is in the form of being an engaged citizen, both locally and globally. Examining the role you can play as an individual and as a citizen in creating a more balanced lifestyle toward a sustainable future, is essential to the continued growth and evolution of the Sustainability Generation.

Questions to consider as you evaluate your individual responsibilities to yourself, family, community, and generation include: Are you currently an "engaged" citizen? What does it mean to be a "successfully engaged citizen"? What belongs to you as an individual? What do you own? What are your rights, privileges, responsibilities? Do you exhibit "entitlement" for goods, services, resources, and other things? What belongs to "us" as society? What do "we" own? And, what are our collective rights, privileges and responsibilities? Does society exhibit "entitlement" over earth's natural resources? What belongs to your "generation"? What impacts on the positive and negative side of the ecologic ledger has your generation made? Does "conformance" in society, either individual or generational, lead to an unbalanced ecologic portfolio? How can modern innovations, technologies, institutions and networks be deployed to help individuals and generations rebalance the ecologic portfolio for long-term sustainment? By listening to your inner voice, identifying and prioritizing what values are most important to you, and by asking some of the above questions periodically, you can begin to reveal the elements which embody your ideals for living a life of balance, fulfillment, accountability, and sustainable impact.

Question the Status-Quo and Conventional Wisdom

Everything has a lifecycle, and tried and true does not equate to efficient or sustainable. Although it is nice to have "systems that work," they only do so for awhile. For example, we have a great deal of legacy infrastructure, systems, products, and processes currently in use (for transportation, information technology, communications, energy, defense, education, healthcare, and so on). Many of these systems are outdated, aging, and deteriorating and in need of a makeover. However, these systems don't just need "new paint"; some of them need a wholesale redesign and redeployment to serve the needs of this, and future generations.

The petroleum industry is a case and point. The United States has built an economy on a one fuel town: petroleum. As a result, the United States and our citizenry are at an economic disadvantage. As consumers of oil, we have to succumb to a myriad of issues impacting oil supply and price. More importantly, as a nation we are at a strategic security and sustainability disadvantage every day we choose to consume more oil. Alternatives exist for us to lessen our dependence on oil. There are domestic reserves of cleaner fuels like natural gas, or more fuel efficient vehicle technology options including fuel cells, electric, and alternative fuel blends that can enable our "one fuel town" to be more balanced in serving our sustainability goals: energy innovation, environmental protection, economic progress, and national security.

Yet, our challenges at a nation (and global economy) do not just reside with infrastructure or technology. There is a need to reassess the laws, policies, and governance structures in the context of the current generation's needs. The policies and laws that exist today were written based out of a socio-political-legal that existed twenty, thirty, or more years ago. However, generational needs change as people age, as advancements in science and technology transform how we do business, and as we become more conscious to the world around us. The Sustainability Generation has to be accountable to itself and to future generations by taking a critical look at its infrastructure, technology, policy and law, market incentives and disincentives, education, research, geopolitical relations, and ask itself:

- Are we, as a generation alive "here and now" aligned toward a common purpose?

- Do barriers exist which artificially inhibit our pursuit of our common goals?

- Is the current generation being held back by past generational context or decisions?

- Are we jeopardizing the future of our children?

Government interference in markets, without direct influence on consumer behavior or trade law modification is futile. It will not affect long-term sustainability in a positive way. The dialog and debate in Washington during the summer of 2011 regarding whether, and to what extent, to raise the national debt ceiling is an example. Pushing out the inevitable financial pain does no generation any good. This also holds true for policy issues on energy and environment. The role of government has traditionally been limited to a focus on environmental protection and human health and safety goals. There is no doubt that this has been an essential and effective role for government to serve. We need our citizenry and natural environment to be protected. But, sustainability is broader in its orientation and potential to address social, economic, and environmental needs. Sustainability is about having the generation here and now ask of itself, how we can live, consume, work, and play within a balanced system. This sounds simplistic, but it is challenging to get people to come together, define needs and goals, and determine how to implement for success.

As a starting place, we need to begin asking the right questions and pushing for the most balanced decisions. Not all decisions are ever going to appeal to everyone or toward all of our needs. As an example, in the case of new technologies and the use of rare earth minerals, we have to be cautious not to simply patch up a wound by stitching it short-term, or while a new wound is being cut. Some rare earth minerals offer great efficiency and promise (lithium for batteries to enable lower emission "cleaner" transport). However in a global supply chain these materials may bring with them huge sustainability issues (economic security, waste, materials handling challenges, and so on). While we may solve some issues (mobile emissions), new ones may be created (hazardous waste, environmental liabilities at mining sites). The question we need to ask as we pursue cleaner technologies is, "are we playing a zero sum game, leveraging technology to buy time?" Or, "are we truly solving our sustainability challenges with well thought out innovation, policies, and products that serve our needs today and into the future?"

By being accountable to ourselves, individuals can be the impetus for great change and transformation. Further, individuals (people) are the lifeblood of business. Taking on complex challenges is where business and commerce thrives, and people are the common denominator and beating heart of that natural convergence in the economy. Business will find the right balanced solutions in aligning technology, its people, and processes toward a more sustainable return on investment, and with products and services that society needs, not just wants. The role of government is also essential; but this role needs to work with a stick-and-carrot across all stakeholders, not just a select few. If business is the only one pressured; and if consumers are incentivized; that is a push pull option, albeit limiting. All stakeholders need push-pull to make change. At the heart of this are our behaviors and perceptions on consumption and stubbornness for change. We need to break free from conventional thinking about the past and how that can affect the future. If we exhaust our natural resources, if the country becomes less secure, if we owe too much money to China, and so on, no one will bail us out. We need to reinvigorate a sense of "get it done" in government and in business. But, that sentiment starts with us as individuals choosing to be a part of the change. This also requires a collective generational focus on goals and strategies that we can all agree to. Getting there comes down to a need for leadership and accountability at all levels of society, beginning with individual, and magnifying to government, business, and greater society.

Discover Balance in Financial Controls, Governance, and Leadership

The Sustainability Generation is evolving, in part, due to inefficiencies in markets, lack of accountability, and an erosion of the public's trust in some business, government and financial systems. For the Sustainability Generation to make progress toward creating a better world it must adopt the right balance of financial controls, policies, and leadership to carry out its goals. A systematic approach of plan-do-check-act is necessary for the Sustainability Generation to be effective. The following questions pertain to business; however they can also be applied to public-private partnerships, government agencies, NGOs and not-for-profit organizations, and individuals seeking to lead their own course of self-discovery to define what it means for them to be a part of the Sustainability Generation.

To understand how policy and governance aligns with your sustainability goals, ask yourself: Does your organization have a sustainability policy and governance oversight role/committee? Has a sustainability vision, mission, roadmap, and implementation strategy/plan been developed? Does the organization have a diverse, inclusive and open learning environment? Does the organization have processes/controls in place to inventory, measure, and report on progress and goals?

Understand and Address Risks

Whether your enterprise is a small sandwich shop or a multinational operating in 180 countries, enterprise risk management (ERM) is an essential element of business strategy and for addressing sustainability. The Sustainability Generation operates in a world consumed with risks: natural hazards, terrorism, geo-political conflict, natural resource constraints, climate change, financial market and regulatory uncertainties, staying in-step or ahead of the rate of technological innovation, energy diversity and security, emerging capital markets, and so on. Thus it is prudent and responsible to incorporate enterprise risk management into the Sustainability Generation's enterprises of today and tomorrow.

The questions below begin to frame an approach to explore and manage "enterprise risks" that affect your life and business: Is there a process for identifying, assessing, and vetting risk? Who is in charge of heading up this process? Should you even be in this business from a sustainability (including unknown health, safety, environmental, economic, or societal risk) point of view? How are emerging sustainability issues, including carbon emissions and the cost and availability of natural resources, water, and energy, a potential impact to your business, operations, and lifestyle? How significant is the "green movement" to business performance and profitability? What is the value your employees and communities in which you operate in today and in the future provide toward addressing risk and sustainability?

Innovate to the Societal Value Shift

We now know that there is a societal value shift (SVS) occurring throughout the world. This value shift is multifaceted, and now being embraced by all sectors of the economy, throughout governments, and among all generations and levels of social-economic status. The societal value shift is being influenced by:

- Government Policy and Regulatory Changes
- Global Competitiveness
- Market Access & Differentiation
- Resource Optimization
- Creativity and Entrepreneurship
- Energy Efficiency and Renewable Energy
- Climate Change
- Managing Environmental Legacies and Liabilities
- Public Distrust in Big Government and Corporate Structures

These drivers of the SVS are transforming how we think, behave, and lead. While society is rooted in the present, we are often diligently focused on defining the future through new innovative technologies, business practices, and public policy. Innovation, much like sustainability, is a difficult concept to define, measure, and report. Like sustainability, innovation goes hand-in-hand with:

- Strong leadership
- Alignment with personal, societal, and strategic goals
- An ability to influence conceptual and technical buy-in
- Skilled/qualified/experienced individuals and teams
- Strong project management discipline
- Strong negotiation, communication, and advocacy skills

Like sustainability, innovation is a journey represented by processes and defined by goals. Innovation is strategic and deliberate, yet flexible to allow for creativity and modification. The pursuit of innovation is not simply the development of new intellectual property (IP) or ideas for the sake of creating something new; it is the creation AND realization of new products and services that address the needs of society. Innovation takes form when value is created. Innovation is not just the identification of a need tied to a potential solution. When innovation occurs, a problem is identified AND solved. The quote below from a May 2010 White House Energy Innovation Conference further embellishes the point that innovation needs to be intrinsically tied to social and market needs, and result in the commercialization of technology, to provide society value.

> *"Acceleration of commercialization requires collaboration and reform at all stages of the energy innovation pipeline, from research and development, demonstration and deployment. In the United States, universities and research laboratories are our major centers of research and knowledge generation. Despite our strength in producing knowledge and new ideas, the current system does not allow for the efficient identification of innovations with the potential for commercialization. Moreover, new technologies and insights will not result in commercial impact unless research aims to address relevant issues in the marketplace ... Communication from investors, early adopters, and mainstream customers is critical to ensuring that the research and resulting designs accurately reflect the market needs."*
> —White House Energy Innovation Conference Summary Report
> Prepared by the Ewing Marion Kauffman Foundation
> May 7, 2010[77]

The Sustainability Generation has a profound opportunity to use innovative tools and technologies to enhance human health and our environment. Advancements in novel sensors, information technologies, optics and imaging, electronics, and renewable energy technologies can provide a foundation for modernizing our technologies or constructing entirely new infrastructures that meet the needs of today, as well as the needs of future generations.

The following sequence of questions can be helpful in understanding the role of technology and innovation in the Sustainability Generation: What social needs are changing (or emerging) that are not being addressed by the current state of government or industry? What are the human, natural, financial, technological, and other resource inputs that can be aligned to address the social needs? What opportunities exist to utilize the resource requirements needed to address social needs in the most efficient and effective manner? What are the desired outcomes toward addressing social needs through sustainable innovation that can be measured? What are the desired impacts that innovation can have on addressing social needs over a short, mid, and long-term time horizon? How can these impacts be measured, reported and accounted for? If impacts are not being achieved efficiently or to the scale or degree of intent, what is required to modify and refine the approach? What is the desired end-state for the innovation? Are there numerous solutions to address the social needs? How can solutions work independently and as a system to achieve the desired impacts? What are the quantifiable and non-quantifiable social, environmental, and economic risks and trade-offs associated with the use of technology or the introduction of a new innovation?

The Need to Embrace Civility for a Sustainable Generation

Our responsibility to ourselves and to future generations includes the comportment of ourselves in our public lives and valuing the importance of social civility during political discourse.

In his *New York Times* op-ed column of January 13, 2010, titled "Tree of Failure,"[78] David Brooks wrote about civility in the wake of reactions of politicians and the public to the Tucson, Arizona shooting tragedy that left Arizona Congresswoman Gabrielle Giffords and five other citizens dead, and several wounded. The immediate response of many Americans was to blame the current negative rhetoric of our politicians for the violence toward the Democratic Congresswoman. Brooks joined the call for a greater civility toward each other during political conversations and describes and defines what he thinks civility is:

> . . .So this is where civility comes from—from a sense of personal modesty and from the ensuing gratitude for the political process. Civility is the natural state for people who know how limited their own individual powers are and know, too, that they need the conversation. They are useless without the conversation.
>
> The problem is that over the past 40 years or so we have gone from a culture that reminds people of their own limitations to a culture that encourages people to think highly of themselves. The nation's founders had a modest but realistic opinion of themselves and of the voters. They erected all sorts of institutional and social restraints to protect Americans from themselves. They admired George Washington because of the way he kept himself in check.
>
> But over the past few decades, people have lost a sense of their own sinfulness. Children are raised amid a chorus of applause. Politics has become less about institutional restraint and more about giving voters whatever they want at that second. Joe DiMaggio

didn't ostentatiously admire his own home runs, but now athletes routinely celebrate themselves as part of the self-branding process.

So, of course, you get narcissists who believe they or members of their party possess direct access to the truth. Of course you get people who prefer monologue to dialogue. Of course you get people who detest politics because it frustrates their ability to get 100 percent of what they want. Of course you get people who gravitate toward the like-minded and loathe their political opponents. They feel no need for balance and correction.

Beneath all the other things that have contributed to polarization and the loss of civility, the most important is this: The roots of modesty have been carved away.

The themes Brooks reveals in these few passages including societal (individual and generational) restraint, the need for balance and correction, a call for modesty, and the importance of conversation in society, are each elements of a civil society that has mutual respect and admiration for one another. I have discussed the need to "rebalance your portfolio" to have greater balance and alignment between individual goals and the external pressures that influence our lives. Rebalancing ourselves toward common goals requires a sense of humility, a shared empathy for others around us, and ability for us to carry on a conversation in a peaceful, nonviolent manner. In my strong opinion, achieving a civility in society is critical for working toward sustainability. This point gets back to the "WE" versus "I" in society. Achieving civility means being more tolerant and open to hearing perspectives from a diversity of other individuals.

Civility starts with individual responsibility for how we carry ourselves in our daily affairs and extends to how these behaviors influence those around us, the organizations we work for, and ultimately the greater construct of society. There will always be a push-pull between individual rights, societal needs, and the role of business, government, and NGOs that envelop modern society. How we communicate and interact with one another to solve complex challenges will be the differentiator between attaining an enlightened future, or one that is unbalanced and unsustainable.

As the Sustainability Generation advances, it will be pitted against tough questions, difficult challenges, and a diversity of opinion and perspective. To be effective in advancing sustainability and improving the world, the Sustainability Generation will need to:

- Embrace and advance civility in all its work.

- Openly communicate and carry out conversations that seek

diversity, inclusion, and broad perspective in an effort to align interests, find common goals and objectives.

- Understand the "I" or individual role in "WE" societal opportunities, challenges, and solutions. The "I" has a critical role to play in helping to advance sustainability, by empowering and enlightening others that attributes including modesty, restraint, and frugality can be incredible forces for achieving a greater balance in personal fulfillment and societal well being.

Embrace Your Personal Journey of Self Discovery toward Sustainable Living

I have had the experience of knowing many people who exemplify leadership, innovation and creativity, entrepreneurship and an ability to accept change and make something beautiful out of things we cannot always control.

I believe everyone has a unique role to play either directly or indirectly in achieving individual and generational sustainability goals. Some members of the Sustainability Generation will take significant leadership roles in government that focus on regulatory issues, public policy, and market incentives. Others will be leaders of new innovation, corporate strategy, and better products that enable economic growth with fewer natural resource damages. And others will be watchdogs, engaged citizens, and savvy consumers. Whatever role you embrace, seek to find a balance between your passion and capabilities for contributing to sustainable development. The following quote by Ken Robinson, educator and author of *The Element: How Finding Your Passion Changes Everything,* sums up for me the importance and urgency to strike that balance between your passion for sustainability and your aptitude so that you can lead an enriched and enlightened life, not one that is unfulfilled and centered on entitlement.

> *"It's interested me for a very long time that most people have no real sense of what they're capable of—of what their talents are ... And a lot of people—in my experience, perhaps the majority—live their lives doing things they're not very much concerned with, or interested in."*[79]

—Ken Robinson, Ph.D.
Educator and author of *The Element:*
How Finding Your Passion Changes Everything

The following ten points summarize ways to embrace the personal journey of life so that you can instill a sense of discovery in yourself and those that you accept during your journey of defining and living sustainably.

1. Seek to discover yourself and the world around you.
2. Learn from experience (yours and others).
3. Allow a curious mind to explore.
4. Seek out like-minded others.
5. Learn from those that are not like-minded.
6. Take calculated risks.
7. Don't be afraid to fail.
8. Build and leverage upon your successes.
9. Be innovative, creative, and entrepreneurial in your personal endeavors,
10. Use the art of improvisation to build your character, leadership skills, and the ability to influence.

And remember, sustainability is subjective. From a corporate point-of-view, in my experience, there are ways to put a value (number/metric) on sustainability performance. However, from an individual and generational point-of-view, sustainability is less about finding the right number, and more about a "way of being" individually and participating in a new cultural value-shift and movement that is gaining acceptance by the current generation. Sustainability is subjective as it expands into a generational context of cultural, social, behavioral, and temporal influences. Sustainability involves "you," "me" and "we," all of which are likely to think, act, behave, and decide differently in a variety of circumstances. The important thing to recognize is that sustainability is not an end-state to be summed up by one action, one number, or one report or outcome. It is a state of being that exemplifies a consensus driven process of finding balance, purpose, and meaning in our individual and collective lives. Sustainability is about people, our interaction with one another, and the planet in which we inhabit.

Some of my contemporaries focus on sustainability exclusively from a competitive perspective. They like to measure, rate, and report-out on who are the leaders and laggards in some fictional "sustainability race" to an unknown finish line. Some consultants will suggest they have the answer to sustainability and others create elaborate programs and PR campaigns. All of this has some use, but if the client and consultant are not on the same page regarding the intent of such efforts, these efforts are fleeting, flawed, and irresponsible. The short and honest answer is that none of us really has the answer to sustainability. The best we can do is to try to remove subjectivity from sustainability by working as a common coalition to define what we collectively feel are the true values, goals, and outcomes we want to achieve with the resources available to us. This requires breaking down real or artificial barriers in communication from geography, age, and politics and to have open dialog and critical thinking about public agendas that we all buy into and support. As individuals and citizens we need to focus our attention on our needs, not just our wants. And, we need to come together to define a common platform for progress and renewal.

The world is not limitless. Our knowledge of waning ecosystem services and exhausted "commons" reminds us of the natural resource constraints upon the 7 billion and growing. But our imagination, creativity, and ingenuity are limitless. Humans are the most "conscious" species on the planet. We have the capacity to envision, empower, evaluate, and evolve. George Lucas envisioned a sci-fi future in Star Wars. Steve Jobs helped us to realize the potential of technology by bringing us a family of social communication and "engagement" innovations. We have the beautiful landscape paintings of Frederic Church, and the eerie foreshadowing of a dystopian society by Ray Bradbury in his famous novel *Fahrenheit 451*. Humans are tinkerers, doers, creators, and destroyers. We represent authors, inventors, business moguls, musicians, heads-of-state, educators, parents, builders, and scrapers. We are resilient, resourceful, and revolutionary. But sometimes we take for granted our most important traits: respectfulness, mindfulness, and a collective consciousness that separates us from the plant and animal species. While we can be as destructive and efficient as ants, or as particular and iconic as a Kermode bear, we separate ourselves entirely by having the capacity to think, reason, and advance our intellect. It is only right that we use our creative skills, ambition, passion, and imagination to envision and create a world full of promise, potential, and a diversity and abundance of life.

I find it interesting that many people spend so much time in a virtual environment today. It presents the question: Are we so starved for better real life experiences or relationships that we have to create fictional universes to modify who we are, what we believe, and how we behave? The Internet and creation of virtual Avatars is human ingenuity and innovation in action, but not necessarily at its finest. I'd love to see more young people taking their passion (and pain) they have to the real world to redefine our physical and political landscape to realize their dreams and address their needs with balanced solutions. This is not to suggest those spending time creating Avatars are not spending their time wisely. But perhaps they could take a pause, a moment of reflection and stillness, to consider if we are living to our fullest potential and with a sense of purpose and accountability. The Sustainability Generation is about finding that stillness in one's mind and connecting with others that share your passion and vision for a better future. Sustainability is subjective, but by working together, we can find a common collective purpose and resolve what addresses all of our hopes and dreams.

A Reflection of Our Past: From Silent Spring to In Bloom

One of my favorite places to visit is the State of Maine. It has a classic beauty, rich from its rocky coasts and northern mountains to its in-land lakes and rivers. My love of Maine was nurtured by my parents who took me and my three sisters there almost every year that I can remember for our summer vacation. I have a great deal of nostalgia from my childhood summers in Maine that includes camping, going to the beach, eating saltwater taffy, going deep sea fishing with my father, catching sand sharks, dreaming of being a world-renowned surfer (that never happened!), and enjoying the simple pleasures of summer. I have been to Maine many times as an "adult" with my wife and now our two sons, Owen and Neal. And of all of the places I have visited, there is something that still draws my desire to be back to Maine. Maine carries with it a sense of possibility, intrigue, and wonder. From its natural beauty to its passionate people, Maine is a unique place on Earth. For years the forest and fishery industries of the state were primary drivers of the Maine economy. When I was in graduate school at Rensselaer Polytechnic Institute (RPI) I immersed myself for more than six months in the study of the issues of one of Maine's most notable and complex natural resource: the lobster fishery of the state. In the late 1990s Maine exported more lobsters than any other location in the world. The industry was and continues to be under profound pressure from a variety of economic, environmental, social and cultural influences. In my study of the lobster fishery in the late 1990s, the State of

Maine under the leadership of then Governor Angus King and the Maine Lobstermen's Association (MLA), was taking very proactive measures toward sustaining their fishery.

In my study of the lobster fishery of the State, one of the issues affecting lobsters and other aquatic life has been runoff from the mainland. Preservation of critical habitat, estuaries, and wetlands that naturally cleanse the environment of toxins, is essential for healthy and vibrant oceans and coastal ecosystems. The ability for natural habitat to provide "ecosystem services" such as cleaning our water, remediating our soils, and supporting biodiversity of plant and animal species is, quite frankly, undervalued. The 14,000 acres of protected habitat set aside by the State of Maine and U.S. Fish and Wildlife Service is a model of resource conservation and protection that is critical to enabling this and future generations to achieve our natural resource stewardship goals. Conservation easements and set-asides by private land-owners, land trusts, or through State or federal jurisdiction are enabling a bigger picture to be seen, managed, understood, and valued. That picture is the recognition that we must balance goals of growth and prosperity with restraint and reflection.

One of the natural treasures of Maine nestled on the coast in the Southern region of the State is the Rachel Carson National Wildlife Refuge. The refuge was established in 1966, almost two years after her death from cancer and four years after the September 1962 release of her seminal book, *Silent Spring*. Through her advocacy, passion, and eloquent communication about the impact chemicals were having in the environment, Rachel Carson is credited with formally launching the modern environmental movement. In the process she created a generation of ecologically concerned and conscious Americans. In 1966 the State of Maine and the U.S. Fish and Wildlife Service created the Rachel Carson National Wildlife Refuge to protect valuable salt marches and estuaries for migratory birds. The refuge will contain more than 14,000 acres once it is complete and is located along 50 miles of southern Maine coastline. According to the U.S. Fish and Wildlife Service,[80] *"the proximity of the refuge to the coast and its location between the eastern deciduous forest and the boreal forest creates a composition of plants and animals not found elsewhere in Maine. Major habitat types present on the refuge include forest upland, barrier beach/dune, coastal meadow, tidal salt marsh, and the distinctive rocky coast."*

Silent Spring was written on reflection that chemicals in the environment, namely DDT, were destroying wildlife and killing birds. Fifty years since the publishing of *Silent Spring* the environmental movement that Rachel Carson began can claim a great deal of success. The spring is not silent. Today a Sustainability Generation is now "in-bloom": flowering, pollinating, and producing results. What began by Rachel Carson as a personal commitment to bring accountability to the environment has spawned fifty years of environmental law, policy, technologies, awareness, consciousness, and achievement, including the legacy of the Rachel Carson Wild Life Refuge that brings more than 300,000 visitors per year.

We can get hung up on giving a definition to sustainability. Or we can spend our time and effort by taking immediate action to work toward a common agenda grounded in shared societal beliefs, values, and intentions for meeting the needs of the present that does not hinder the ability of future generations to meet their own needs. A common criticism of sustainability is that it is a "gray" word, difficult to visualize and define. The challenge and responsibility for the current generation of people on earth is to come together to identify, define, and prioritize the clear-cut vision, goals, and objectives of the first "Sustainability Generation" to advance what Rachel Carson began half a century ago.

Chapter Summary

- A generational intelligence grounded in a philosophy of sustainable practices has taken root. With more than forty years of development, this new societal intelligence is beginning to infiltrate our daily decisions, behaviors, and culture in every facet of the economy and personal lifestyle. This new generational intelligence is accelerating the evolution of the Sustainability Generation.

- Change is hard. Trying to define and measure sustainability with so much happening in the world is extremely challenging. But, with deliberate planning and collaboration the current generation can simplify sustainability and make significant strides toward a better future.

- Achieving sustainability is as much a personal journey as it is a societal journey. Just as much as big corporations and government, Individuals need to, assess their role as citizens and stakeholders that can have a direct and profound impact on sustainable development and their quality of life.

The collective "WE" of society, the citizenry of the U.S. and throughout the world, are the underlying common denominator to all global and local sustainability issues. Better technologies, processes, and policies can have a positive impact on sustainability metrics and outcomes. However, people are the ultimate driver and recipient of more balanced sustainability solutions. Together, WE have the intellect, passion, power, and potential to envision and realize a better world.

7

Developing Leadership Skills to Address a New Era of Economic, Environmental, and Social Accountability

The type of personality required to address complex sustainability challenges today and into the future is dynamic. There is no particular academic or professional lineage that will generate the right mix of attributes and qualities sought in sustainability professionals. Working in the field of sustainability is challenging because it takes on different meanings among individuals, stakeholders, organizations, and ecosystems. Developing the skill set and experiences to become a "sustainability professional" has some common elements, but by no means are these professionals all alike. Most sustainability professionals that I have worked with or encountered come from a variety of academic and professional backgrounds. There are however, common traits that exist among the most effective sustainability leaders: an innate desire to learn by questioning the world before them, a goal to lead by taking action on accountability in their own lives, and an ability to leverage by building upon and replicating success. I believe these common personality traits are what differentiate those sustainability professionals who are change-agents from those who are comfortable with the status quo.

These leaders address sustainability from different points-of-view. Presidents of universities and chief sustainability officers for Fortune 500 companies think of leadership in the context of addressing complex systems challenges, including sustainability. A common theme emerges among the following leaders profiled here and among other leaders interviewed in the preparation of this book. Sustainability leaders have personal accountability, strong conviction to their values and morals, and unwavering commitment to supporting the pursuit of excellence and success in their peers and enterprise/organization.

Further, these leaders also balance their professional endeavors with the accountability they have to themselves, their families, and the communities in which they live and work. Leadership, as I have come to understand, is about being *true* to oneself and allowing that truth to infiltrate all that you do and all whom you influence. That *truth* comes in the form of sincerity and authenticity of character, integrity and honesty to oneself and others, and a selfless desire to have the ability to take action to improve the world and those around you.

Table 7.1 presents a sample of the top traits and characteristics that embody both leaders and sustainability professionals:

Table 7.1

Leadership Traits Most Commonly Exhibited by Sustainability Professionals
• A love for complexity • Thirst for learning: curious and inquisitive • Tolerance and ability to manage ambiguity • Desire to share knowledge • Self-starter • Good Listener • Ability to empower those around them • Honesty and humility • Systems thinking • Strong personal values, ethics and morals • Humanistic—a love of people • Ability to define personal goals • Prepared for success • Prepared for risk and failure • Operate knowing change happens • Ability to take action • Accountability to self • Accountability to others • Constancy toward a purpose • Continuous investment • Multidisciplinary and holistic thinking • Empathy and understanding of others • Ability to frame the discussion • Drive others for success and leadership roles • Focused, diligent, and customer minded • Salesmanship

Leaders that are enabling the transition and evolution of a Sustainability Generation through their personal accountability to manage change also share the following characteristics:

- A need for "connecting the dots" in ideas and concepts and in relationships and people and toward igniting their full potential toward new innovation

- Fostering a culture and ethic for taking action, beginning with themselves

- A burning desire to live life with purpose, consequence, and a focus on individual and global betterment

"The best corporate leaders never point out the window to blame external conditions; they look in the mirror and say , 'We are responsible for our results!' Those who take personal credit for good times but blame external events in bad times simply do not deserve to lead our institutions. No law of nature dictates that a great institution must inevitably fall, at least not within a human lifetime. That most do fall—and we cannot deny this fact—does not mean you have to be one of them."

—Author Jim Collins
From *FORTUNE* Magazine, June 6, 2008

The following pages highlight perspectives on sustainability from leaders in industry and academia. The leaders interviewed for this book were deliberately selected because they represent, in my mind, the fundamental building blocks of our society: education and innovation. I begin with perspective from the President of the Rochester Institute of Technology (RIT), William Destler.

The Role of Universities in Creating a More Sustainable World: William (Bill) Destler, President, Rochester Institute of Technology (RIT)

Background: RIT, Innovation & Leadership

Founded in 1829,[81] the Rochester Institute of Technology (RIT) is a privately endowed, coeducational university with nine colleges[82] and institutes emphasizing career education and experiential learning. As of 2010, more than 17,000 students (graduate and undergraduate[83]) were enrolled at the university. And RIT employs more than 3,600 people. The current campus occupies over 1,300 acres in suburban Rochester, the third-largest city in New York. The RIT campus consists of 243 buildings total (5.6 million sq. ft.). RIT is well recognized for its academic programs and reputation (see vignette on RIT Rankings & Recognition) including its 2011 *Princeton Review* ranking RIT fourth nationally for "Top Schools for Video Game Design for 2011"; and its 2011 *U.S. News & World Report* ranking RIT #2 in the North as a "Great College, Great Price."

I began working at RIT in April 2004. Prior to RIT I worked for the New York State Energy Research and Development Authority (NYSERDA) in Albany, New York. My wife Aileen and I share the same hometown, Auburn, located in the Finger Lakes region of New York State. We chose to move from Albany to Rochester in 2004 since the move brought us closer to family, particularly at a time when we were more serious about starting a family. When I began working at RIT I was struck by how applied the university was. RIT has one of the oldest coop programs in the country. The faculty and staff are focused on students, ensuring that they have high quality real-world experiences before they graduate. RIT has grown a great deal during the years I have worked there. New academic programs, buildings, institutes, research thrusts and alliances, and global partnerships churned as if the university were on an all-out drive to demonstrate that it is a world-class institution with global reach, consequential and innovative academic and research programs.

William W. Destler became RIT's 9th president[84] on July 1, 2007. Prior to his inauguration, Dr. Destler was senior vice president for academic affairs and provost of the University of Maryland at College Park. Dr. Destler began his tenure with a vision to take RIT to the next level by transforming it into the nation's first "Innovation University." Dr. Destler succeeded Albert Simone who was RIT President for fifteen years (1992–2007), during which time he left an impressive legacy including: helping to launch Ph.D. programs in microsystems engineering (2002), computing and information sciences (2005) and color science (2007); and spearheading the addition of the Gordon Field House and Activities Center and approved RIT's move to Division I men's hockey (we love our hockey at RIT!).

In his first four years at RIT Dr. Destler made incredible progress elevating RIT's internal assets and external reputation around innovation. Under Dr. Destler's leadership, the "Imagine RIT: Creativity and Innovation Festival"[85] has become an annual phenomenon for the university. In 2011, its 4th consecutive year since it began, the "Imaging RIT" festival brought 32,000 to campus to immerse themselves in the experience of more than 350 exhibits showcasing creativity, entrepreneurship, and innovation. The "Imagine RIT" festival has grown in popularity and attendance year-over-year, and draws a diversity of people, from RIT students, faculty and alumni to others just interested in learning about how universities proactively engage in the advancement of science, technology, and innovation.

The Role of Universities in Advancing Sustainability

I do not recall exactly when I met Dr. Destler for the first time. Our paths crossed on a number of occasions in his first couple years at RIT. In general, I would describe Dr. Destler as a very accessible person, particularly as the president of the 11th largest[86] private university in the United States (measured by student enrollment). He is, in my opinion, a man with great curiosity about the world around him, decisive and deliberate in his actions, very personable and approachable, and engaging and encouraging to students, staff, and faculty. In his inaugural speech November 2007 President Destler began to emphasize the importance of engaging the entire university community toward the critical mission of developing our youth. President Destler stated,

> *"How do we encourage the development of their minds, their hearts, and their souls in such a way that we ensure that the next generation of humans can grow and flourish on this planet? As we work to make RIT a real 'Innovation University,' we will have to come up with good answers."* ...

> ... *"These questions do not have easy answers, but if we can positively address them, the rewards for these efforts for RIT, for the Rochester region, and for our nation will be great, indeed. And the greatest beneficiaries of all will be our students, who will, by virtue of the experiences they have at RIT, become better world citizens while they gain the edge they will need to compete against the world's best. The university that best addresses these*

questions will capture the new 'high ground' in higher education. Given our head-start in so many of these areas, why shouldn't that institution be RIT?"

—William W. Destler
President of Rochester Institute of Technology
November 2007 Presidential Inaugural Address, RIT

Around 2007 RIT began a new academic and research initiative focused on sustainability. The concept was originally envisioned by Dr. Nabil Nasr, a world-renowned expert in the field of sustainability and environmental issues and catalyst in building RIT's expertise in sustainable product design and environmentally conscious manufacturing. Plans formed to create a new "institute for sustainability," a multidisciplinary effort to advance the research, technology, and academic programs for sustainable production of goods and services. In September 2007, with a generous gift of $10 million from billionaire philanthropist B. Thomas Golisano,[87] RIT announced the formation of the Golisano Institute for Sustainability (GIS).[88] At the announcement, B. Thomas Golisano commented on his desire to initiate this new imitative at RIT:

"It is imperative that we accelerate strategies to promote a sustainable society and ensure future generations the opportunity to address their own needs ... For that reason, it is my desire for The Golisano Institute for Sustainability to produce the first generation of professionals with the vision and know-how to deliver on the promise of sustainability, and I am very proud to be associated with this exciting endeavor."

—B. Thomas Golisano
September 12, 2007, RIT

Prior to his $10 million gift to RIT, Thomas Golisano also contributed to other initiatives focused on global natural resource and sustainability issues. For example, he had provided support to the William J. Clinton Foundation, and had been a sponsor of the Clinton Global Initiative.[89] Regarding Thomas Golisano's gift to establish the Sustainability Institute at RIT under his name, President Clinton remarked:

"For the past few years, I have been very proud to have Tom's support for the Clinton Global Initiative, which works to inspire innovative solutions to some of the

world's most pressing challenges . . . One of our most significant ones is the threat of climate change, and I'm very glad Tom is continuing to look for a solution through the creation of this institute for sustainability."

President Bill Clinton[90]

Today the Golisano Institute for Sustainability (GIS), http://www.rit.edu/gis/, is a thriving enterprise well on its way to realizing the original vision of Dr. Nasr. The GIS academic program now has three anchor programs, a Ph.D. in Sustainability, M.S. in Sustainable Systems, and a Master of Architecture. GIS has students in all three programs. In 2011 GIS awarded its two first Ph.D.s[91] in sustainable systems and sustainability. GIS has also anchored itself with state-of-the-art applied technology and research in thrusts including remanufacturing, sustainable production, sustainable mobility, nano-power research, and pollution prevention. Further, GIS is currently constructing a 75,000 sq. ft. building which will be LEED certified (GIS is targeting LEED Platinum certification) and designed to demonstrate sustainable building technologies and energy systems. The GIS building will incorporate a unique infrastructure, a smart microgrid, and computing data center as it envisions being a "living laboratory" of sustainable building integrated technologies and solutions that intersect academic learning, technology research, deployment, proof-of-concept/realization, and acceleration.

I mention the GIS program because it is just one shining example, of how universities, and RIT in particular, are now taking action on sustainability both in their intellectual and research pursuits, and in transitioning student academic programs for a future that is defined by natural resource constraints and a need to do more with less.

From 2008–2010 I was one of eight members that served on the RIT Campus Environmental Committee (CEC), a standing committee of the RIT Academic Senate.[92] During this time the CEC worked on specific charges each year. One of the CECs recommendations during this time period was to have the academic senate and university consider hiring an "environmental coordinator." RIT was experiencing what I would call a ballooning of environmental committees, sustainability working groups, and wide-variety of initiatives focused on sustainability. It seemed between 2006 and 2011 the "green" movement had been reinvigorated at colleges and universities, and in a more substantial way than ever before.

Historically, "green" initiatives at colleges and universities were driven by a small fraction of professors and engaged students.

Grassroots activities often aligned themselves with issues surrounding recycling or "sit-ins" focused on a specific global challenge or issue. But in the past five to ten years something has changed. Universities (as well as corporations, government, and others) have begun to see the value in taking ownership and responsibility for their environmental footprint, and in the process, yielding significant economic and reputational value. In response to growing interest in sustainability on university campuses, the Association for the Advancement of Sustainability in Higher Education (AASHE)[93] was formed in 2006. That same year AASHE held its first conference in Tempe, AZ, with over 650 attendees. By 2008 attendance at the AASHE conference had tripled to over 1,700 participants. AASHE has become a very significant and influential organization. AASHE's mission is *"to empower higher education to lead the sustainability transformation. We do this by providing resources, professional development, and a network of support to enable institutions of higher education to model and advance sustainability in everything they do, from governance and operations to education and research."*

AASHE also led the development of the American College and University Presidents' Climate Commitment (ACUPCC) and was recognized by the U.S. Green Building Council in 2009, along with eco-America and Second Nature (co-developers of ACUPCC) with an award for Leadership in Non-Governmental Organization (NGO) Sector. Sustainability in higher education is not fringe business; it is core strategic business. Universities now recognize that they must compete on sustainability in their operations, reducing their economic spending on energy, water, waste transport, etc.; for reputation, by attracting talented staff, faculty, and students with sustainability focused curriculum and engagement opportunities; in governance, as policies, controls and procedures that foster a sustainability ethic take root at all administrative levels of the university; in reporting, including the internal and external reporting of metrics and progress toward sustainability goals; and in innovation, the ability to leverage the university as leading adopter and integrator of sustainable best practices, technologies, and processes which are also communicated and transferred into the broader community.

The brief summary on AASHE provides additional context to my statement that a "ballooning" of initiatives and programs on sustainability were influencing RIT internally and externally. A recommendation of the CEC was to have RIT hire an individual to take stock of all of these programs, prioritize which ones were the most important, and help RIT define its sustainability mission, goals, and strategy. Further, the CEC envisioned that the individual would begin by aligning all of the great things that were happening internally at RIT together so that the university "story could be told and made transparent to the RIT community" to leverage and expand their efforts for greatest impact.

Parallel to the CEC's charges and external forces like AASHE, there were other significant events happening at RIT. For example, on April 22, 2009, RIT President William W. Destler signed the American College and University Presidents' Climate Commitment (ACUPCC). The ACUPCC commitment is a pledge by academic leaders to move their campuses toward more sustainable programs and practices. Under Dr. Destler's leadership, on April 22 RIT volunteered to take deliberate steps in the pursuit of climate neutrality:[94]

RIT's Steps for Pursuing Climate Neutrality with the ACUPCC

Source: RIT

1. Initiate the development of a comprehensive plan to achieve climate neutrality as soon as possible.
   a. Within two months of signing this document, create institutional structures to guide the development and implementation of the plan.
   b. Within one year of signing this document, complete a comprehensive inventory of all greenhouse gas emissions (including emissions from electricity, heating, commuting, and air travel) and update the inventory every other year thereafter.
   c. Within two years of signing this document, develop an institutional action plan for becoming climate neutral, which will include:
      i. A target date for achieving climate neutrality as soon as possible.
      ii. Interim targets for goals and actions that will lead to climate neutrality.
      iii. Actions to make climate neutrality and sustainability a part of the curriculum and other educational experience for all students.
      iv. Actions to expand research or other efforts necessary to achieve climate neutrality.
      v. Mechanisms for tracking progress on goals and actions.
2. Initiate two or more tangible actions (see sidebar) to reduce greenhouse gases while the more comprehensive plan is being developed.
3. Make the action plan, inventory, and periodic progress reports publicly available by providing them to the Association for the Advancement of Sustainability in Higher Education (AASHE) for posting and dissemination.

The efforts of the CEC to create awareness on the need for a full-time "environmental coordinator" combined with President Destler's signing of the ACUPCC, and other influences led to a decision by President Destler to form a committee in the fall of 2010 to hire a Senior Sustainability Advisor to the President. In October 2010 President Destler asked if I would chair the committee, and I agreed. After meeting with Dr. Destler to hear and clarify what his desires were for the newly created position and his goals and objectives for the Committee. He views sustainability as a strategic element of RIT's future, both in terms of working on the operational context, and to prepare the institute and students for a more competitive future.

A sixteen-member Committee representative of all major segments of the university, including academics, research facilities, human resources, students, and administration convened from November through March. The committee was charged with creating the position announcement, marketing the announcement, developing review criteria for applicants, reviewing applications, selecting candidates for phone and video conference interviews, and ultimately recommending at least three candidates for the president's review. The committee met at a minimum every other week, and toward the end of the process, met every week as final candidates were being reviewed. The process was deliberately made as transparent and open as it could be for candidates. More than fifty applications were received, and the committee ultimately recommended three finalists to Dr. Destler.

In his review of the committee selections, Dr. Destler believed the committee had accomplished the goals he set forth. He and his staff met with the three finalists and ultimately a finalist was selected and hired. Ms. Enid Cardinal[95] accepted the RIT offer to be the Senior Sustainability Advisor to the President and she formally began her position in July 2011. Ms. Cardinal exemplifies the characteristics of sustainability professionals. For the position at RIT the committee sought and found in Ms. Cardinal the following characteristics:

Characteristics of a Sustainability Leader (A university perspective)

- **Leadership**
    An ability to leverage and bring to the university, good external knowledge and professional networks
    Skill at dealing with conflicts, negotiations, and finding common-ground and common-sense solutions for being good influencers and advocates

- **Strong Communication**
  Excellent speaking and writing skills
  Appreciation and expertise in communication and Public Relations
- **Strategic/Tactical**
  Experience with STARS rating system which seems to be the rating system upon which all are converging
  Particularly attracted to the university position because of the reporting structure and ability thereby to optimize their effectiveness
  Resourcefulness in leveraging existing resources to develop programs from the ground up
- **Charisma and Passion**
  Likeable and engaging
  Passionate commitment to sustainability which motivates them to take the initiative to develop programs;
- **Strong Understanding of Sustainability and in the Context of a University Environment/Ecosystem**
  Technical and sustainability literacy
  Appreciation of the potential of the campus to evolve as a "sustainability living lab" and the opportunity of engaging students to move the campus forward, collect data
- **Community Engagement**
  Connection and familiarity with community engagement including desire to understand and collaborate with other leaders in Upstate New York and its singular virtues

  Summarized from the RIT Senior Sustainability Advisor to the President Committee Transmittal Memo to Dr. Destler, spring 2011

Leadership Views on the Convergence of Sustainability & Innovation: An Interview with RIT President Dr. Destler

In July 2011 I sat down with Dr. Destler at his office to catch-up on campus sustainability and to brief him on this book. I began by summarizing my goals and intentions for this book, and what ensued was a great forty-five-minute exchange. Dr. Destler is, in my view, one of those rare leaders that bridges passion with aptitude and vision. With his academic background in applied physics, and professional career spanning thirty years in academia in several leadership roles, he understands "systems dynamics" and the how establishing boundary conditions plays a crucial role in the success or failure in how science and technology can converge as solutions to everyday challenges. His left and right brain collide in his office, and while it is a "president's office" at a university, one feels a sense of warmth and creativity exuding from the walls. And quite literally; a wall of banjos hangs from the west facing wall in his office. Dr. Destler is an avid collector of banjos; however, he would say he is a hobbyist. His collection can be viewed at: http://www.billsbanjos.com/, a website he created to share photos and descriptions of banjos in his collection, along with other vintage instruments he has collected. Dr. Destler, himself, is like a banjo. He's got a bit of twang; a lot of character, attention to detail, and somehow listening to him just feels right.

Dr. Destler spoke about the role of universities in sustainability. Referencing how innovation and sustainability are converging at this point in history, Dr. Destler stated that universities can be the ultimate inflection point of more sustainable technology, practices, and lifestyles. He said, "... take RIT for example: *"On any given day we have 20,000 to 24,000 staff, faculty, students, visitors and others on our 1,300 acre campus. We know the system boundaries of our operations and we have the ability to influence and control this system in a more sustainable manner."*

Dr. Destler was referring to the capacity and potential of a university to be a fixed system that could very deliberately and directly influence its own footprint and demonstrate to the world that sustainable policies, practices, and products could be deployed and work to provide a more enriching experience for all whom interact at the university. As an example of the potential, he described how the university centralized its physical plant for heating hot water and distributing it on campus for enhanced energy efficiency. Further, he pointed out that the magnifying effect of influencing 20–24,000 people is enormous. As universities take leadership roles in a more sustainable future, they will influence the communities around them, and ultimately the broader region and world.

When asked how leaders can influence the behavior of others he said, *"... you have to walk the talk ... take for example the electric Chevy Volt I drive. I could drive almost anything, a Cadillac, an SUV, or something else, but I want to set an example, so I choose to drive a Chevy Volt that uses one-third the energy of a typical sized car. Further the Chevy Volt is an example of how ingenuity and innovation have been brought to bear on a product that focuses on delivering a more sustainable solution to our transportation challenges. Ingenuity, innovation, sustainability, each of these has become pillars of our vision for quality research and academics at RIT. It is important for those that see me to understand that is also what I practice in my daily life."*

The discussion became more focused on the human behavior side of sustainability (or why people exhibit unsustainable behaviors). On one hand, people may not have access to the right data, information or options to make better decisions or have alternatives to a behavior that could be unsustainable. On the other hand, there are underlying and fundamental behaviors that are exhibited, simply because they can be. I asked Dr. Destler what his impressions were of "entitlement" being one of the root causes of unsustainable behavior. I prefaced the question by stating that I was not referring to "entitlement programs" like Social Security or Medicare, but focused on the idea that perhaps past generations and the current generation of citizens, particularly in the United States, have behaved with a sense of entitlement over the environment, natural resources, and even financial institutions.

Dr. Destler agreed stating, "*. . . everyone thinks they are entitled to things like clean water, natural resources, oil and gas, etc. beyond what we really should consume. Right now somebody is eating away at our freedom because we are a society of consumers and not necessarily always thinking about the impact our decisions today have on our future potential to provide a good standard of living to future generations. Europeans don't suffer from this notion of entitlement as much as Americans. They (Europeans) have understood constraints better than we (Americans). Further, there may be an interesting dynamic between male and female perspectives on entitlement. For example, males have associated success with buying a bigger house, more expensive car, and paying for more expensive colleges for their children. Women on the other hand are less affected by the dynamics of success and material goods. They tend to be more in tune with the experience and spirituality side of success than men. Society is a complex thing. There is a level of ignorance in all societies. Take for example the 10 second media blitz where we are fed the most important news feeds in small segments. We try to understand the world around us in simplistic terms, but reality is society is much more complex than that. There is a need for this generation and for leaders in all institutions to do a better job of framing the issues and discussion if we are to move beyond sense of entitlement and toward a more sustainable way of interacting with one another and world around us.*"

Dr. Destler then discussed how the United States has become a society of specialists; and while that is very useful in certain fields like medicine, it can also be a deterrent to having broad knowledge and systems-level perspective of how, for example, clean energy technologies can be deployed as an integrated system that achieves more than any one of the technologies could achieve singularly. He pointed out that there are no silver bullets for sustainability or technology solutions for complex challenges associated with water quality and availability, clean energy, or alternative processes for cleaning up hazardous wastes and producing more sustainable goods and services. Dr. Destler stated that he believes that the solutions will be multifaceted, and require both strong technical and specialty expertise, but also a broader understanding and context of how systems can be tied together. When asked how universities can help develop the next generation of leaders, and sustainability practitioners at that, Dr. Destler said *"we have to incorporate more thinking into course materials in a multidisciplinary way. Right now universities don't do a good enough job of providing multidisciplinary approaches. There is still a great deal of compartmentalized thinking and programs that can inhibit the true potential for universities to provide society with the right answers and perspective when needed."*

Regarding what makes a great leader; Dr. Destler pointed out that *"leaders need to be broadly trained. It is useful for them to have strong backgrounds in technical disciplines and the sciences, however they also must understand and know how to manage the pressures of social sciences, society, statistics, and have an ability to evaluate what is true from untrue."*

Dr. Destler also noted that there is a challenge and dilemma between what is a good leader and a good sustainability practitioner. He said it is a question of balance, ingenuity and personal conduct. He pointed out that in some organizations the sustainability leader should have deep knowledge of the enterprise, the technical and societal challenges, and the array of potential solutions. He said however, the traits of the sustainability professional may be different than other organizational leaders. He stated, *".. there can be a danger putting technology in charge of social scientists."*

The time with Dr. Destler was nearing an end, and the conversation had been very informative, lively, and with great tempo, perhaps much like one of his banjos might sound when played to a favorite song. Dr. Destler summarized by stating, *"... you cannot ignore the real and complex issues of our time. Simple solutions often sound appealing, but more often than not, the issues warrant more than a simplistic view. There are realities that we can sometimes see; like the way a hockey player can skate to wear his teammate will move the puck next without even hesitating. If we know where the puck is moving, we should be staking and moving early."*

I took to heart this last nugget of my time with Dr. Destler on a summer day. I felt the wisdom of a leader whom you get the sense has caught up with the proverbial hockey puck several times in his career. Leadership is in part, sensing the external world to know where it is moving and when, and positioning yourself and your enterprise to make contact with that puck at the right time.

"Truth Speaking" on Sustainability: Insights and Perspective from GP's Chief Sustainability Officer, Bill Frerking

In 2007 Bill Frerking was named by Georgia-Pacific LLC to lead the "development and implementation of sustainability strategies, goals, measurement and reporting across the Georgia-Pacific enterprise."[96] Three years into his tenure as Chief Sustainability Officer, Bill invited my colleague Denny Minano and me to see what he and the Georgia-Pacific team had accomplished, what challenges remained, and where the Company was heading into the future regarding sustainability. What we learned about GP was very impressive. The journey Bill and his team had begun and continues to be on is, in a word, transformational. This profile in sustainability leadership summarizes how the one of the world's largest tissue products producers and one of the largest U.S. forest products manufacturers has created a culture of change, innovation and accountability toward sustainability.

Georgia-Pacific (GP) is one of the world's leading manufacturers of tissue, pulp, paper, packaging, building products, and related chemicals. The company has approximately 300 locations across North America, South America, and Europe, ranging from large pulp, paper, and tissue operations to gypsum plants, box plants, and building products complexes. Some of GP's well known brands include Quilted Northern® and Angel Soft tissue; Dixie® cups and tableware; Mardi Gras®, Vanity Fair® and Dixie® napkin brands; Brawny®, Sparkle®, Mardi Gras® and So-Dri® brands of paper towels; and a suite of recognized and leading brands in the building/remodeling, home and office papers, wood and fiber, gypsum, packaging, chemicals, and professional product sectors.

GP believes in creating long-term value for the company, its customers, and society. Having been acquired in 2005 by Koch Industries, one of the largest private companies in the U.S.GP is now a private company. As such, not a great deal of data is available on GP's financials, but key competitors of the company include International Paper and Kimberly-Clark whose gross revenues for 2010 were $25.1 billion and $19.7 billion, respectively. GP's 40,000 employees are guided by its Market Based Management® principles, which are based on integrity and compliance. GP states, ". . . these principles challenge us to achieve world-class excellence by constantly finding new and better ways to manufacture products and support the needs of our customers."[97]

In December 2010 Denny and I were invited by Bill to brief his team on a variety of external indicators/trends focused on corporate sustainability and enterprise risks. In my experience, the best leaders are always looking for what is on the horizon and have external speakers and thought leaders brief them and their staff. Some call this "kicking the tires"; others simply want a conversation to "true-up" their internal assumptions with the knowledge and expertise of others who experience the world differently from them. This gets at another useful (and in my personal view, critical) trait of sustainability leaders: the ability to conduct external sensing and analysis of multiple stakeholder perspectives to sharpen and refine your sustainability goals, objectives, and metrics.

After arriving at GP's corporate headquarters at 133 Peachtree Street in Atlanta, Denny and I were brought to the 51st floor to meet with Bill Frerking. As Bill greeted us we entered into a shared sitting area, overlooking the streets of Atlanta below. The day was clear and a view could be seen for miles. As Bill talked about Georgia-Pacific, and the view from the 51st floor, I could not help but think about the view from Olana[98] in Hudson, New York. Olana was the home of Fredrick E. Church, one of the famed Hudson River School Painters.[99] Olana sits on 250 acres in what is called an "integrated environment of famed Hudson River School painter Frederic E. Church: Art, Architecture, Landscape, Farm and Views." The Olana estate is now managed by New York State, and was one of the many picturesque locations used by the Hudson River School to create their mid-1800's landscape paintings that were "characterized by fidelity to nature; clarity of detail; skies sometimes glowing at sunrise or sunset, sometimes shining a sunny, clear blue; nearly invisible brushstrokes; an overall feeling of tranquility; and a presentation of the American landscape as a new Eden in a benevolent universe, blessed by God and providing an uplifting moral influence."[100]

There was something about the way in which Bill Frerking spoke about GP's history in the context of the view from the 51st floor that was much like looking at the past through one of the beautiful landscape paintings by Church or one of his Hudson River School colleagues. In Bill's words there was attention to detail, incredible vision, a story of American innovation and ingenuity, and a company steered by the morals and values of leaders that understand that their products are rooted in natural resource stewardship. Since their founding in 1927, GP has understood and respected the essence of value in sustaining its primary commodity, wood fiber. The long-term stewardship of renewable resources like trees is and has been an essential pillar of GP's corporate strategy since their founding in 1927 to today; and a pillar of growth and sustainability into the future.

Looking out at the Atlanta landscape from the GP headquarters, Bill rhetorically asked, *"What do you guys see?"* He went on to add, *"... there are trees, and many of them."* And he was right; the surrounding area had a good density of mature trees. Bill pointed out that the land use surrounding Atlanta, and throughout the U.S. has changed numerous times in the past century. In fact, much of the land we were looking at out of the GP headquarters was once used for agriculture, namely cotton fields and working plantations. But, by the mid-1950s, tree plantings had begun to take over many vacant, dormant, or underutilized agriculture lands. According to researchers of the Warnell School of Forestry and Natural Resources at the University of Georgia,[101] "under the 1956 to 1960 Soil Conservation Reserve Program (Soil Bank) 693,499 acres of new pine plantations (afforestation) were planted on former cropland in Georgia ... and under the 1986 to 1992 Conservation Reserve Program (CRP) 645,931 acres of new pine plantations (afforestation) were planted on former cropland in Georgia." Further, University of Georgia researchers note, "... since 1981, Georgians have replanted nearly 5 million acres in trees to ensure that future forests will continue to support our economy and environment in this sustainable use." Additional facts on U.S. forests are shown in the vignette.

Facts about U.S. Forests

- One-third of the United States is forested—751 million acres.
- Sixty percent of all forestland in the U.S. is privately owned.
- Privately-owned forests supply 91 percent of the wood harvested in the U.S. State and tribal forests supply approximately 6 percent and federal forests supply only 2 percent of the wood used by the forest products industry.
- Over 25 percent of private U.S. forestland is certified to one of three sustainable forestry management certification systems: the Sustainable Forestry Initiative, Forest Stewardship Council, or American Tree Farm System, as compared with 10 percent of forestland worldwide.
- Insects and disease threaten 58 million acres of America's forests.

- A single tree can absorb more than 10 pounds of CO2 each year.
- In the U.S., forests and forest products store enough carbon each year to offset approximately 10 percent of the nation's CO2 emissions.
- Private landowners in the U.S. plant about 4 million trees each day— five trees each year for every man, woman and child in America.
- Two-thirds of the nation's drinking water comes from forests.

Source: American Forest & Paper Association (AF&PA), http://www.afandpa.org/

Bill reflected the trend from GP's point of view, noting that companies which are dependent upon fiber (trees, pulp, and wood) resources learned to grow their businesses in step with the availability, growth rates, and renewable resource potential of forests and trees. Thus it is in the short-and-long-term interest of companies and communities to be good stewards of their natural resources.

Bill noted that there are many dimensions of sustainability for businesses. At a basic level is our ability to meet the current generations' needs with the resource constraints we have today. Bill pointed out that businesses dependent on fiber resources have developed their own standards for sustainability, long before the word took on a contemporary meaning or justification. GP's current "Statement on Forest Protection and Sustainable Practices,"[102] shown below summarizes the comprehensive governing principles that the company holds itself to in conserving forests and fostering sustainable forestry practices.

Georgia-Pacific Statement on Forest Protection and Sustainable Practices

FEBRUARY 2008

http://www.gp.com/aboutus/sustainability/forestry/forest-policy/downloads /GP_Statement_Forest_Protection_Sustainable_Practice_2008.pdf

Georgia-Pacific believes in creating value by making its customers' and consumers' lives better and contributing to prosperity in society. Georgia-Pacific strives to manufacture needed products while consuming fewer resources and maintaining a healthy environment. Through collaboration with customers, suppliers and environmental non-governmental groups, Georgia-Pacific has been able to update its policies to incorporate practices that are consistent with its desire to act responsibly and remain a good corporate citizen.

Forest Protection: Georgia-Pacific supports the value of preserving the world's unique and endangered forests and maintaining forest diversity. Accordingly Georgia-Pacific makes the following commitments:

- Georgia-Pacific will work actively on the definition and mapping of endangered forests and special areas. As endangered forests are identified, Georgia-Pacific will not source fiber from these areas. Georgia-Pacific will prioritize its efforts to identify endangered forests and special areas in its key supply regions, including the Southeastern United States.
- Georgia-Pacific will not procure pine fiber from plantations established after July 1, 2008, on sites that were natural hardwood forestlands immediately prior to their conversion. Additionally, Georgia-Pacific will continue to offer information and education on natural regeneration options to forest landowners.
- Georgia-Pacific will closely monitor its supply chain so that customers can be assured that wood and paper products are not sourced from endangered forests or plantations established on sites that were natural hardwood forests immediately prior to their conversion as set forth above.
- Georgia-Pacific agrees with the principles set forth in the Canadian Boreal Framework (CBI) as a long-term, collaborative, and science-based approach to identify, map and protect endangered forests in the boreal region.
- Georgia-Pacific will encourage its Canadian suppliers to participate in the CBI.
- Georgia-Pacific will not procure fiber from the Tongass National Forest until Roadless Areas, identified there in the 2001 Roadless Area Conservation Rule, are permanently protected.
- Georgia-Pacific will support initiatives to address conservation, restoration, education and promotion of sustainable communities and wise stewardship in the Cumberland Plateau region.
- Georgia-Pacific will not knowingly purchase illegally harvested or traded fiber and will maintain procedures to communicate this to our suppliers and will require documentation of the legal origin of imported wood products.
- Georgia-Pacific will not purchase native tropical wood products from sources in Indonesia until measures providing Georgia-Pacific assurance of legal harvesting and endangered forest protection are in place.

Sustainable Practices: Georgia-Pacific supports credible forest certification programs and is committed to sustainable practices. Accordingly, Georgia-Pacific makes the following commitments:

- Georgia-Pacific will continue regular third-party certification of its wood and fiber procurement practices across all of its operating areas. Summary results of audits will be periodically made public and available to interest groups and stakeholders.

- All things being equal, Georgia-Pacific will give preference to wood certified by established and recognized certification systems.
- Georgia-Pacific will continue to require its timber suppliers to be trained in sustainable forestry practices.
- Georgia-Pacific will continue to require adherence to both mandatory and voluntary state Best Management Practices (BMPs) during the harvest of any timber supplied to Georgia-Pacific facilities.
- Georgia-Pacific will continue efforts to increase the use of post-consumer content in its products, to the extent it meets consumer needs, to a goal of 50% post-consumer recycled fiber within Georgia-Pacific's total recycled fiber supply system.

Georgia-Pacific will continue to participate in the industry effort to recover 60 percent of paper consumed in the United States by 2020.

GP's corporate history and current market position exemplify Bill's points. In 2001 GP sold its timberland assets. It now sources its wood and fiber supplies from private, institutional, industrial and public entities. One of the ways in which GP continues to grow and achieve its fiber needs in a decentralized fiber supply model is by balancing the use of virgin and recycled fiber while meeting the needs of its customers in a superior fashion. GP is one of the largest makers of tissue products from virgin and recycled fibers. The price and availability of virgin and recycled fiber directly impacts GP's growth, but by having large capacity to work within both commodity streams the company is able to remain competitive and balance the trade offs, opportunities, and limits of the market.

GP is the one of the nation's largest recyclers of paper products. The Company is a member of, and working with, the American Forest & Paper Association (AFPA), on an initiative to recover 70 percent of the paper consumed in the United States for recycling, by 2020[103]. According to AFPA, in 2010, 63.5 percent of U.S. paper consumed was recovered. The GP Harmon Recycling[104] division is strategically helping the Company achieve new growth through opportunities in recycled fiber markets. For example, GP has two of the largest recycled mills in the world. And, these assets are paying off.

As the conversation with Bill advanced, he provided what I personally believe is one of the more succinct and eloquent definitions of sustainability that I have heard. I have heard Bill speak before and since, at executive workshops and conferences, and each time I hear him, I am reminded of this eloquent definition I paraphrase below:

> *Sustainability is largely based upon one's world view, which is what is available to a person at one point in time. And, it is also rooted in a philosophical orientation of individuals, which drives many different points-of-view on what sustainability is and is not. From a social dynamic and point-of-view, Maslow's hierarchy of needs has a great deal to do with sustainability, and the current world view someone might have. Sustainability, at least as considered in industrialized countries, is a wealthy society priority. A key question we have to always consider, as citizens and corporations is—who gets to decide what is sustainable? . . . For example, who has a better knowledge and interest in managing forest/fiber resources? . . . accountability is essential in defining and pursuing sustainability, and it comes down to this . . . sustainability is about finding the balance between the trade-offs associated with managing the three classic dimensions most commonly cited: social (people), environmental (planet), economic (profit/equity) . . at any given point in time, we need to ask ourselves as citizens and companies, what is the balance of these three dimensions? . . . From GP's point-of-view we ask of ourselves, what is our role in helping society balance these three dimensions? How do we look ahead and ask the most probing questions? And how do we get the organization to see the change that is happening in the marketplace and take a position on taking action?*

This brings many rich ideas together. The clarity and most consequential concepts involve the idea that sustainability is about finding the right balance between the trade-offs associated with different decisions we as consumers, citizens, corporations, governments and others face. Given that sustainability is largely subjective and depends upon one's world-view, economic status, or relationship to Maslow's hierarchy of needs, there is not a one-size-fits-all definition, approach, or solution for all sustainability-related questions. There is often not a right or wrong answer, just different points-of-view. The challenge for the Sustainability Generation is to find ways to reach a balance in how we work together, and in the pursuit of shared options that address the trade-offs that come with every challenging sustainability decision. With the myriad of social and environmental issues linked to hydrofracking in the Finger Lakes and other regions, responsibility for stewardship of end-user products, management of carbon and climate, development of Alberta's oil sands, management of fishing rights in the North Atlantic, the use of agriculture (food) products for biofuels, there are no shortage of complex challenges that impact the three dimensions of sustainability.

As Bill Frerking put it, "finding that balance" in the context of the current generation's needs and with an outlook to the needs of future generations is essential when working toward sustainable solutions. GP's perspective on balancing the three sustainability dimensions is further defined below:

GP's Three Dimensions of Sustainability

"Georgia-Pacific believes sustainability has three dimensions—social, environmental and economic. In making business decisions, we try to find the right balance among the three dimensions and achieve the following outcomes.

Social dimension Helping make people's lives better through the products we make, supporting the communities in which we live and work, maintaining quality work environments, and sourcing responsibly.

Environmental dimension Using resources wisely, complying with laws, minimizing the impact of our facilities by operating in a safe, responsible and efficient manner, and reducing the adverse impact of our products in use.

Economic dimension Maintaining profitability; managing the cost to customers and consumers to use our products; making products that are preferred in the marketplace; positively impacting our communities through local purchases of goods and services, taxes, and other community support.

Source: GP, http://www.gp.com/aboutus/sustainability/introduction/sustainability-overview/

Bill also stated that there is a need for more "truth seekers" in all facets of sustainability: government, industry, NGOs, citizens, and foundations. He noted that there are organizations and people that focus their time and effort exclusively on shaping and positioning around a "point-of-view" (POV). While POVs are necessary, they do not always seek to find that shared and common "balance" of competing resources or trade-offs. In my experience working with hundreds of people working on "sustainability" from corporate, government, NGO, academic, consultant, and other perspectives, Bill is 100% correct. Too often projects come to a halt because stakeholders cannot come to a balanced common agreement. When one POV is pushed too strongly, and is not in line with a balanced solution, decisions can be delayed, or even ended altogether. Truth seekers spend their time, skills, and leadership striking the balance between the three sustainability dimensions. They point out information or data deficiencies, and also prepare themselves and their teams to have the most respected and validated information available when making decisions. Truth seekers are not "yes" people or "no" people—they are "we" people that try to use their ability to ask the right questions so that stakeholders can agree to a common vision and goals, and then work toward a balanced decision-making.

> **"Georgia-Pacific creates long-term value by using resources efficiently to provide innovative products and solutions that meet the needs of customers and society, while operating in a manner that is environmentally and socially responsible and economically sound."**[105]

In a conversation about "the role of corporations in enabling sustainability in society" Bill stated that companies, including GP, play a significant role toward three objectives:

1. **Identifying Choices (balance of options)** Helping navigate and determine the most optimal choices, considering all of the trade-offs, in a dynamic marketplace.

2. **Aligning Stakeholders, Innovating and Partnering** Helping align those interests that are best positioned, based upon sustainability trade-offs, to provide, or innovate if necessary, the best solutions toward societal needs.

3. **Competing for the Right to Do Business** Competing on marketplace needs while continuously striking the balance between the sustainability dimensions and trade-offs.

In Bill's POV, the marketplace is the arena in which needs will be balanced with the suite of products, services, policies, etc. that infiltrate citizens everyday lives, particularly from a sustainability perspective. He states, *"... in a free society, the role of citizens as consumers and decision makers is the ultimate expression of social value ... in a sense, consumers vote with their pocketbooks, and the marketplace and price of goods and services will strive for balance."*

From my POV, the role of government, industry, research organizations, foundations, and other stakeholders are critical within this context. While the role of government can be viewed as unbiased, objective, and in the interest of the public, this is only true to an extent. Checks and balances work. However we have all seen how partisan politics can dilute, divert, and restrict the true role of government and intent of its citizenry. Some might point to the Obama administration's health care legislation as a case-in-point of a highly partisan legislation that will have a significant impact on society, yet it does not fully achieve the outcomes intended for recipients that many wish government could have provided in a more balanced, even transparent way.

Bill also stated that corporations, including their people, products, and policies, are largely a reflection of larger society. He noted that *"the companies that provide consumers with the most value, most efficiently will be the most profitable and sustainable."* Figure 7.1 presents this as a formula for competitive and sustainable success.

Figure 7.1
Quantifying the Value of Business Sustainability
Leadership & Performance
Created by Mark C. Coleman

most value **+** greatest efficiency **= Superior long-term profitability**

⸻⸻⸻⸻⸻⸻▶ time ⸻⸻⸻⸻⸻⸻▶

Bill stated that understanding the marketplace and determining the best way to create the highest value for society in our products, is part of corporate strategy for GP and other successful corporations. Because the marketplace is dynamic, its needs are continuously changing. Under Bill's leadership in sustainability, GP is continuously sensing the external marketplace, ensuring the value they build into their products is in check with the expectations of its customers. If it is not in check, then products are not purchased, market share declines, earnings expectations are not achieved, and revenue and income are lost to another company that more fully addresses the current marketplace needs. The Enron debacle is a classic example of the checks and balances that exist within the marketplace. Frerking stated, *"Enron was built upon the illusion of value. For corporations to fully appreciate their role in sustainability they need to have their virtues in place, and the right mix of talent to work toward balancing the trade-offs of growth and long-term sustainability."*

I have often believed that the marketplace and interrelationships of corporations and their supply chains is much like an ecosystem. That ecosystem is always in flux, changing, inventing, and becoming more efficient. Ecosystems seek, like Bill's reference to sustainability, a certain amount of balance. In balanced ecosystems there are producers and consumers, checks and balances, and a system that tries to achieve continuity, not always by design, but through its efficient functioning. Bill noted that manufacturers are very well positioned in the marketplace because they are the ones that must balance the trade-offs associated with the three dimensions of sustainability. If manufactures are well-positioned, they will do well, if not, they will do poorly.

Again, Frerking noted, "... manufacturers deal with contamination, safety, resource use, liabilities and risk, financial and human capital, and other elements that need to be balanced if they are to provide value in the marketplace, and remain in check with the social expectations of the current generation ... at GP we identify value-drivers of sustainability in key markets and then look across the manufacturing enterprise for opportunities to align with that value including in the design of new products, sourcing of raw materials, manufacturing footprint of our operations, packaging and logistics of getting products to market, and in the consumer use phase of our products."

In retrospect, while the past 100 years of industrialization has had many environmental challenges, the "corporate" ecosystem is, in my view, becoming more efficient and balanced with (reflective of) the needs and morals of society. As one dimension, more companies are ISO 14000 certified than ever before. Companies are also defining their corporate sustainability vision and goals, and in many cases, like GP, taking specific actions to achieve its vision. And, there are more and more companies designing and commercializing products and services that seek to optimize the use of natural resources, reduce energy consumption, and minimize environmental risks and impacts. Examples of how GP has begun to take action on sustainability in its products and operations are presented below. It is impressive to see how this privately held company continues to innovate toward market needs and expectations and in many cases, above and beyond competition.

Taking Action on Sustainability: Examples of Balancing the Sustainability Dimensions at GP

- Georgia-Pacific Wood I Beam™ joists use 40 to 50 percent less wood fiber than 2x10 or 2x12 dimension lumber without sacrificing performance. Constructed from oriented strand board and sawn or laminated veneer lumber (LVL), engineered products like Wood I Beam joists, GP Lam® LVL, FiberStrong® rim board and other engineered lumber products are excellent for floor and roof systems. They also use wood from smaller trees, resulting in more efficient use of forest resources.
- Georgia-Pacific's unique dispensing systems for paper towels, tissue, napkins and soap have been proven to reduce consumption in away-from-home environments. The enMotion® towel and soap systems, EasyNap napkin and SmartStock cutlery systems work by controlling the amount and format of towels or product dispensed. The enMotion "touchless" towel dispenser reduces waste at the source, improves hygiene for consumers and reduces paper waste by 30%.
- Georgia-Pacific is the largest producer of recycled away-from-home tissue products, offering a broad array of products that contain up to 100 percent recycled fiber. The company's Envision® line of washroom and tabletop products meets or exceeds the U.S. Environmental Protection Agency's recommended guidelines for total and post-consumer recycled fiber content.
- Georgia-Pacific's Recycled Copy and Print paper and Spectrum® Recycled Multi-Use paper contain 30% post-consumer fiber.
- Consumers who want paper towels and napkins with recycled content can choose Georgia-Pacific's Mardi Gras® brand.
- Georgia-Pacific's Toledo, Ore., containerboard mill is recognized as being better than 90% of similar mills in the nation when it comes to efficient water use. Yet, in response to a drought, the mill additionally reduced water consumption by 2 million gallons/day.

Source: Georgia Pacific

Bill and I also broached the subject of employee engagement and empowerment, and how employees (and everyday citizens) can take action toward sustainability. We spoke about the need for instilling not just "knowledge" but also "behavioral norms" in society. Bill noted that in the United States we have many cultural/societal norms, but we have much further to go to instill norms that can have a positive impact on our generational sustainability. Bill came back to the idea of "truth seeking" and noted that it is important for citizens and society to try to stay away from the "myths of sustainability," as he put it.

He gave the example that many Americans may feel, based upon mis-information and perception, that use of recycled fibers is always more sustainable than the use of virgin fibers. In reality, recycled fibers are a processed raw material that has additional value in a number of applications. However, life-cycle assessments have shown that neither recycled fiber nor virgin fiber is significantly environmentally advan-taged over the other for use in paper products.

Frerking also aptly noted that taking action on sustainability does not always have to mean that all parties have to compromise their goals to achieve balanced decisions all of the time. He pointed out that there are limits to the information any citizen or company will have, and that while we ultimately seek balance in the decisions we make, sometimes one has to look at how real-value is crated over the long-haul. And that may go beyond consumers' ability to articulate their needs into the future. Thus Bill noted, *"Focusing on long-term profitability and working to create long-term value means that sometimes our business isn't aligned with the popular view, tide of public opinion or current trend in the market. It requires that we do our homework, challenge our assumptions and points of view, and be willing to accept that some people aren't going to be happy with our positions. Alternatively, humility, intellectual honesty and expe-rience require that we acknowledge that our positions could be incorrect, and we can't predict the future any better than others can—our competitors, customers, non-governmental organizations and governments. But honestly striving for long-term value creation is what sustainability requires us to do, and understanding what purchasers' value long-term is very important."*

It is Bill's belief that *"empowering people to take action as they see fit, within the rules of the law"* is an essential element of helping a culture of sustainability take root within business enterprises, and throughout general society. Bill has done an incredible job of empow-ering his staff and others at GP, which has resulted in fostering the culture of change within the company.

In reflection about the time spent with Bill and learning from oth-ers at GP, I see clearly the role personal accountability has played in their journey and transformation. While sustainability has been part of this nearly century-old company since its origins, the company has taken a new-age approach to sensing marketplace needs and ensuring value is portrayed throughout its portfolio of products and services. GP employees are engaged, empowered, and happy to be personally accountable to the success of the company for the long-term. Balancing the three dimensions of sustainability is becoming more complex (and critical) as large companies like GP try to deliver high quality value-added products to society in the face of energy price volatility, heightened demand and competition for natural resources, and shifting consumer behaviors and preferences. To ensure long-term competitiveness, personal accountability is required more than ever at the corporate employee level to sense, analyze, and take action on marketplace drivers and trends impacting the future viability of the modern corporation. Sustainability leaders like Bill Frerking are change-agents, helping their organizations leverage their key assets, their people, to be a critical part of serving the needs of the current generation. The reward at the end of the day is the ability (because the market allows for it to happen) for the employees to reengage and continue their evolution with the marketplace.

What Bill has accomplished at GP is as picturesque as one of those Fredrick Church paintings. When I visited him in Atlanta in 2010 it was clear that his vision and leadership extended throughout the GP organization, into corporate communications, business units, operations/ production, supply chain, executive management, and beyond. If achieving sustainability were measured by the authenticity, "truth telling", and value creation it can bring to an enterprise (and society), Bill's efforts and team within GP would be first in class in many regards. In the past decade I have visited many companies and met with several chief sustainability officers of public and private corporations. Some companies are very flashy with their public relations and programming about sustainability. However, when you look for the depth within the painting, one finds very little behind the public positioning of these masters of persuasion and perception. Yet there are firms like GP that are strategic, tactical, and focus first and foremost on delivering value to its customers, employees, and society.

The pursuit of sustainability is not an altruistic endeavor for companies like GP. It is a fundamental business strategy. GP understands that earning the social license to operate is the first dimension of sustainability, and essential to the long-term competitiveness of its brands, businesses, and capacity to serve the marketplace. And it is the marketplace (individual citizens) that ultimately determines which companies to continue to support, or not, with their hard-earned dollars.

GP wants to be around for another 100 years, and it wants to be a part of choosing its future. As Bill Frerking summed up, *"GP wants a sustainability story it chooses to have, not one it gets stuck with."* His point is well noted. The depth behind GP's sustainability journey is real, tangible, and grounded in strong morals and values that come from leaders like Bill Frerking and the management at GP's parent, Koch Industries. Creating a culture of change in any organization is very challenging. Many small-and-large corporations are, like GP, going through their own sustainability journey with their eyes wide open. What I like about GP's approach is their enterprising and market-driven culture that understands the who, what, why, and how of value creation as a necessary requirement for earning society's trust and delivering products and services that meet the needs of today and address the growing constraints on future generations.

Xerox: Ready for Real (Sustainable) Business: a Conversation with Patty Calkins, Vice President, Environment, Health and Safety

A Personal Reflection on Xerox

I have a strong personal affinity for Xerox as a company. I don't want that statement to bias this profile in sustainability leadership, but it is true. During graduate school at Rensselaer Polytechnic Institute (RPI) I completed a coop experience with Xerox in their Environment, Health and Safety (EHS) division, and what was called their Market Leadership Group. The opportunity was located in Xerox's Webster, New York large manufacturing complex outside of Rochester.

At Xerox, I spent my time in the Market Leadership Group doing research, analysis, and internal reporting on global eco-labeling programs, emerging and stakeholder issues, and a variety of special projects that aided the Market Leadership team's goals and objectives. The experience was very rewarding for me and my first real-world understanding of how large corporations operate, behave, and innovate. I did not pursue any employment with Xerox after I graduated from RPI. At that time in my career I felt a need to understand the inner-workings of government, and thus took an opportunity to work for the New York State Energy Research and Development Authority (NYSERDA). I would not return to the Rochester region of New York for five years when I chose to take a position with Rochester Institute Technology (RIT) working within their Center for Integrated Manufacturing Studies (CIMS), an applied research and technology organization focused on enhancing the competitiveness of manufacturers in New York and the nation. Like my desire to obtain experience in government, my career led to RIT because I also wanted to spend time under-standing the research and applied technology world. Being at RIT brought me closer to Xerox again, and in the years since living in the Rochester region, I have watched Xerox struggle and succeed.

As have many corporations, Xerox has undergone corporate restructuring and change to position itself to be as competitive as possible in a global marketplace. Xerox has a long history in the Rochester region of New York, and given my personal experience, appreciation of, and affinity for the company, I have chosen to pro-file them and their sustainability leadership in this book.

Xerox: Ready for Real Business

All companies and organizations update their branding and image from time-to-time, particularly to reflect any changes in their culture or the marketplace. Dating back to 1906, Xerox has gone through many iterations of reinvention in its approach to branding. It's most current slogan, "Xerox: Ready for Real Business" reflects the compa-ny's recent integration new businesses into its portfolio, and which have a heavier focus on information technology (IT) services. The global economic meltdown impacted all companies in the 2008–09 timeframe, and Xerox was not immune. However, due to strategic business acquisitions, cost-control measures, and a commitment to delivering high quality products and services, the Company boosted sales by close to 30% in 2010, helping it curtail the 14% decline from a year prior. For example, in 2010 Xerox acquired business process outsourcing, IT service and financial management company ACS for approximately $6.4 billion. The acquisition paid-off, tripling Xerox's service-based revenue, from $3.5 billion in 2008 to approximately $10 billion in 2010.[106] While Xerox is best known for its color and black-and-white copiers, 80% of its revenues actually derive from post-copier sale sources, including maintenance, consulting, docu-ment management and outsourcing services, consumable supplies, and financing. In recent years, Xerox has been putting much more emphasis on its portfolio of multifunction devices which can have a profound impact for its customers with regard to financial spend, environmental footprint, efficiency and productivity.

On September 28, 2007, I published an article on my blog, *"World Inc. For Better or For Worse?"* titled, *"Looking for Social Response Leadership? You Might Consider 'Copying' Xerox."*[107] I replicate the blog posting here as it captures the essence of Xerox's entrée into multifunctional devices that save energy, money, and material resources. I wrote the article after hearing Xerox's Vice President for

Environment, Health, and Safety, Patty Calkins, talk at a leadership breakfast series called "Liberty Hill" put on by the president of Rochester Institute of Technology. After hearing Patty's talk, I knew Xerox was entering a new age of growth and profitability based upon how they were (and continue to be) positioning to compete for sustainability. In 2007 I was working with colleague Bruce Piasecki, who had published his 6th book, *"World Inc.: When it Comes to Solutions —Both Local and Global—Businesses are Now More Powerful than Government,"* on researching and writing case examples where companies were beginning to align their business strategy toward competing on sustainability and what Piasecki calls "social response."

This is just one dimension of how Xerox is creating new value for its shareholders, customers, and society and in the context of advancing innovative products and services to address the resource constraints of today's generation. My conversation with Patty Calkins, in the late summer of 2011 and summarized below, helps reveal other dimensions in which the Company is embracing sustainability as a core ethic and business strategy.

Xerox: Ready for Real (Sustainable) Business

It was a delight to catch-up and talk with Patty Calkins in the summer of 2011. Our conversation covered a lot of ground, from how to engage the younger generation to filling a void in talent within large corporations, to how to create corporate sustainability strategy that has internal buy-in and accountability and external marketplace action and value for customers and society. The thread throughout the conversation however comes back to accountability at the individual, organization (corporate) or generational (societal) levels.

In 2011 I published an excerpt from this book with GreenBiz.com titled, *"The Silver Tsunami vs. the Green Wave"*[108] which focused in on the projected large-scale of retirements that are anticipated to occur between 2010 and 2020 as Baby Boomers get to their retirement age. My assumption in the article, qualified by many within industry and government, is that mass retirements may leave a gap, or void in knowledge and experience within many major institutions and critical business sectors (including energy, chemicals, infrastructure, transportation, etc.). If this gap truly exists, how much of an impact will it have on the economy, environment, and society at large? Is it really an issue or just a perception that is being fueled by fear of the unknown?

Looking for Social Response Leadership? You Might Consider "Copying" Xerox

Originally published, September 28, 2007,
http://worldincbook.blogspot.com/2007/09/looking-for-social-response-leadership.html

The company is best known for its copier machines, making its brand synonymous with photocopying, much like Kleenex is synonymous with tissues. Xerox is a "document company" with high-end printing and publishing and multifunctional devices with can print, copy, scan and fax. Xerox also develops the consumable supplies like toner, paper and ink as well as value added services like software and workflow services. Key competitors of Xerox include Canon, HP, Hitachi, IBM, Lexmark, Ricoh, Sharp and Toshiba.

Xerox has a long history of innovation, social responsibility and environmental excellence. Just recently the company announced that they provide $1 million to the National Academy Foundation's Academy of Engineering Initiative through the Xerox Foundation to support the study of math and science in grades 9–12, with the goal of preparing students for advanced study in engineering disciplines. The National Academy Foundation (NAF) is a partnership between business leaders and educators to prepare students for professional careers. The Xerox Foundation also recently announced that they are funding fellowships for a three year period at MIT with a $1 million grant in the areas of green innovation, imaging and smart document technology and nanotechnology. With a focus on the future of engineering, Xerox's investments in our youth are socially responsive gifts, and ones that will likely yield future innovators.

Like many companies, in the 1980's Xerox was very focused on risk mitigation. But during that time they were also an innovator as the company introduced the first "power down" photocopying machine in the industry to save their customers electricity. Xerox also launched a toner health study to better understand the long-term health impacts of toner on employees, customers and tech representatives. In the 1990's there was a big focus on eco-efficiency. Xerox launched their comprehensive remanufacturing program and working to get their products back to place into new products. Xerox also became ISO 14001 certified during the 1990's. In the mid-1990's the company implemented chemical restriction standards (1995) and integrated EH&S into their product development process (1996). In the 2000's the company made more of a transition toward "Global Sustainable Growth" and began implementing paper supplier requirements (2003). They have also established GHG reduction targets (2005), signed the electronic industry code of conduct to ensure they are not causing global issues, and have partnered with the Nature Conservancy (2006) on sustainable forestry practices.

According to the World Wildlife Foundation, more than 36 million acres of natural forests are lost per year. Xerox is one of the world's largest brand distributors of cut-sheet paper. So Xerox has established a paper sourcing policy (2000) and committed to sound EHS practices and sustainable management in their own operations and those of their paper and product suppliers. Xerox works with its paper suppliers to focus-in on forestry practices (adhere to sustainable forest management standards). In paper mills they certify that environmental practices are managed and that they operate free of chlorine. In the product use phase the company ensures that paper is used efficiently by manufacturing machines have duplex capability, and that reliably operate with recycled paper. Xerox focuses in on sustainable forestry through performance requirements, third party assurance and certifications (e.g., FSC, SFI, CSA).

Xerox, like most multinational firms with global supply chains, vast manufacturing operations and stakeholders, is impacted by several environmental and social drivers. For Xerox these include: (1) climate change and energy, (2) preservation of clean air and water, (3) preservation of biodiversity and the World's forest resources, and (4) waste prevention and management. To address these global challenges Xerox has:

- **Innovated** a high-yield paper that reduced pressure on forests because more of the tree goes into the paper. The paper (and product process) uses less total energy, uses fewer chemicals and water, is lighter weight and contributes to lower GHG emissions and hazardous air pollutants.
- **Partnered** with The Nature Conservancy through a $1M three year partnership to strengthen practices to conserve the world's forests. Goals of the partnership include demonstrating measurable progress in protecting forests and providing lasting solutions for environmental sustainability.
- **Reduced** air emissions from operations by 93% from 1991 to 2005. Xerox products sold in Europe now meet the European Union's RoHS standard, and all of the company's global manufacturing facilities are certified to the environmental management standard, ISO 14001.
- **Designed** Waste Free Products and Waste-Free Facilities through reduce, reuse, and recycle strategies. Xerox designs products for recovery and remanufacture with the objective being zero landfill. In doing so the company has achieved in diverting more than 2 billion pounds of material from landfill. In addition, Xerox's energy efficient design of products and manufacturing processes reduce economic costs and mitigate climate change risks. Xerox was the first in its industry to launch remanufacturing strategies for its products resulting in asset recover, waste minimization and conservation of natural resources.
- **Enabled** efficient paper use and paper sourcing leading to a more sustainable paper cycle through design and sale its multifunction and copier technologies and global Paper Sourcing Policy.

All of this resource conservation, asset recovery, recycling and product stewardship result in minimizing environmental risks and impacts and save Xerox several hundred million dollars per year. In addition Xerox's environmental strategy promotes positive brand awareness and serves to ensure full market access, resulting in more bids & tenders and more product/service sales. By incorporating energy saving and environmental features into their products and services Xerox is able to help their customers achieve their own corporate environmental goals.

According to Patricia Calkins, *Vice President of Environment, Health and Safety*, Xerox's environmental commitment is central to their sustainable development approach. Xerox seeks to reduce their environmental footprint along their supplier value chain as well as meeting regulatory compliance and reduced footprint of their manufacturing operations. In doing so the company has a top line focus on providing sustainable value to customers and stakeholders. The company seeks top line growth with products and technology services that solve environmental challenges, social problems and that improve economic conditions in the developing world. The company invests in their people and their communities and also nurtures a [better] world through more sustainable investment, innovation and market leadership that builds shareholder value.

In a world that loves documents, Xerox products and services continue to serve a growth market. The company is innovating new products, services and manufacturing operations to continually stay competitively relevant, but just as important, **socially responsive**. Seeing the social need in products is an innovative trait of a company. And, Xerox portrays the traits of what we call a "World Inc." company, one that recognizes social response product development through strong leadership and governance.

In fact, Anne M. Mulcahy, CEO notes "To Xerox, sustainable development is a race with no finish line. It requires leadership that sets high expectations and clear direction. It takes employees that embrace Xerox values and innovation that constantly pushes the frontier of what is possible."

Xerox has found success in leading a greener revolution in the document management industry, and its strategy and implementation are worth copying ... on recycled paper of course!

Some of these issues were raised with Patty during our conversation. She is of the belief that there is a gap in knowledge that comes with retirements, and perhaps the uncertainty associated with that gap is a risk factor that all institutions need to address. She noted that many companies in the United States have not been growing in the past decade as briskly as in the 1980s and 1990s. And, for those companies not growing, Patty noted that many were actually retracting, decreasing their workforce. She said when companies retract; it can be a double edged sword. On one hand, many companies need the experience of mid-career professionals to remain competitive,

yet they have cut many positions and talented individuals. She pointed out that new college hires don't yet have the experience to replace
seasoned executives. As companies lose their talent and fail to fill
that void, they can become more vulnerable, perhaps less competitive. If companies are not seeding themselves with younger talent
while growing within, ultimately the chasm between the older generation and younger widens, perhaps making the "silver tsunami
effect" (impact of mass retirements) a much bigger impact than it
needs to be for some enterprises.

Suggesting that part of the challenge are the incentives and structure of the U.S. education system, Patty stated, *"for so long in the
U.S., the educational system and pay structure (within companies)
have valued MBA's ... those completing more difficult curriculum
requirements in engineering and sciences have not traditionally
been valued as much by the market."*

Patty's point was that the marketplace can sometimes distort its
own needs, and if that distortion perpetuates, true innovation and
competitiveness within corporations and for the nation as a whole,
will suffer. Students have choices as they map out their futures
including what degree(s) to earn at colleges and universities. And
enrollment figures and graduations rates of certain degrees (MBAs,
attorneys, healthcare professionals) often mimic market demand,
and where the market is willing to pay more. But as Patty suggests,
this market-based approach to education can have negative impact
on the knowledge and skill set required for companies to compete in
a global economy. If the market is flooded with MBAs, and companies
need to innovate through science and technology, a gap in our competitiveness potential is created. Patty suggested that as incentives
and pay structure better align with the needs of society (companies
and government), perhaps more graduates with a solid background in
science, mathematics, and engineering will result. This is not to suggest that the value of an MBA is diminished, but that a core challenge
in the past decade and longer has been building a strong capacity in
science and engineering graduates—which U.S. companies need
more than ever to enable innovation and new products and services.

When I asked whether she felt if the younger generation was
more or less ready to take on critical sustainability challenges of its
time, Patty noted *"the younger generation is more sensitive to
social, environmental, and economic issues, and at what seems to
be an earlier age .. the awareness of young adults on sustainability issues is there, but there remains a naiveté with them ..
that is true of any younger generation, it is human nature to be*

more altruistic and have a desire to take on the world when you are younger."

Similar sentiment has been shared with me by educators in K–12, colleges and universities, and hiring managers in government and industry. The younger generation is, through social media, the Internet, and their social circle, seemingly more aware of the world around them, particularly certain sustainability challenges. But, as a K–12 teacher once told me of her 6th grade students, *"the awareness is there, but the knowledge can be superficial. The students understand that renewable energy may be less polluting that coal fired power plants, but they don't yet see that renewable energy also has costs, impacts and challenges. It is as they see the quick fix, but don't yet draw out a level of critical thinking to further justify their judgments."* College and university professors have shared similar anecdotes of their incoming classes of freshmen. It is as if the one-dimensional solution clouds the younger generation's ability to dissect the real issues.

Patty also went on to add, *"there seems to me, less of the younger generation willing to roll-up its sleeves and put in the time to learn today . . . there are so many distractions to their attention and time; we need talented individuals that know not just how to access information, but what to do with it once they have it."* There is no doubt that each generation has a different way of learning, engaging with society, and demonstrating action and value. Generational research conducted by the Pew Research Center in 2009 noted that 70% of older people believe they have better moral values, and 74% of older people believe they have a better work ethic than those younger than them (see Figure 7.2). A February 2010 report, *"Millennials: A Portrait of Generation Next,"* by the Pew Research Center characterized these differences, *"Not only do most Americans agree that young and old are different when it comes to values and morals, but most people feel that older people are superior in this regard. Regardless of age, about two-thirds or more of the public believes that, compared with the younger generation, older Americans have better moral values, have a better work ethic and are more respectful of others."*[109]

Patty also noted that she is seeing more of the Baby Boom generation begin to ask themselves things like: What matters to them the most? What defines their lives? What meaning are they getting from their career and daily activities? There is much written on the psychology of aging and transitions we experience in life as we age. My conversation with Patty made me visualize this with the help of the following Figure 7.2.

Figure 7.2

The Values Gap between Young and Old
Who has better values ... ?

Source: Pew Research Center Social &
Demographic Trends survey report, "Forty Years
After Woodstock, A Gentler Generation Gap,"
August 12, 2009.

As shown in Figure 7.3 , as we transition through life through age our needs change, as do our thoughts, behaviors, and consciousness about the world around us. The Sustainability Generation is alive and exists in all phases of life. Understanding life transitions can aid in bringing all generations together to understand each other's perspectives, needs, and purpose ... and to advance our collective goals toward a more sustainable lifestyle.

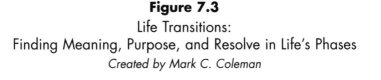

Figure 7.3
Life Transitions:
Finding Meaning, Purpose, and Resolve in Life's Phases
Created by Mark C. Coleman

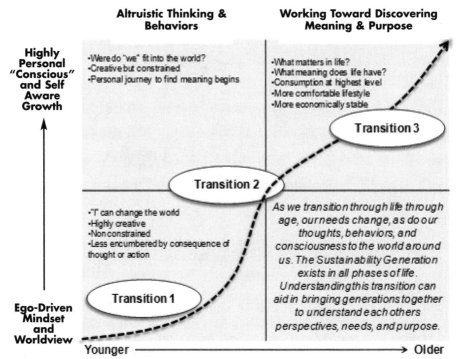

There are challenges the Sustainability Generation needs to acknowledge and address, like engaging our youth to embrace their personal accountability as citizens and students to develop the skills to think more critically about themselves, their futures, and the world around them. I'm of the belief that the younger generation has to go beyond the glamour, sound-bite, and façade of contemporary issues like sustainability, and dive deeper into accountability and personal action. This statement by the way holds true for all generations, as those in power are often the biggest offenders of this as they seek out paths to stay in power, focusing only on short-term gain, often dismissing long-term agendas and needs. Imagine the impact the younger generation could have if they chose to go beyond the "2-or-4 year election cycle" or the "24–7 consumer mentality" or the "breaking news coverage" political and media blitzes that infiltrate a typical day in America. Freeing up the mind from the onslaught of reactionary media and attention seeking is one way we can instill more critical thought, discovery, and action toward societal needs with positive consequence.

With the younger generation in mind, I asked Patty her perception of the traits and skills of a sustainability leader. She noted, *"sustainability leaders embrace ambiguity and different ways of thinking ... those that are successful can integrate multiple variables and stakeholder inputs into their thinking and actions, further they have a strong ability to incorporate systems thinking and dynamics internal and external to the organization, understand life-cycle perspective, and are always working toward organizational effectiveness"* Patty went on to add, *"... sustainability professionals have a love of complexity, but can translate that into workable elements so that those that don't understand the complexity can more readily see where they add value ... successful sustainability professionals need to do both, they need to translate complexity into workable elements and deliver on value for the enterprise. They have the ability to translate complex concepts into simple actionable components."*

Patty noted that in many ways the translation of marketplace, regulatory, and societal complexity into business strategy is the beating heart of sustainability for corporations. She went on to state, *"... corporations want to be in it (serving the needs of society through their products and services) for the long-haul. For this to happen society has to be around, the economy has to be around, natural and human resources have to be around ..."* Her point is well taken. It is self-fulfilling and necessary for companies to have markets (customers), resources to grow, and a social license to operate. Without any of these elements the company will not succeed. Thus, at a very fundamental level, sustainability is ensuring the elements by which a corporation exists, are functioning well (if not abundant), and balanced. Patty also noted that most large companies that have been in existence for the past thirty years resonate with environmental, health, and safety issues and programs. She stated however, *"... the social dimension of sustainability is an element that people are just starting to understand."*

I asked Patty how Xerox has begun to define, take action on, and embed sustainability as a core ethic within its changing business structure. She said the Company has been very engaged and accepting of sustainability conceptually, and as it has been defined toward the Company vision, values and strategy, sustainability has taken on a new dimension. Patty noted that in the 2009–10 timeframe she took some of Xerox's executives through "... *a journey to begin thinking about the business differently.*" She pointed out that senior leadership at Xerox was supportive of the effort, from the CEO to the sustainability council that was appointed assembled to explore how the Company would address sustainability. Patty noted, "... *getting your peers to think about this new, seemingly ambiguous topic in the context of their respective part of the business groups, the internal value change, and brought clarity that sustainability is both a risk and opportunity for Xerox ... once others saw how the complexity of sustainability could be disaggregated and simplified, and that it fit within how they saw the world, conversations on how the Company could more tightly integrate into business strategy began.*"

Patty went on to define the approach she took. She said that a sustainability council was convened comprised of executives from a cross section of the company. The council agreed on a three phased approach: (1) Coaching Workshops that brought the council and others up to speed on sustainability, trends, emerging issues and implication to their current business strategies; (2) Scenario Planning workshop that immersed executive in one of four very different worlds and culminated with identifying common moves/themes that traversed all four worlds (3) Evaluating potential moves and prioritizing efforts to tightly integrate critical sustainability dynamics into the business.

In facilitating this internal strategy process Patty was pleased to discover that there was no shortage of interest to participate within the company. The net result of Patty's internal leadership and facilitation efforts was a clearly defined sustainability agenda and action plan for the Company, and an executives engaged and ready to be accountable toward a new strategy that would integrate sustainability throughout the Xerox enterprise including its supply chain and through to customers. Some of the areas of emphasis in which Xerox has begun to integrate into its sustainability program include:

- Compliance & Risk Management
- Meeting Stakeholder Expectations
- Creating and Delivering on a "Shared Value" Approach to Business

- Integrating Sustainability into Strategy and throughout the Service Side of the Business

Patty reflected that there are many exciting initiatives underway with the company and that *". . . integrating sustainability into the service side of the business is the Holy Grail . . . services can enable decoupling of revenue from material streams, provide new capabilities for customers without adding more stuff, and an ability to do more with less."* As an example, Patty summarized how Xerox is now getting into the transportation market with its information technology and other business service products that can help reduce traffic congestion, make parking easier and more efficient, and enable better asset and resource utilization, particularly in large transport markets like New York City. Patty said this is all part of the rebranding and refocus of Xerox to be "Ready for Real Business." By freeing up resources (internally and for customers), and by leveraging and extending the company's existing "culture of innovation," Xerox is not just "Ready for Real Business," but "Ready for Real Sustainable Business."

Patty's sustainability journey at Xerox is significant and cannot be understated. People, through their personal accountability, leadership, and influence, are the reason change is embraced or pushed away. Xerox is lucky to have Patty and her team as their internal anchor to understand and translate ambiguity into workable elements. They guide others make sense of market changes as they facilitate dialog and influence and enact strategy to enable the company flourish in this new economy. I'm eager to see how Xerox advances in the IT space, particularly as it helps customers improve their efficiency, productivity, and sustainability footprint.

Strategic Succession Planning: Addressing Enterprise Risks While Developing the Next Generation of Innovative Companies and Sustainability Leaders

Introduction

The number one asset for organizations competing in a global economy is its people. But typically the value of human resources is diluted as current affairs, emerging issues, and the woes of the marketplace cloud critical and strategic (deliberate) planning to maintain and enrich these critical assets. As companies try to save money in this global recession, many are opting to not replace senior staff when they retire, or hire staff with less experience. In some industries, the short term gain from lower operating expenses may be a net long-term competitive disadvantage.

I have pointed out that beginning this year, every day 10,000 Baby Boomers will turn 65 and will continue to do so for the next for 20 years; and by 2030, almost one out of every five Americans—some 72 million people—will be 65 years or older. There is a simple fact alarming to many organizational leaders reaching retirement age: a large portion of senior leadership within government, corporate, and non-government-organizations (NGOs) will be transitioning out of their positions in the next five years. How can these organizations and their existing leadership develop a strategic succession plan to embrace the new generation of leaders needed to address issues of constraint, growth, enterprise risk, innovation, and sustainability?

People Make Business Go

Numbers and statistics can paint many pictures, often causing undue anxiety about the state of the present and our fate in the future. Over-simplification of certain trends like the aging workforce is equally dangerous. A lack of care and concern over the impact of organizational change in the wake of retirements could leave many companies ill-equipped to effectively achieve their business strategy. In a nutshell, the transition of the older generation out of certain careers and the advancement of the younger generation into their shoes is an enterprise risk that can impact reputation and image, business continuity, and fundamental pillars of business value like quality, performance, price, and overall competitiveness.

The beating heart of every organization is its people. People innovate and make these complex systems work, providing them purpose and life, enhancing their value and reputation, and working to ensure safety and compliance so that their enterprise continuously earns the right to do business in the eyes of society. Many people I work with are in leadership positions, Vice President's of Environment, Chief Sustainability Officers, CEOs, CFOs, and others. The leaders in these positions, from early-stage innovative companies going to market for the first time, or very mature multi-billion dollar Fortune 500 companies, share a certain amount of concern over succession planning, and what the next five years will bring. Their concern is for their own positions and who will fill their shoes, but also for the entire enterprise, where for some companies thousands of highly skilled employees that have been with a company for twenty, thirty, or more years will be retiring. This issue transcends senior management, mid-level management, and all operational employees of the organization. And, the issue is not just about the loss of technical and highly skilled labor, but also a loss in corporate knowledge, culture, and identity; and in worst case scenarios, deterioration of product/service quality and value to customers.

Managing Enterprise Risks: The People Factor

As an ever-present enterprise risk, managing the talent of the organization is essential to do as frequently as possible, to minimize or altogether avoid crisis events with the long-tail of uncertainty that crisis management that can cause. Obtaining concrete data and information on the enterprise vulnerability and resiliency to changes in workforce status is essential to curtail any "crisis event" that could occur with the loss of knowledge and practical experience when employees transition to retirement. Too often "perceptions" of what is happening in the enterprise rule out analysis grounded in data, facts, and active "sensing" of the employee base.

Companies can skirt some challenges working in a world of perceptions; but those perceptions become a hard reality if when triggered by crisis events. During times of an industrial accident, natural resource damage, product liability, or financial and governance concern, it is essential to tap the institutional knowledge of experienced staff and executives. The long-tail of crisis management (see Figure 7.4) is often best managed by those who have had a great deal of exposure to enterprise risks, stakeholder relations, and crisis management in their career. This supports the need to have a balance of knowledge, experience, and ingenuity throughout the organization at any given time.

Many of the risks associated with projected exodus of a knowledgeable workforce can be addressed with strategic succession planning for every level and responsibility within the enterprise. Through the use of strategic succession planning and action plans, organizations can dramatically reduce their enterprise risks associated with the retention or loss of their human capital. Further, succession plans can ensure continuity in business operations during times of growth and constraint.

Figure 7.4

When "perceptions" matter most

Created by Mark C. Coleman

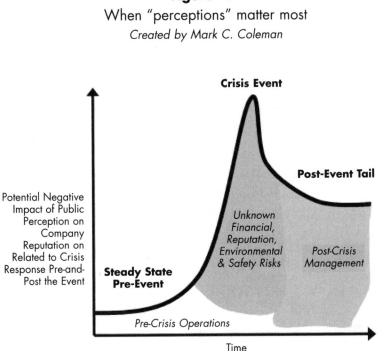

Strategic Succession Planning: Strategy and Sustainability

No one-size-fits-all approach to strategic succession planning exists. However, there are general ground rules and context that organizations can put into their plan to fully assess their human resource needs and requirements and define what their needs will be in the context of their corporate strategic plan. Figure 7.5 summarizes three essential corporate elements to consider when defining succession plans: governance, processes and people.

Corporate governance policies and procedures help to define and ensure the enterprise is working within the rules that ensure compliance, accountability, and transparency. Senior management has much of the responsibility for governance. However organizations need to continually reinforce governance procedures throughout the enterprise, particularly during times of business transition or vulnerability, and in particular, during times of employee turnover. Corporate processes involving data, metrics, reporting and disclosure, and compliance are also susceptible to disruption during transitional periods. These essential processes need to be made transparent, accessible, and teachable so that the next generation of employees can quickly and effectively work within these processes to ensure business continuity and growth. Finally, strategic succession planning envelops the people side of the enterprise, perhaps the most important asset of all.

Figure 7.5
Strategic Succession Planning
Created by Mark C. Coleman

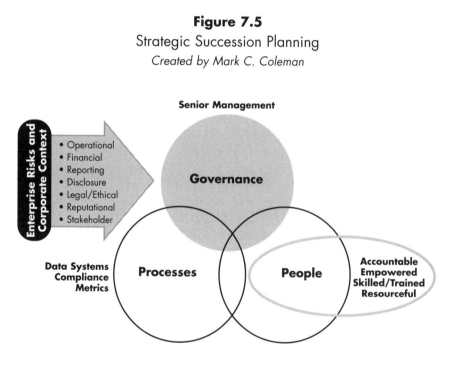

Without the right people, governance and processes fail to function as intended. People need to be knowledgeable and experienced, but they also should carry values and traits that enable them to be accountable, resourceful, resilient, and empowered to effectively work cross-organizationally and with external stakeholders. The nature of business has become more complex. Enterprise risks transcend operational, financial, reporting, legal, ethical, reputational, and stakeholder influences, opportunities and challenges. As such, the skill set for high-functioning employees is shifting.

Many hiring mangers I have interviewed for this book tell me that they continue to seek highly candidates with disciplined technical expertise (candidates with strong backgrounds and academic degrees in science, engineering, mathematics, etc.) The hiring managers also are looking for individuals that are systems thinkers, strong communicators, and natural collaborators with tolerance for ambiguity, and who have strong values and judgment to work independently and in cross-functional roles. Hiring managers seeking "sustainability talent" are looking for a strong balance of skills, capabilities, personal motivation and values in their new strategic hires. This comes as no surprise, not just because the internal and external drivers influencing modern business are transforming and in some cases more complex, but also because organizations are constrained by capital and seek multi-faceted talent that can effectively do many jobs.

The evolving pursuit of sustainability within organizations also supports the need for active and ongoing strategic succession planning. Sustainability has taken a front-and-center role in defining new markets, products, and competitive differentiation within many corporations. Companies including GE, BMW, Xerox, Green Mountain Coffee, Method Products, FedEx, CSX and Duke Energy have incorporated strategic sustainability planning and market facing innovation and technology into their business. For some companies, their strategy is directly tied to the employee experience and their leadership development. For example, through their Smarter Planet and Corporate Social Responsibility (CSR) initiatives, IBM engages the talent of their workforce on specific societal issues and in an effort to have tangible resources impacting change. IBM's CSR website notes:

> "We focus our community engagement and corporate service programs on specific societal issues, including the environment, community economic development, education, health, literacy, language and culture. These are areas of urgent societal needs where we can apply IBM's technology and talent to solve problems, rather than simply making cash donations. We believe that direct action and collaboration, not spare change, are the path to real change." [IBM, http://www.ibm.com/ibm/responsibility/]

In 2011 IBM celebrated its 100th year in business. In recognition of this achievement and demonstration of its commitment to global service, the company is aiming to have all of its employees, some 400,000, donate a minimum of one day toward community service. IBM has also deliberately tied global service to leadership development programs. Since 2008 the company has operated its "Global Enablement Teams (GET)." The GET initiative matches four to five senior IBM executives with local IBM management in developed and developing countries with the goal to advance their strategic focus, leverage corporate knowledge, and develop regional expertise networks. The IBM GET program is one example of several internal initiatives they are using to educate and train the next generation of sustainability leaders, and by leveraging the existing capabilities, know-how, and knowledge of their senior executives.

Many companies have also begun to define senior management and mid-level management "sustainability officer" roles to ensure their pursuit of sustainability is seeded with the best and brightest talent, and with capabilities to ensure maximum benefit and success from their investments.

Competitive Advantage and Succession Planning

The reasons corporations seek out these leadership traits in new talent in sustainability and other corporate functions is deliberate and grounded in competitive differentiation and advantage. Strategic succession planning is about finding, acquiring, training, and supporting the right people for the right positions during the right times in the evolution of the organization. Figure 7.6 summarizes, from a "strategic sustainability" viewpoint, how competitive advantage can be achieved. While governance controls and the best processes can create and define the steps for achieving differentiated business strategy, people are the means by which competitive advantage is truly achieved or not. Thus, integrating succession planning, within the current and projected operating environment for the company should be tied to strategic business planning to balance the minimization of any adverse impacts from enterprise risks tied to people while maximizing the potential for competitive differentiation.

Enterprise risks are often thought of external factors impacting the current and future state of the business. But, enterprise risks are also internal, and can be tied to the "perceptions" people have about their span-of-control and influence within the business. For example, in the first third-to-half of the past three decades corporate environment, health, and safety (EHS) professionals did a monumental job demonstrating their value, role, and purpose to senior management. Originally criticized as a cost-center, EHS has now evolved to a high functioning center of service and in some cases, technology excellence that support all elements of the business: product developers, supply chain, business units, customers, finance and reporting, etc. In the past decade sustainability has taken precedence for many corporations.

The skill set, training, and experience for chief sustainability officers is much different than that of those in "more traditional" corporate EHS roles. However, many EHS professionals feel their value to the company has been proven, tested, and validated and that their role maps directly to sustainability. This perception is somewhat true.

Figure 7.6

Enterprise Opportunity:
Achieving Sustainable Competitive Advantage

Created by Mark C. Coleman

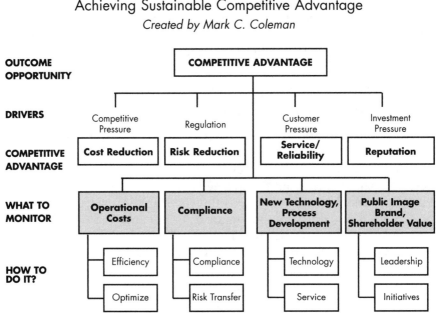

Their value may have been demonstrated, but there may be a gap in how senior management views the traditional role of EHS compared to the more dynamic nature of sustainability on the company. Thus, corporate EHS professionals that feel they have a distinct advantage to envelop corporate sustainability have to, as they did in the past three decades, demonstrate to senior management why they are the inhouse organization to lead this newer corporate charge. There are systematic processes and options for EHS, or other corporate organizations (i.e., HR, Legal, CIO) to determine whether they have the right mix of talent in place to address current and future organization human resource needs. Options for being accountable to Strategic Succession Planning needs and requirements:

- ***Assess Organizational Needs*** This requires alignment with the strategic business plan and strong consideration of external drivers on the business, including risk factors, shifts in the global regulatory environment, volatility in commodity markets and supply chain, trends in transparency and reporting, and greater requirements for stakeholder engagement and achievement of voluntary standards or customer requirements.

- ***Identify Talent Gaps*** This requires a review of existing position responsibilities, titles, scope of influence, pay and benefits in the context of talent development and management. As the enterprise transitions through the economic recession, internal staff can be developed so that the enterprise has the right balance of critical and leadership skills to position sustained long term growth.

- ***Partner for Long Term Talent Development*** A number of organizations can aid the enterprise in managing and developing its talent pool including trade associations, professional development organizations, colleges and universities, peer-to-peer knowledge and leadership networks. Partnering, for example, with universities to design and develop customized training and education modules to serve your enterprise growth needs can be a strategic way to help ensure retention and development of top talent.

- ***Develop and Take Action on the Strategic Succession Plan*** Establishing a strategic plan requires organizational buy-in and commitment at all levels of management. Taking action requires accountability and follow-through.

- ***Evaluate, Forecast, and Refine*** Succession planning and talent management require ongoing review and resolve. The marketplace, stakeholder needs, role of technology, regulatory environment, and pursuit and execution of innovation are never static; these business influences are always changing and evolving with society. By evaluating, forecasting, and refining succession planning in context with existing and expected enterprise risks can keep organizational human resources efficient, effective, and timely.

Summary on Leadership Development

A global convergence is occurring between science, technology, policy, and market opportunity. This convergence is challenging the current generation to work toward more efficient utilization of financial and natural resources throughout industry and government. As this convergence evolves, the external influences on corporations intensify. Internal capacity to manage these influences in-step with their development is a business priority. A major society shift is underway. Mass retirements pose an enterprise risk as well as an opportunity for corporations to ensure they have the right talent to deliver on the strategy of the corporation today and also keep the company competitive into the future.

The timing of this sea-change comes at a vulnerable, critical time. Globalization, economic pressures, the uncertainty around carbon and natural resource availability, and global development concerns all circle the future disposition, strategy and requirements of the modern corporation. Businesses are made efficient by technology and processes, are compliant through policy and controls, and are competitive through relevant and value-added products and services. Front-and-center in this business context is the need to have the right people in the right positions at the right time.

Chapter Summary

- If people are the beating heart of the Sustainability Generation, then strong leadership is mind, passion, and vision.

- Leadership, as I have come to understand, is about being true to oneself and allowing that truth to infiltrate all that you do and all whom you influence. That truth comes in the form of sincerity and authenticity of character, ability to take-action, integrity and honesty to oneself and others, and a selfless desire to improve the world and those around you.

- Leadership in sustainability comes in many forms, personalities, and people. There are numerous traits that are generally shared however among leaders, and in particular, sustainability leaders. These traits are not prerequisites for those seeking careers in sustainability. But, these traits are common threads in those that demonstrate leadership, tact, and success over time.

- There is a continual need to educate, train, and foster leadership skills development in all facets of society and the economy.

- The greatest risk to our society, economy, and modern institutions is a lack of and educated, trained, and socially conscious workforce and citizenry. For the Sustainability Generation to be successful, it will require strong leadership in government, in politics, in business, in not-for-profits, and from everyday citizens choosing to live a life full of purpose, passion, and curiosity.

Endnotes

FOREWORD ENDNOTES

1 http://gbo3.cbd.int/.

2 www.unreasonableinstitute.org.

3 http://www.nytimes.com/2011/11/07/opinion/krugman-here-comes-solar-energy.html.

4 http://www.wind-works.org/articles/DardesheimGermanys RenewableEnergyCity.html.

5 http://energybusinessdaily.com/renewables/san-francisco-to-have-100-renewable-energy-by-2020/.

6 GS Sustain 22 June 2007 http://www2.goldmansachs.com/ideas/environment-and-energy/gs-sustain/index.html.

7 Nidumolu, Ram, Prahalad, C.K, Rangaswami, "Why Sustainability is Now the Key Driver of Innovation," *Harvard Business Review,* Sep - tember 2009, Reprint R0909E.

8 http://www.unglobalcompact.org/news/42-06-22-2010.

9 http://sloanreview.mit.edu/feature/sustainability-advantage/.

10 https://api.twitter.com/#!/BardMBA.

PREFACE ENDNOTES

11 Epinephrine injection is used to treat life-threatening allergic reactions caused by insect bites, foods, medications, latex, and other causes. Symptoms of allergic reaction include wheezing, shortness of breath, low blood pressure, hives, itching, swelling, stomach cramps, diarrhea, and loss of bladder control. Epinephrine is in a class of medications called sympathomimetic agents. It works by relaxing the muscles in the airways and tightening the blood vessels. To learn more see, http://www.ncbi.nlm.nih.gov/pubmedhealth/PMH0000211/.

INTRODUCTION ENDNOTES

12 Source: Thomas L. Friedman. From his Op-Ed *New York Times* Column, "This I Believe." Published December 1, 2009. http://www.nytimes.com/2009/12/02/opinion/02friedman.html.

13 Source: Quoted in Richard Kostelanetz's 1988 book, *Conversing with Cage.* (New York: Limelight Editions, 1988).

14 The Conservation of Natural Resources; From Theodore Roosevelt's Seventh Annual Message to Congress Dec. 3, 1907. http://www.pbs. org/weta/thewest/resources/archives/eight/trconserv.htm, also see, http://www.presidency.ucsb.edu/ws/index.php?pid=29548#axzz1i2I EoqGg.

15 For more information on David Gershon and the Empowerment Institute see, http://www.empowermentinstitute.net/Default.htm.

16 Source: CNN Wire Staff. October 9, 2011. "As 'Occupy' protests spread, some politicians rebuke," http://www.cnn.com/2011/10/09/us/occupy-wall-street/index.html?hpt=hp_t1.

CHAPTER 1 ENDNOTES

17 Source: CNN Wire Staff. October 3, 2011. "As Wall Street protest enters 3rd week, movement gains steam nationwide.
CNN, http://www.cnn.com/2011/10/02/business/wall-street-protests/index.html?hpt=hp_t2.

18 Source: CNN Wire Staff. October 3, 2011. "As Wall Street protest enters 3rd week, movement gains steam nationwide." CNN, http://www.cnn.com/2011/10/02/business/wall-street-protests/index.html?hpt=hp_t2.

19 Source: Pratt, Mark. October 3, 2011. "Boston Protesters: End Corporate Control of Govt." Associated Press. http://www.boston. com/news/local/massachusetts/articles/2011/10/03/boston_protesters _fight_corporate_greed/.

20 For additional information on Patricia Aburdene and "Megatrends 2010: The Rise of Conscious Capitalism," see, http://www.patriciaaburdene.com/.

21 Source: Social Investment Forum Foundation. "2010 Report on Socially Responsible Investing Trends in the United States." Available at: http://ussif.org/resources/research/.

22 Source: Clean Edge, http://www.cleanedge.com/.

23 The Equator Principles (EPs) are a credit risk management framework for determining, assessing, and managing environmental and social risk in project finance transactions. Project finance is often used to fund the development and construction of major infrastructure and industrial projects. The EPs are adopted voluntarily by financial institutions and are applied where total project capital costs exceed US$10 million. The EPs are primarily intended to provide a minimum standard for due diligence to support responsible risk decision-making. The EPs, based on the International Finance Corporation (IFC) Performance Standards on social and environmental sustainability and on the World Bank Group Environmental,

Health, and Safety Guidelines (EHS Guidelines), are intended to serve as a common baseline and framework for the implementation by each adopting institution of its own internal social and environmental policies, procedures and standards related to its project financing activities. Equator Principles Financial Institutions (EPFIs) commit to not providing loans to projects where the borrower will not or is unable to comply with their respective social and environmental policies and procedures that implement the EPs. In addition, while the EPs are not intended to be applied retroactively, EPFIs will apply them to all project financings covering expansion or upgrade of an existing facility where changes in scale or scope may create significant environmental and/or social impacts, or significantly change the nature or degree of an existing impact. The EPs have become the industry standard for environmental and social risk management and financial institutions, clients/project sponsors, other financial institutions, and even some industry bodies, refer to the EPs as good practice. Currently 72 adopting financial institutions (70 EPFIs and 2 Associates) in 27 countries have officially adopted the EPs, covering over 70 percent of international project finance debt in emerging markets. The EPs has greatly increased attention and focus on social/community standards and responsibility, including robust standards for indigenous peoples, labor standards, and consultation with locally affected communities within the project finance market. They have also promoted convergence around common environmental and social standards. Multilateral development banks, including the European Bank for Reconstruction & Development (EBRD), and export credit agencies through the OECD Common Approaches are increasingly drawing on the same standards as the EPs. The EPs have also helped spur the development of other responsible environmental and social management practices in the financial sector and banking industry (for example, Carbon Principles in the U.S. and, Climate Principles worldwide) and have provided a platform for engagement with a broad range of interested stakeholders, including NGOs, clients and industry bodies. Additional information on the Equator Principles is available at: http://www.equator-principles.com/.

24 Loomis, Carol J., FORTUNE editor-at-large. June 25, 2006. "Warren Buffett gives away his fortune." *Fortune Magazine.* http://money.cnn.com/2006/06/25/magazines/fortune/charity1. fortune/.

25 Source: Bill and Melinda Gates Foundation, http://www.gatesfoundation.org/Pages/home.aspx.

26 Source: Clinton Global Initiative, http://www.clintonglobalinitiative.org/.

CHAPTER 2 ENDNOTES

27 Sources: http://news.xinhuanet.com/english2010/world/2011-08/15/ c_131050757.html; http://www.cnn.com/2011/WORLD/europe/08/15/uk.riots/; and http://www.reuters.com/article/2011/08/15/us-britain-riot-idUSTRE77E2XJ20110815?feedType=RSS&feedName=topNews&rp c=71.

28 MA Governing Board statements were extracted from the *"Statement of the MA Board: Living Beyond Our Means: Natural Assets and Human Well-being:"* available at http://www.millenniumassessment.org/en/BoardStatement.aspx.

29 Source: Bloomberg Energy, http://www.bloomberg.com/energy/.

30 The December 15, 2012 NYMEX Crude Futures price per barrel was $93.48. Source: Bloomberg, http://www.bloomberg.com/energy/.

31 Source: Wikipedia, http://en.wikipedia.org/wiki/List_of_social_networking_websites, and http://en.wikipedia.org/wiki/Facebook

32 Source: Pew Research Center, http://pewsocialtrends.org/files/2010/10/millennials-confident-connected-open-to-change.pdf.

33 Source: Pew Research Center, http://pewsocialtrends.org/files/2010/10/millennials-confident-connected-open-to-change.pdf.

34 Source: HP, http://www.hp.com/hpinfo/newsroom/press/2003/ 031002a .html.

35 Source: NY Times and Reuters, http://www.nytimes.com/reuters/ 2011/01/24/technology/tech-us-pope-facebook.html?_r=1&hp.

36 Source: Industry Week, http://www.industryweek.com/articles/ rare_earth_materials_facing_supply_chain_crisis_21599.aspx.

37 Source: Fast Company and DOE, http://www.fastcompany.com/ 1710110/doe-it-will-take-15-years-to-break-american-dependence-on-chinese-rare-earth-materials.

38 Source: Rockwood, Kate. November 1, 2010. "Rare Earth: How a Handful of Countries Control the Earth's Most Precious Materials." FastCompany. http://www.fastcompany.com/magazine/150/rare-earth.html.

CHAPTER 3 ENDNOTES

39 Source: Stanisław Jerzy Lec (1909-1966) from his work, "More Unkempt Thoughts" [Myśli nieuczesane nowe] (1964).

40 Finn, Kathy, Longstreth, Andrew, and Tom Bergin. March 3, 2012. "BP's $7.8 billion deal may speed payments for U.S. spill". Reuters. http://www.reuters.com/article/2012/03/03/us-bp-trial-idUSTRE8 2205N20120303.

41 Source: Gulf Coast Claims Facility, http://www.gulfcoastclaims
facility.com/.

42 The Brundtland Commission Report, *"Report of the World Commission on Environment and Development: Our Common Future"*
is available at, http://www.un-documents.net/wced-ocf.htm.

43 For additional information on *"Green to Gold: How Smart Companies Use Environmental Strategy to Innovate, Create Value, and
Build Competitive Advantage"* by Daniel Esty and Andrew Winston
see, http://www.eco-advantage.com/book.php.

44 Bestselling books by Eckhart Tolle include *A New Earth: Awakening
to Your Life's Purpose and The Power of Now: A Guide to Spiritual
Enlightenment*. Additional information about Eckhart Tolle including publications, web, and television appearances, and his thinking
is available at, http://www.eckharttolle.com/.

45 A portion of the "Silver Tsunami" in Chapter 3: Personal Accountability was originally published as an excerpt on June 18, 2011. See,
http://www.greenbiz.com/blog/2011/06/18/weekend-reading-silver-
tsunami-vs-green-wave.

46 Source: Alliance for Aging Research, http://www.agingresearch.org/
content/article/detail/826.

CHAPTER 4 ENDNOTES

47 Source: Huffington Post. "GM Earnings 4q 2011: Automaker Records
Its Highest Profit Ever." http://www.huffingtonpost.com/2012/
02/16/gm-earnings-4q-2011_n_1281349.html.

48 For additional information on The Conference Board see, http://
www.conference-board.org/.

49 Source: GMCR, http://www.gmcr.com/csr.

50 Source: GMCR, http://www.gmcr.com/csr/WorkingTogetherFor
Change/SupplierEngagement.aspx.

51 Source, GMCR "Partnering with Supply-Chain Communities Scorecard," http://www.gmcr.com/csr/PartneringWithCoffeeGrowing Com
munities/~/media/70D91B3340014C08831D7B02D8D4500D.ashx.

52 Source: GMCR, "Building Demand for Sustainable Products
Scorecard," http://www.gmcr.com/en/CSR/~/media/1C7B91D81B
8C4BCF99061F7135677067.ashx.

53 Source: GMCR, 2009 Corporate Social Responsibility Report,
http://www.gmcr.com/PDF/gmcr_csr_2009.pdf.

54 Source: GMCR, 2009 Corporate Social Responsibility Report, http://
www.gmcr.com/PDF/gmcr_csr_2009.pdf.

55 Source: GMCR, "Purpose and Principles," http://www.gmcr.com/en/
CSR/~/media/6B5C7347A3774DEEB3E7041336898E55.ashx.

56 Source: GMCR, "Creating a Great Place to Work Scorecard,"
http://www.gmcr.com/en/CSR/~/media/5F53C6FD3334442E99C22A
B97C2475BF.ashx.

57 Source: SCORE, http://www.score.org/small_biz_stats.html.

58 Additional information on the "Small Business Economy" is available from the Small Business Administration including their annual research reports and summaries available at: http://www.sba.gov/sites/default/files/files/rs347.pdf and http://www.sba.gov/sites/default/files/files/sb_econ2009.pdf.

59 About SCORE: http://www.score.org/explore_score.html.

60 SCORE is the premier source for small business advice and mentoring in America. SCORE celebrates 46 years of volunteer service in 2010. Established October 5, 1964, SCORE is a nonprofit association dedicated to entrepreneur education and the formation, growth and success of small business nationwide. More than 13,000 volunteers at 350 chapters provide individual mentoring—in person and online—and business workshops for aspiring entrepreneurs and small business owners. SCORE is a resource partner with the U.S. Small Business Administration (SBA). SCORE has served more than 9 million entrepreneurs since 1964. SCORE currently serves more than 350,000 entrepreneurs annually. Based on the findings of the 2009 SCORE Client Outcomes Survey by Gallup Consulting, SCORE helped create more than 30,000 new jobs nationwide in 2009. One in seven clients created a job. SCORE also helped create 68,452 new small businesses in 2009, according to an SBA report sent to Congress.

60 Source: Harbec Plastics, http://www.harbec.com/about-us/mission-values-vision/

61 Source: Bureau of Labor Statistics (BLS). *"Supersector/Industry: Manufacturing. State and Area Employment, Hours, and Earnings.* http://www.bls.gov/.

62 For further information on Harbec Plastics eco-environmental values, sustainability strategy, initiatives and impacts see:
http://www.harbec.com
http://www.harbec.com/sustainability/energy-management-solution/.
http://www.harbec.com/sustainability/eco-economics/
http://www.harbec.com/sustainability/green-molder/
http://www.harbec.com/sustainability/work-environment/
http://www.harbec.com/about-us/history/.
http://www.harbec.com/sustainability/biopolymer-information-center/
http://www.harbec.com/about-us/mission-values-vision/#_self.
http://www.harbec.com/video/
http://www.harbec.com/media/uploads/websterherald08222001.pdf
http://www.harbec.com/media/uploads/rbj04262002.pdf
http://www.harbec.com/media/uploads/dginsight11012002.pdf
http://www.harbec.com/inside-harbec/design-guides/

http://www.harbec.com/about-us/in-the-news/

http://www.harbec.com/media/uploads/er-03-4x.pdf

http://www.ucsusa.org/global_warming/solutions/big_picture_
solutions/efficiency_profitable_strategy.html

63 Source: Harbec Plastics, http://www.harbec.com/about-us/in-the-news/#_self.

64 Source: Mongabay News, http://news.mongabay.com/2008/0807-hance_pope.html.

65 Source Winfield, Nicole. August 18, 2011. "Pope demands greater ethics in economic policy." Associated Press, http://www.ajc.com/news/nation-world/pope-demands-greater-ethics-1119336.html.

CHAPTER 5 ENDNOTES

66 Source: LMI Government Consulting. "TRANSFORMING THE WAY DOD LOOKS AT ENERGY AN APPROACH TO ESTABLISHING AN ENERGY STRATEGY."

67 Ralph Waldo Emerson. "Essays and Lectures: Nature: Addresses and Lectures, Essays: First and Second Series, Representative Men, English Traits, and the Conduct of Life: (Google eBook). Digireads.com Publishing, Jan 30, 2009.

68 Source: Meier, Deborah, *The Power of Their Ideas: Lessons for America from a Small School in Harlem.* (Beacon Press, 2002).

69 The 2008 freshman norms are based on the responses of 240,580 first-time, full-time students at 340 of the nation's baccalaureate colleges and universities. The data have been statistically adjusted to reflect the responses of the 1.4 million first-time, full-time students entering four year colleges and universities as freshmen in 2008. Source: Higher Education Research Institute. "The American Freshman: National Norms, Fall 2008." http://www.heri.ucla.edu/pr-display.php?prQry=28.

70 Source: MSN, "10 Jobs of the Future," http://msn.career builder.com/Article/MSN-2520-Job-Info-and-Trends-10-jobs-of-the-future/.

71 The results are based upon W.P. Carey School of Business at Arizona State University Professor Kevin Dooley's analysis of about 100 job postings related to sustainability, interviews with corporate sustainability managers, and survey results from about 200 managers and executives from small, medium and large companies. Source: http://asunews.asu.edu/20110615_business_sustainabilityjobs

72 Source: http://asunews.asu.edu/20110615_business_sustainability jobs.

73 For more information on the AHC Group, see, www.ahcgroup.com.

74 Source: Enolia Ventus, http://www.enoliaventus.com/en/.

CHAPTER 6 ENDNOTES

75 As a follow up to the 2005 survey, the 2008 survey is regarded as the most comprehensive conducted on this subject to date. In addition to the Global Fortune 250, the sample also included the 100 largest companies by revenue, in 22 countries. The survey presents historical data where possible, drawing from 5 previous surveys conducted by KPMG firms since 1993. Only information available in the public domain was used for the survey, such as company websites, corporate responsibility reports and annual reports issued in 2007-2008. Source: KPMG International Survey of Corporate Responsibility Reporting 2008. http://www.kpmg.com/cn/en/issuesandinsights/articlespublications/pages/corporate-responsibility-survey-200810-o.aspx.

76 James Cameron, February 2010 TED talk, "Before Avatar, a curious boy". http://www.ted.com/talks/james_cameron_before_avatar_a_curious_boy.html.

77 The report, "White House Energy Innovation Conference Summary Report" May, 7, 2010 was compiled by the Ewing Marion Kauffman Foundation. The report is available through: http://www.energyinnovationnetwork.org/.

78 Source: Brooks, David. January 13, 2011. "Tree of Failure" Op-Ed. NY Times, http://www.nytimes.com/2011/01/14/opinion/14brooks.html?_r=1&nl=todaysheadlines&emc=tha212

79 For additional information on Sir Ken Robinson, PhD and author of "The Element: How Finding Your Passion Changes Everything" (Penguin/Viking 2009), see, http://sirkenrobinson.com/skr/.

80 Source: U.S. Fish & Wildlife Service, http://www.fws.gov/northeast/rachelcarson/.

CHAPTER 7 ENDNOTES

81 For a summarized history of RIT, see http://www.rit.edu/overview/history.html.

82 For a summary of RIT Colleges, see http://www.rit.edu/overview/colleges.html.

83 For a summary of RIT academic and professional programs, see, http://www.rit.edu/overview/programs.php.

84 For a summary of RIT's past Presidents' see, http://www.rit.edu/president/history.html.

85 For additional information on the Imagine RIT: Creativity & Innovation Festival see, http://www.rit.edu/imagine/about_imagine.html.

86 Source of "11th largest private university" statistic, http://www.rit.edu/provost/sites/rit.edu.provost/files/provosts_update_march_2011_0.pdf.

87 B. Thomas Golisano is founder and chairman of Paychex Inc. and owner of the National Hockey League's Buffalo Sabres. He also serves as a member of RIT's Board of Trustees.

88 Source for Golisano Institute for Sustainability launch, http://www.rit.edu/news/story.php?id=45789.

89 For more information on the Clinton Global Initiative, see, http://www.clintonglobalinitiative.org/.

90 Source of quote, RIT, September 12, 2007 article by Paul Stella "RIT Launches The Golisano Institute for Sustainability," see, http://www.rit.edu/news/story.php?id=45789.

91 Groundbreaking Grads Featured at RIT Commencement Ceremony May 20: Diplomas awarded to RIT's first-ever degree recipients in sustainability and sustainable systems. See, http://www.rit.edu/news/story.php?id=48369.

92 For more information on the RIT Campus Environmental Committee, see, http://www.rit.edu/academicaffairs/academicsenate/standing/campusenvironment/charges.php.

93 For more information about AASHE see, http://www.aashe.org/about.

94 Source: extracted from, http://www.rit.edu/fa/ritgreen/pcc.html.

95 For more information on Enid Cardinal and RIT, http://www.rit.edu/news/story.php?id=48309.

96 Source: Atlanta Business Chronicle, http://www.bizjournals.com/atlanta/stories/2007/11/05/daily2.html

97 Source: Georgia-Pacific, http://www.gp.com/aboutus/companyOverview/index.html.

98 For more information on Olana, see, http://olana.org/index.php

99 For more information on the Hudson River School Painters, see, http://olana.org/learn_hudson_river_school.php.

100 Source of quotation: Hudson River School Painters, see http://olana.org/learn_hudson_river_school.php.

101 Source: Beckwith, Julian R. III, et.al. "Forest Resources One-liners with Georgia Highlights." Warnell School of Forestry and Natural Resources, University of Georgia. November 1996. http://warnell.forestry.uga.edu/service/library/index.php3?docID=126&docHistory%5B%5D=10.

102 For more information on GPs Statement on Forest Protection and Sustainability Practices see, http://www.gp.com/aboutus/sustainability/forestry/pdf/policy_statement.pdf.

103 Source: AFPA, http://www.afandpa.org/whatwebelieve.aspx?id=1897.

104 For more information on GP Harmon Recycling, see, http://www.harmongp.com/index.asp.

105 Source: Georgia-Pacific, http://www.gp.com/aboutus/sustainability/.

106 Source: Hoovers, a Dun & Bradstreet Company. www.hoovers.com.

107 Coleman, Mark C. "Looking for Social Response Leadership? You Might Consider Copying' Xerox." September 28, 2007. http://worldinc book.blogspot.com/2007/09/looking-for-social-response-leadership. html.
108 Source, GreenBiz.com, http://www.greenbiz.com/blog/2011/06/18/ weekend-reading-silver-tsunami-vs-green-wave.
109 Source: Pew Research Center, http://pewsocialtrends.org/files/2010/ 10/millennials-confident-connected-open-to-change.pdf.

Additional Sources of Learning and Information

American College & University Presidents' Climate Commitment (ACUPCC)

http://www.presidentsclimatecommitment.org/

The American College & University Presidents' Climate Commitment (ACUPCC) is a high-visibility effort to address global climate disruption undertaken by a network of colleges and universities that have made institutional commitments to eliminate net greenhouse gas emissions from specified campus operations, and to promote the research and educational efforts of higher education to equip society to re-stabilize the earth's climate. Its mission is to accelerate progress towards climate neutrality and sustainability by empowering the higher education sector to educate students, create solutions, and provide leadership-by-example for the rest of society.

The ACUPCC provides a framework and support for America's colleges and universities to implement comprehensive plans in pursuit of climate neutrality. The Commitment recognizes the unique responsibility that institutions of higher education have as role models for their communities and in educating the people who will develop the social, economic and technological solutions to reverse global warming and help create a thriving, civil and sustainable society.

ACUPCC institutions have agreed to:

- Complete an emissions inventory.
- Within two years, set a target date and interim milestones for becoming climate neutral.
- Take immediate steps to reduce greenhouse gas emissions by choosing from a list of short-term actions.
- Integrate sustainability into the curriculum and make it part of the educational experience.
- Make the action plan, inventory and progress reports publicly available.

American Forest & Paper Association (AF&PA)

http://www.afandpa.org/

The American Forest & Paper Association (AF&PA) is the national trade association of the forest products industry and advances public policies that promote a strong and sustainable U.S. forest products industry in the global marketplace.

The U.S. forest products industry accounts for approximately 5 percent of the total U.S. manufacturing GDP. Industry companies produce about $175 billion in products annually and employ nearly 900,000 men and women, exceeding employment levels in the automotive, chemicals and plastics industries. The industry meets a payroll of approximately $50 billion and is among the top 10 manufacturing sector employers in 48 states.

AF&PA's member companies make more than 75 percent of the U.S.'s pulp, paper, paper-based packaging and wood building materials—essential products used every day that are made from renewable and recyclable resources that sustain the environment. The Association's membership represents the diverse spectrum of the forest products industry—from independent forest owners, to family-owned mills, to large multi-product, publicly-owned companies that manufacture pulp, paper, paperboard and wood products.

Association for the Advancement of Sustainability in Higher Education (AASHE)

http://www.aashe.org/

AASHE is helping to create a brighter future of opportunity for all by advancing sustainability in higher education. By creating a diverse community engaged in sharing ideas and promising practices, AASHE provides administrators, faculty, staff and students, as well as the business that serve them, with: thought leadership and essential knowledge resources; outstanding opportunities for professional development; and a unique framework for demonstrating the value and competitive edge created by sustainability initiatives.

AASHE defines sustainability in an inclusive way, encompassing human and ecological health, social justice, secure livelihoods, and a better world for all generations. AASHE is a member-driven, independent 501(c)(3). Institutional membership in AASHE includes every individual at an institution.

Business for Social Responsibility (BSR)

http://www.bsr.org/

http://www.bsr.org/files/About_BSR_2010.pdf

A leader in corporate responsibility since 1992, BSR works with its global network of more than 250 member companies to develop sustainable business strategies and solutions through consulting, research, and cross-sector collaboration.

With offices in Asia, Europe, and North America, BSR uses its expertise in environment, human rights, economic development, and governance and accountability to guide global companies toward creating a just and sustainable world.

Ceres

http://www.ceres.org/

Ceres is a non-profit organization that leads a national coalition of investors, environmental organizations and other public interest groups working with companies to address sustainability challenges such as global climate change and water scarcity.

At Ceres, our mission is to integrate sustainability into day-to-day business practices for the health of the planet and its people. Changing capital market practices to incorporate long-term environmental and social risks instead of merely relying on short-term returns as a measure of economic health is a key component of our work. To accomplish our goals, we work with leading companies, investors, public interest groups, policymakers and other economic players to advance sustainable solutions that will reduce carbon emissions and other pollutants, protect vital natural resources like water supplies, ensure safe and just working conditions for employees and reduce our reliance on fossil fuels while transitioning to a clean energy economy.

Clean Edge, Inc.

http://www.cleanedge.com/

Clean Edge, Inc., founded in 2000, is the world's first research and advisory firm devoted to the clean-tech sector. The company, via its publications, events, and online services, helps companies, investors, and governments understand and profit from clean technologies. Clean Edge, with offices in the San Francisco Bay Area and Portland Oregon, integrates timely clean-tech data from dozens of sources with expert analysis to provide critical insights quickly and cost effectively. The firm's offerings include:

- *The U.S. Clean Energy Leadership Index*—The leading advisory service for clients looking to gain a competitive advantage in the U.S. clean-energy marketplace via state-based leadership data, rankings and analysis; market insight reports; and related consulting services
- *Sponsored Publications*—including our annual Clean Energy Trends and Clean Tech Job Trends report series
- *NASDAQ® Clean Edge® Stock Indices*—benchmark indices tracking U.S. clean-energy and global wind and smart grid infrastructure companies

- *The Clean-Tech Investor Summit*—the premier clean-tech conference and networking opportunity of the year

Clinton Global Initiative (CGI)

http://www.clintonglobalinitiative.org/

The mission of the Clinton Global Initiative (CGI) is to inspire, connect, and empower a community of global leaders to forge solutions to the world's most pressing challenges. By fostering partnerships, providing strategic advice, and driving resources toward effective ideas, CGI helps its members—organizations from the private sector, public sector, and civil society—maximize their efforts to alleviate poverty, create a cleaner environment, and increase access to health care and education.

Since CGI was established in 2005 by President Bill Clinton, its Annual Meetings have brought together nearly 150 current and former heads of state, 18 Nobel Prize laureates, and hundreds of leading CEOs, along with heads of foundations, major philanthropists, directors of the most effective nongovernmental organizations, and prominent members of the media. These CGI members have made nearly 2,000 commitments, which have already improved the lives of 300 million people in more than 180 countries. When fully funded and implemented, these commitments will be valued in excess of $63 billion.

The Conference Board

http://www.conference-board.org/

The Conference Board is a global, independent business membership and research association working in the public interest. Our mission is unique: To provide the world's leading organizations with the practical knowledge they need to improve their performance and better serve society. The Conference Board is a non-advocacy, not-for-profit entity holding 501 (c) (3) tax-exempt status in the United States.

Founded in 1916, The Conference Board is an objective, independent source of economic and business knowledge with one agenda: to help our member companies understand and deal with the most critical issues of our time.

The Conference Board works within and across four main subject areas—Corporate Leadership; Economies, Markets & Value Creation; High-Performing Organizations; and Human Capital—to create a unique, enterprise-wide perspective that helps business leaders respond today, anticipate tomorrow, and make the right strategic decisions every day.

Empowerment Institute

http://www.empowermentinstitute.net/

Empowerment Institute is the world's premiere consulting and training organization specializing in the methodology of empowerment. Its state-of-the-art empowerment tools have been applied over the past thirty years to achieve measurable behavior change at the community and organizational level. Its clients consist of public sector agencies, corporations and non profits. Empowerment Institute's programs have received many awards including Renew America's top honor for community participation, EPA's environmental quality award, and citations from the President's Council on Sustainable Development, U.S. Department of Energy, Oregon Department of Energy and a number of state environment and energy offices.

Go Green Initiative

http://www.gogreeninitiative.org/

The mission of the Go Green Initiative is to provide schools, homes, businesses and organizations of all kinds with the tools and training they need to create a "culture of conservation" within their community. Our goals are to conserve and protect natural resources for future generations, and to protect human health through environmental stewardship.

The Go Green Initiative Association is a non-profit organization that seeks to provide every school the opportunity to protect the environment and children's health through environmentally responsible behaviors. The GGIA provides training and resources for Go Green schools and serves as a clearinghouse for information on environmental education programs throughout the country.

Golisano Institute for Sustainability (GIS)

http://www.rit.edu/gis/

The Golisano Institute of Sustainability (GIS) is a multidisciplinary academic unit of Rochester Institute of Technology, Rochester, NY USA. The mission of GIS is to undertake world-class education and research missions in sustainability.

GIS academic and research programs focus on sustainable production, sustainable energy, sustainable mobility, and ecologically friendly information technology systems. These programs are led by a multidisciplinary team of faculty and researchers who collaborate with organizations locally, nationally, and internationally to create implementable solutions to complex sustainability programs.

Imagine RIT: Innovation & Creativity Festival

http://www.rit.edu/imagine/

Imagine RIT: Innovation and Creativity Festival is a campus-wide event that showcases the innovative and creative spirit of RIT students, faculty and staff. Visitors experience the breadth and depth of RIT through interactive presentations, hands-on demonstrations, exhibitions, and research projects set up throughout campus. Inflatables, games and multiple performance stages with live music and entertainment are also a hit with visitors of all ages. Held annually each spring, Imagine RIT is the kickoff to Rochester's rich festival season.

Institute for Sustainable Communities (ISC)

http://www.iscvt.org/

ISC's mission is to help communities around the world address environmental, economic, and social challenges to build a better future shaped and shared by all. We are in the business of unleashing the power of people to transform their communities. Our approach ensures solutions emerge from within the community, rather than being imposed from the outside. By combining technical expertise and leadership training with strategic investments in local organizations, we are sparking creative solutions and lasting change.

Since our founding in 1991 by former Vermont Governor Madeleine M. Kunin, ISC has led transformative community-driven projects across the globe. We garnered early recognition for connecting civic participation with environmental problem solving, and over the years we have developed an approach that accelerates a community's ability to meet challenges head on.

Whether the challenge at hand is halting air and water pollution, catalyzing HIV/AIDS prevention campaigns, or training new civic leaders, our work is making a real difference in millions of lives across the world. We get people involved in shaping their future and cultivate local talent—enabling people to become strong advocates and effective leaders in their communities.

ISC defines Sustainable Communities in the following way: A sustainable community is one that is economically, environmentally, and socially healthy and resilient. It meets challenges through integrated solutions rather than through fragmented approaches that meet one of those goals at the expense of the others. And it takes a long-term perspective—one that's focused on both the present and future, well beyond the next budget or election cycle.

Leonardo Academy

http://www.leonardoacademy.org/

Leonardo Academy is a charitable nonprofit organization dedicated to advancing sustainability by leveraging innovative tools and information to motivate the competitive market. By utilizing an interdisciplinary approach to sustainability strategies, education and implementation, we strive to make sustainability practical for everyone.

We develop integrative sustainability solutions designed to enhance the environmental stewardship, social responsibility and economic prosperity of organizations, corporations and individuals. We see a world filled with sustainable opportunities that can transform the way we live today and ensure the prosperity of future generations.

Leonardo Academy provides comprehensive sustainability services that help companies and organizations understand, quantify, manage and report their overall sustainability including all three legs of sustainability. Leonardo Academy specializes in LEED consulting, Enterprise Sustainability, Emissions Services, Land Management Services and Sustainability Training.

Leonardo Academy works with organizations, corporations, families and individuals to evaluate their current impacts and to develop effective, measurable strategies to enhance sustainability. Leonardo Academy works to develop innovative tools that leverage the competitive market so both buyers and sellers can drive increased sustainability and create sustainability opportunities that promote a thriving planet and transform the way we live.

Make It Right
http://www.makeitrightnola.org/

The Mission of Make It Right is clear: It is to be a catalyst for redevelopment of the Lower 9th Ward, by building a neighborhood comprises of safe and healthy homes that are inspired by Cradle to Cradle thinking, with an emphasis on a high quality of design, while preserving the spirit of the community's culture. The goal is to accomplish this quickly, so that the first residents can begin returning to their homes as soon as possible.

On August 29, 2005, Hurricane Katrina flooded 80 percent of the City of New Orleans and killed 1,577 people. Hardest hit was the Lower 9th Ward where more than 4,000 homes were destroyed by the storm and the surge of water caused by the breach of the Industrial Canal levee.

Two years later after Katrina when actor Brad Pitt toured the city, no progress had been made in the Lower 9th Ward. Still, the community was determined to rebuild. After meeting with local families, Pitt established Make It Right to build 150 green, affordable, high-quality design homes in the neighborhood closest to the levee breach.

Make It Right kicked off in December 2007 with the Pink Project—an art installation designed to bring attention to the challenges and possibilities of rebuilding the Lower 9th Ward. The Pink Project raised 12 million dollars. 21 local, national and international architects donated designs for single family and duplexes to Make It Right. Today, Make It Right has built 75 sustainable, LEED Platinum certified homes for Lower 9th Ward families. According to the U.S. Green Building Council, Make It Right is the "largest and greenest community of single-family homes in the world."

Natural Capital Solutions
http://natcapsolutions.org/
Natural Capitalism Solutions is recognized internationally for its work in the field of sustainability. Formed by Hunter Lovins, co-author of the acclaimed book "Natural Capitalism: Creating the Next Industrial Revolution," Natural Capitalism Solutions is led by Lovins, who has over 40 years experience in business, sustainability, and change management.

Together with their network of best in class sustainability professionals, the Natural Capitalism staff has an impressive record in developing innovative and practical ways to increase efficiency and environmental practices, as well as economic sustainability, for a long list of government and corporate clients.

Natural Capitalism Solutions' mission is to educate senior decision-makers in business, government and civil society about the principles of sustainability. Natural Capitalism Solutions shows how to restore and further enhance natural and human capital while increasing prosperity and quality of life. In partnership with leading thinkers and groups, Natural Capitalism Solutions creates innovative, practical tools and implementation strategies for companies, communities and countries. Natural Capitalism Solutions (NCS) is a 501(c)(3) non-profit organization.

The organization is based on the principles presented in the acclaimed book Natural Capitalism: Creating the Next Industrial Revolution. Natural Capitalism Solutions builds on the original Natural Capitalism Principles, a leading whole-system sustainability framework. Since the book's publication in 1999, Hunter and her colleagues have gained a wealth of experience in helping companies and communities use these principles to capture the economic advantages of sustainability. The principles have evolved to identify opportunities to reduce capital investment and operating costs and generate market leadership advantages.

Pew Research Center
http://pewresearch.org/
Pew Research Center is a nonpartisan "fact tank" that provides information on the issues, attitudes and trends shaping America and the world. It does so by conducting public opinion polling and social science research, by analyzing news coverage, and by holding forums and briefings. It does not take positions on policy issues. Its work is carried out by seven projects:
• Pew Research Center for the People & the Press
• Pew Research Center's Project for Excellence in Journalism

- Pew Internet & American Life Project
- Pew Forum on Religion & Public Life
- Pew Hispanic Center
- Pew Global Attitudes Project
- Pew Social & Demographic Trends Project

It provides its research and data— free of charge—as a public service to policymakers, researchers, journalists and the general public. All publications and datasets can be accessed via PewResearch.org, which is a portal to a network of Pew Research websites.

Rachel Carson National Wildlife Refuge

http://www.fws.gov/northeast/rachelcarson/

Rachel Carson National Wildlife Refuge was established in 1966 in cooperation with the State of Maine to protect valuable salt marshes and estuaries for migratory birds. Located along 50 miles of coastline in York and Cumberland counties, the refuge consists of eleven divisions between Kittery and Cape Elizabeth. It will contain approximately 14,600 acres when land acquisition is complete. The proximity of the refuge to the coast and its location between the eastern deciduous forest and the boreal forest creates a composition of plants and animals not found elsewhere in Maine. Major habitat types present on the refuge include forested upland, barrier beach/dune, coastal meadows, tidal salt marsh, and the distinctive rocky coast.

Resources for the Future

http://www.rff.org/

The mission of Resources for the Future (RFF) is to improve environmental and natural resource policymaking worldwide through objective social science research of the highest caliber. RFF is a nonprofit and nonpartisan organization that conducts independent research—rooted primarily in economics and other social sciences—on environmental, energy, natural resource, and environmental health issues.

Although RFF is headquartered in Washington, D.C., its research scope comprises programs in nations around the world. Founded in 1952, RFF was created at the recommendation of William Paley, then head of the Columbia Broadcasting System, who had chaired a presidential commission that examined whether the United States was becoming overly dependent on foreign sources of important natural resources and commodities. RFF became the first think tank devoted exclusively to natural resource and environmental issues.

For more than 50 years, RFF has pioneered the application of economics as a tool to develop more effective policy about the use and conservation of natural resources. Its scholars continue to analyze critical issues concerning pollution control, energy and transportation policy, land and water use, hazardous waste, climate change, biodiversity, ecosystem management, health, and the environmental challenges of developing countries.

SRI World Group Inc.

http://www.sriworld.com/index.html
http://www.socialfunds.com/

SRI World Group Inc. is a leading provider of social investing and corporate social responsibility information. We pride ourselves at being independent and objective sources of information that empower individuals and institutions.

Originally called SocialFunds.com, SRI World Group was founded in 1999 by Jay Falk. SocialFunds.com was an idea that was born during Jay's 15 years in the social investing industry to bring information to individual investors. SRI World Group now also serves institutional investors with news, research, consulting and other services that can be found at www.institutionalshareowner.com.

The Earth Institute, Columbia University

http://www.earth.columbia.edu/

The Earth Institute brings together the people and tools needed to address some of the world's most difficult problems, from climate change and environmental degradation, to poverty, disease and the sustainable use of resources. The Institute, under the direction of Professor Jeffrey D. Sachs, comprises more than 30 research centers and some 850 scientists, postdoctoral fellows, staff and students. Working across many disciplines, we study and create solutions for problems in public health, poverty, energy, ecosystems, climate, natural hazards, and urbanization.

Earth Institute experts work hand-in-hand with academia, corporations, government agencies, nonprofits and individuals. They advise national governments and the United Nations on issues related to sustainable development and the Millennium Development Goals. They are educating the next generation of leaders in basic sciences and sustainable development.

The Madrone Project

http://www.madroneproject.com/
http://www.facebook.com/madroneproject

The Madrone Project is a non-profit educational team that brings greater depth and scale to sustainability education by delivering advanced modular curricula curated for digital media. Madrone works with academic institutions, companies and citizens who want high quality education on the challenges facing the planet and the new research developments that will impact the future of sustainability.

The New Creed of Greed: Going Green is Good, but also Fraught with Near Term Risk
http://www.environmental-expert.com/Files/19530/articles/17597/4.pdf

In June 2007 I published, through Environmental-Expert (www.environ mental-expert.com), a 31-page article "How Irrational Greenness Could Result in Unintended Consequences for Consumers, Corporations & Policy Makers in this New Century of Social Responsibility & Sustainability." Portions of the article are replicated in this book to articulate care and caution on the future regarding constraints in our use of natural resources and a need to realign our thinking toward our rate and state of consumption. The June 2007 article represented early thinking on my behalf which ultimately led to the ideation of The Sustainability Generation as a book concept.

The Shift Report by Conscientious Innovation (Ci)
http://ci-shift.com/the-shift-report/
http://ci-shift.com/

The SHIFT Report is a strategic research tool specifically designed for innovation, business success, and positive change. The SHIFT Report is Ci's proprietary market intelligence tool and represents best in class insight and research on the relationship among consumers, brands, sustainability, and culture. SHIFT was launched in 2006 with a North American qualitative research study with mainstream and trendsetter consumers via twenty-four focus groups in six markets, in-depth interviews, ethnography, secondary quantitative data and trend analysis. Additional SHIFT studies have included studies on people's relationship with locally based business versus multinationals, relationships between sustainability and the home, CEO and Corporate Leaders' relationship with sustainability, relationships between sustainability and procurement, and with sustainability and food, and more.

Unreasonable Institute
http://unreasonableinstitute.org/

Another example and evidence that the Sustainability Generation has taken root is through the evolution and ongoing action of the Unreasonable Institute. The mission of the Unreasonable Institute is to "give high-impact entrepreneurs wings." Their vision is to "accelerate ventures that future generations will remember as having defined progress in our time." Since 2010 the Unreasonable Institute has united 25 entrepreneurs per year with 50 world-class mentors in an intensive 6-week training and relationship building program. The Unreasonable Institute differentiates and prides itself on "accelerating unreasonable entrepreneurs and their ventures." Organizations like the Unreasonable

Institute are only as good as the people who are dedicated to making the enterprise effective. One of the impressive forces behind its work are the 50 world-class mentors the Institute has recruited to interact with each class of unreasonable entrepreneurs. The mentors are, in their own right, successful entrepreneurs, social change agents, environmental and energy leaders, and sustainability professionals. Further information about the 50 mentors and current and past entrepreneurs of the Institute is available at: http://unreasonableinstitute.org/our-mentors/.

Us Foundation
http://www.usfoundation.org/
Our mission is to raise the awareness of and to promote and create action to support the highest common good, and the interconnectedness of all. Us Foundation serves as a network and consultant for people, organizations and businesses that are aligned with this mission, so they can unite their energies to further the transformation to a mutually responsible and cooperative global society. Our focus is on the rebalancing of our values, to encourage the integration of head, heart, and spirit in all our interactions. We seek to address the overemphasis on technology to solve all problems, many of which have been caused by technology itself. We use electronic communications to reach large numbers of people, and also sponsor action oriented forums for people who have large spheres of influence to effect change.

Us is the vision and dream of many. It was founded in January of 1996 by Marilyn Tam and Jana Saunders. Since then, many people from all walks of life: social and environmental activists, artists, corporate leaders, educators, lawmakers, and spiritual leaders, have joined in building this vision of a better tomorrow. A tomorrow that acknowledges, celebrates, and builds on our diversity and treats each being with respect.

We believe that the present imbalance in life is a result of the overemphasis in technology, the devaluing of personal and spiritual relationships, and the neglect of our relationship with the planet. Education is a tool to adjust this imbalance. We recognize that change comes from understanding and resolving the cause of the problems, not repairing the symptoms. We know that true change occurs when people are intellectually, emotionally, and spiritually committed to the change, which can only come from understanding and accepting the rationale for change.

US SIF: The Forum for Sustainable and Responsible Investment
http://ussif.org/about/
US SIF, Formerly the Social Investment Forum (SIF), is the U.S. membership association for professionals, firms, institutions and organizations engaged in socially responsible and sustainable investing. US SIF and its members advance investment practices that consider environ-

mental, social and corporate governance criteria to generate long-term competitive financial returns and positive societal impact. Our vision is a world in which investment capital helps build a sustainable and equitable economy.

US SIF's members include investment management and advisory firms, mutual fund companies, research firms, financial planners and advisors, broker-dealers, banks, credit unions, community development organizations, non-profit associations, and pension funds, foundations and other asset owners. US SIF members practice SRI through methods such as portfolio selection analysis, shareholder advocacy and community investing.

World Inc. Blog

http://worldincbook.blogspot.com/

In 2006–2009 I wrote a blog, "World Inc.: For Better or For Worse?" The blog was written when my colleague and prolific writer Bruce Piasecki was publishing his seventh book, World Inc.: When It Comes to Solutions—Both Local and Global—Businesses Are Now More Powerful Than Government. I used a play on words and mimicry in the blog to align with Bruce's book because it helped advance my writing and thinking about the topics of globalization, innovation, and sustainability and in the support of his book release. There are excerpts contained within this book which I originally wrote for the World Inc. Blog. I chose to use certain excerpts from the blog to add emphasis or articulate specific points within this book.

Acknowledgments

I once heard an author say, ". . . writing a book is like a prison sentence." I feel sorry for this writer, but understand his sentiment. Writing a book can be a lonely, self imposed process. No one tells you to write, or what to write. It is something you choose to do, and seek to perfect. I have not once thought of writing this book as anything other than a delight. If anything, I wish I had more time to dive even deeper into the many branches of where this book could extend.

Writing this book was not like writing a research paper or contemporary article, both of which I have spent hundreds if not thousands of hours doing in my career. Instead, the writing was a three-year process of a lot of hard work to find the right words and phrasing to tell the story within. I feel a sense of privilege and pride for having worked on this book for that duration. A great deal of time, effort, passion and energy goes into writing a book. This book was no different. And, like most other authors who have released their first books well before me, there are a great many people to recognize and graciously thank for their support, wisdom, cheerleading, and critical reviews. Without their support, this book would not be published today.

I dedicate this book to my wife Aileen and our two sons, Owen Patrick and Neal Garrett. They are the inspiration, love, and joy of my life. When I met Aileen over seventeen years ago I would have never imagined how incredible our life would be today. Thank you Aileen for your unconditional love and support as ideas drifted their way onto the page as written words, then into structured thoughts, and eventually into the hands of books agents and publishers that saw the wisdom of what I wanted to accomplish in this book, and which you saw and believed in from the start. You have had an incredible hand in shaping this book. Thanks for believing in me and inspiring me to keep at this project.

Over the two-year book writing process Aileen and I had our two sons, and also discovered that she had ovarian cancer in 2011 and multiple sclerosis (MS) in 2012. It has been a challenging time for Aileen, and our family. I know of no braver person in my life than Aileen. For all that she has been through, taken-on, and conquered, she represents resiliency and strength. Bravery is not the act of writing words on the page; it is in living them day-to-day in the face of uncertainty and change, and finding meaning and purpose in that. Aileen is a gift of life, and her encouragement toward this project during one of the toughest chapters of her life is nothing short of miraculous.

Thank you to Owen and Neal, my two beautiful boys. While you won't realize it until I tell you some day, Owen and Neal, you were an incredible inspiration for this book. Something profoundly changes when you have children. You almost lose a bit of yourself, but gain a fuller appreciation and understanding of a higher consciousness that is beyond you. They are the younger generation, our future. It is not just my (our) job to teach them, but to be their guides, mentors, and advisors into a world of promise. This book is in many ways an attempt to show my sons this: you can achieve your dreams and live a life of integrity, strong values, and personal accountability.

I am very grateful and honored to have been introduced to Bill Gladstone of Waterside Productions. After spending close to a year trying to get a publisher to read my book proposal, I asked my friend and colleague Bruce Piasecki if he could connect me with his book agent, Bill Gladstone. Bruce did, and shortly thereafter Bill Gladstone and I began working together. Within four months (and after several rejections) Bill lined me up with SelectBooks, Inc. in New York City. Thank you Bill Gladstone to living up to what Bruce Piasecki and others have termed you, "the super agent." You saw value in what I wanted to do with this book. And, from day one you helped me guide the message, shape the core themes, and dive deeper than I thought I would go with this project. Thank for working with me Bill. It has been a pleasure; and I hope this book is the first of more to come.

Very special thanks to Kenzi Sugihara and his team at SelectBooks, Inc. Without your support, guidance, and hard work I would not be a published author. You saw the wisdom and potential in my concept, and took the risk on this project and in me as a first-time author. Your shared vision and enthusiasm allowed me to deliver a product; however, the coaching, guidance, support and passion you and the entire SelectBooks team provided enabled the product to come to life as a book. For all of this, I am eternally thankful and grateful. It was a pleasure working with you, Kenzi and the SelectBooks team. I hope this book is successful so that we can continue this relationship in years to come.

I could write a separate book about my life experience with Bruce Piasecki. I first met Bruce around 1997–98, when I was searching for the right graduate school. At the time Bruce was the Director of the

Environmental Management and Policy Program at Rensselaer Polytechnic Institute (RPI). In the late 1990s there was only a handful of high quality Masters level programs focused on Environmental Management that tied classical business school MBA training with multi-disciplinary elements of engineering, science, and social sciences together. I chose to study with Bruce at RPI. I then supported, as a Senior Research Associate, his management consulting firm AHC Group, Inc. I'm grateful for our years together, and the guidance, access, personal and professional growth my relationship with him has fostered. Honestly, if I had not met Bruce, I likely never would have written and published this book. That is one of the amazing things in life— how we connect the dots and work with others to achieve things greater than ourselves.

Thanks to my parents, Mark and Elizabeth (Betsy), and my three sisters: Rebecca (Becky), Maureen, and Erin for their support. Where writing this book was not a prison sentence, growing up with three sisters was! Becky is the oldest, three years older than I am. Then there is Maureen four years younger than I am, and Erin, five years younger. Honestly, I poke fun, but I am grateful for having grown-up with three sisters. The experience taught patience, sense of humor, and tenacity. These traits were needed, and came out several times throughout the development of the manuscript.

There are too many people to thank and recognize for helping to make this book a reality. The momentum for writing this book picked-up when I realized the more I reached out to others for their personal insights and critical reviews, the more willing most people seemed to be to share information, data, and knowledge. I received many kind words of encouragement throughout this process, and a few who thanked me for attempting to tackle this tough subject in earnest. Thank you to the following individuals who, in my mind, exemplify leadership and personal accountability in their own lives. Without your time and support I could not have brought this work together in its final form.

Many thanks to my colleagues and friends of the AHC Group and its Corporate Affiliate program, past and present, whom embody "The Sustainability Generation" as they work tirelessly to influence and transform the world around them: Bruce Piasecki, Jonathan Ellerman, Denny Minano, Dwight Bedsole, Steve Percy, Steve Willis, Steve Wolff, Ken Strassner, Frank Weaver, Marti Simmons, Steve Myers and others. I have had the pleasure working with all of you in a variety of capacities and cherish the wisdom, leadership, and guidance you each envelop and project daily.

Most gracious thanks to those that I interviewed for this book, and to others that I spoke with across time but whom helped me shape the framework, phrasing, and message of what I was trying to accomplish including: L. Hunter Lovins, Marilyn Tam, Paul DeCotis, Jill Buck, Nabil

Nasr, Jamie Winebrake, Rebecca Johnson, Tim Engstrom, Bart Alexander, Jill Dumain, Enid Cardinal, Tod Arbogast, Bill Shireman, David Witzel, Stacey Winter, Joel Makower, Carole Inge, Ron Green, Manmeet Chhabra, Rajiv Ramchandra, and David Gershon.

A very special thank you to Bill Destler, President of Rochester Institute of Technology; Bill Frerking, Chief Sustainability Officer for Georgia-Pacific; Patricia Calkins, the Vice President of Environment, Health and Safety for Xerox; Bob Bechtold, President of Harbec, Inc.; and Stelios Voyiatzis, CEO of Enolia Ventus, SA, for their incredible contributions in time and resources, and for providing specific personal reflections within this book. Their stories encapsulate real world perspective and breathe life into this challenging subject of sustainability. I also thank organizations including the Pew Research Center and Inside Washington Publishers for their support, research, and content they supported this project with.

I am incredibly honored by the foreword to this book provided by L. Hunter Lovins. I cannot think of a more prolific advocate and action-oriented leader of sustainability than Hunter. For more than thirty years Hunter has been a thought leader and social change agent driving progress toward sustainable development. Hunter is president of Natural Capitalism Solutions, a 501(c)3 non-profit in Longmont, Colorado and the Chief Insurgent of the Madrone Project, a new initiative she references in the Foreword, and which she is bringing to life with some other leading thinkers. The Madrone Project is a way to bring sustainability solutions to a greater, worldwide audience. Integrating knowledge and the latest in education tools and technologies, the Madrone Project is one shining example of the type of integrated efforts to foster greater empowerment and engagement.

Throughout her career Hunter has also taught at various universities, consulted for many citizens' groups, governments and corporations. She was the co-founder (with her then-husband Amory Lovins) of the well known Rocky Mountain Institute (RMI) which she led for 20 years. Hunter has received many awards and accolades including being named a Hero of the Planet by *Time Magazine* in 2000. To her credit, she has co-authored nine books including *Climate Capitalism: Capitalism in the Age of Climate Change* (2011), *Natural Capitalism: Creating the Next Industrial Revolution* (1999), and *The Natural Advantage of Nations* (2006), *Green Development* (1998).

I asked Hunter to consider the Foreword to this book because I feel she brings more than four decades of learning, wisdom, perspective, and field experience related to sustainable development. Hunter represents the Baby Boomer generation, whereas I am part of Generation X. I believe it is critical for all generations, old and young, to collaborate on a going forward basis if the collective "we" of society is to make strides toward a more balanced (sustainable) world. I hope that you see the logic and balance of having L. Hunter Lovins provide the insightful kick-start to this book.

This book also represents my personal and individual accountability to myself to ensure that I also reach out and work with the leading critical thinkers of our time to accelerate the momentum of what I call The Sustainability Generation. Thank you Hunter for the guidance and wisdom you provided this project. You are an incredible motivator and force in this world. I look forward to where this book brings our dialog, whether in the mountains of Colorado or the pubs of London!

Finally I need to thank all of the individuals that have had profound influence in my life, from teachers and friends, to colleagues and family members. A life is shaped by many things. I have come to understand and appreciate the interpersonal relations between people as much more complex than what we might interpret them to be on the surface. When I connect many of the dots in my past, it leads me to today. We should never take for granted those around us, and how they influence you. Those which we allow to enter into our lives are a very special group of people. There is something magical about that. Thanks to all whom have been a part of my world: past, present and future! I hope that you find some magic and reward in reading this book.

Mark C. Coleman

Index

About the Author

Throughout his career Mark C. Coleman has developed a strong focus on the critical areas of energy, environment, and sustainability. His career has spanned strategic and leadership positions in government, applied research, technology development, and management consulting organizations. This rich and diverse experience has enabled Mr. Coleman to have access to, engage, and work with a broad range of regional, national, and international leaders at every stage of his career, and in the writing of this book.

As an independent sustainability strategist and management consultant, Mr. Coleman has advised start-up and small businesses as well as Fortune 500 and global firms in the areas of strategic business planning, sustainability, enterprise risk, social responsibility, financial and security risks, product stewardship, and innovative practices for achieving business growth. Mr. Coleman has led numerous research studies and has contributed to many publications related to energy, environment, and sustainability.

Mr. Coleman has also led the development and facilitation of numerous executive benchmarking and knowledge-sharing workshops. He also serves as a business coach and mentor to small-and-midsized businesses, supporting the development of their business strategy for day-to-day and long-term growth, profitability, and sustainability.

Early in his career, Mr. Coleman worked as an energy analyst with the New York State Energy Research and Development Authority (NYSERDA). Since 2004 he has been supporting the growth and development of several well respected organizations within Rochester Institute of Technology (RIT), including the Center for Integrated Manufacturing Studies (CIMS), the Golisano Institute for Sustainability (GIS), the Clean Energy Incubator (CEI), and the Venture Creations Incubator (VCI).

During this time he has helped these organizations secure more than $20 million in funding awards toward their development and focus on strategic research, technology, innovation, and sustainability initiatives. In addition to his work at the university, he serves on the board of a not-for-profit organization involving global water development concerns.

Mr. Coleman is a graduate of Rensselaer Polytechnic Institute with a Master of Science degree in Environmental Management and Policy from the Lally School of Management and Technology. He received a Bachelor of Arts degree in Geography and Environmental Studies from Binghamton University. He resides in Fairport, New York with his wife Aileen and sons Owen Patrick and Neal Garrett.